1/10/75

THE GOD OF BUDDHA

THE GOD OF BUDDHA

JAMSHED K FOZDAR

ASIA PUBLISHING HOUSE,INC· New York

© 1973, Jamshed K Fozdar

Library of Congress Catalog Card Number: 72-87303

ISBN 0-210-22395-2

Printed in the United States of America

To

Maitrya

But For Whom This Book Would Never Have Been Written

There is, O monks, an Unborn, Unoriginated, Uncreated, Unformed. Were there not, O monks, This Unborn, Unoriginated, Uncreated, Unformed, there would be no escape from the world of the born, originated, created, formed.

Udana, 80-81

Who denies God, denies himself. Who affirms God, affirms himself.

Taittiriya Upanishad, II.6.i

CONTENTS

PREFACE

As with every task, so also with this thesis, the path towards the goal must be trod on the two feet of discovery and the analysis of that discovery, or, as in our specific quest, verification and interpretation of the recorded utterances of the Buddha on the basic principles as well as the more abstruse concepts of His Message.

Within the limits of possibility available to our time, the verification of the quotations listed in this book has not presented any great difficulty. However, since we have nothing reliable concerning His teachings which could be accurately dated less than 250 years after His passing, the other side of the coin—interpretation of His sayings—can be correct to any reasonable degree only if His utterances are examined within the context of His origins as regards both geography and time. It is towards accomplishing this and eliminating centuries of misunderstanding and erroneous representation of the Buddha's Message that parallel quotations from the Hindu* scriptures have been presented, and the reader, so that he may have a better perspective for coming to his own conclusion, is urged to recognize that the Buddha was very familiar with most, if not all, of these Hindu Scriptures. It is hoped, therefore, that both types of readers, those interested in the subject only for 'talking purpose' as well as those more scholarly inclined towards details, may find in it not only points of interest but also food for thought on a fresh perspective.

In order to ensure a balance between the Sanskrit and Pali names given to the various terms, the reader is requested to treat as identical in meaning such words as Dharma and Dhamma; Nirvana and Nibbana; Gautama and

---

*While recognizing that each and every major religion has identical teachings on the various aspects of its Message, the writer has, for the sake of brevity, refrained from presenting such quotes from the scriptures of the other great Faiths.

Gotama; Arahat and Arahant; Sutra and Sutta; Sangha and Samgha; Karma and Kammana; Samsaras and Sankharas; wherever they occur in the text, as being mere differences of spelling, to account for the slight variation in their pronounciation (Sanskrit, as given by the first, and Pali, by the latter spelling). This rule holds both for the text as well as for the glossary which, it is hoped, will be of some assistance to the reader in obtaining a general concept of some of the terms he may come across in the text. Of course, it should be clearly recognized that the meaning in English of some of those terms will fall far short of the complete idea expressed by the original. This is the problem faced in any translation. The use of capital letters for all nouns such as Religion, Founder, Message, God and the pronouns pertaining to these great spiritual concepts, while fully justifiable in deference to the sacred meaning which these words imply for all of us, has nevertheless been kept to a minimum to avoid difficult reading. To those mentioned in the bibliography and other translated works from which quotations are listed and to my wife Parvati for her help in editing these, I owe a special debt of gratitude.

The number of chapter titles has been kept to a minimum while, wherever necessary, in order to deal with distinct yet related subjects within the format of the chapters, sub-titles have been included for the sake of clarity and ease of study. The chapters themselves have been so arranged as to appear as stepping stones in a gradual approach to the goal of our quest, the God of Buddha.

El Cerrito, California   JAMSHED K. FOZDAR
February, 1973

INTRODUCTION

While minds, both modern and ancient, may have been enamoured by the purely theoretical possibility that righteous behavior, reflection and meditation can emanate from our intellect without the desire of the human psyche to probe the nature of the eternal to gain assurance for its own immortality, yet, in all recorded history, there is no basis for such fanciful conjecture in the real world. If selfishness is merely the product of our ignorance concerning Reality, then, unless we attain to 'omniscience,' we cannot completely shed the love of self and the desire to preserve the self into eternity. As the Buddha says, *this self is our samskaras, and however and wherever they are impressed, that also is the condition of our self.* This may be a novel manner of describing the same entity which human beings wish to have preserved into immortality, but, as to the intrinsic concept of the real self or soul to the minds of men, these words of the Buddha denote no basic change. Because, if that assurance of immortality for the individual consciousness is taken away, there is nothing left to work towards, no reason to strive, nothing to look forward to by being either good or evil, even living or dying. Hence, those who say that the Buddha abolished the self and discredited its quest for immortality of 'itself,' have simply misunderstood both the nature of man and the essence of the Buddha's Message. For, the Buddha knew and taught differently: *Dharma is a door to the eternal.* This is that eternal secret, the 'open sesame,' the Aladdin's lamp, to make men prick up their ears and listen, for it touches their strongest desire. Selfish though that may be, yet it is in the very core of them. And He proclaimed more glad tidings: *I shall fill with joy all the beings whose limbs languish; I shall give happiness to those who are dying from distress; I shall extend to them succour and deliverance. ... Look upon the world as a bubble; look upon it as a mirage. Him who looks thus upon the world the king of death does not see. .... The doctrine of the conquest of self, O Siha, is not taught to destroy the souls of men, but to preserve them.* It was this glorious assurance of eternity for the human soul (or 'mind' as the Buddha preferred to call it, although He also called it soul) that cut across the rigid strata of the Hindu caste system which had begun to stifle the hopes of humanity for salvation and gave birth to a new spiritual dynamism, which was to revitalize the souls of men with a renewed vision of immortality and, thus, once again propel them to dare and risk their all. The 'all,' that would in any event perish—so as to attain 'the imperishable state.' It is said that the essence of the wisdom imparted by Religion is to inspire us to exchange that which we cannot keep (all worldly possessions) in return for that which we cannot lose (our immortal souls):

If, by surrendering a pleasure of little worth one sees a larger pleasure, the wise man will give up the pleasure of little worth and look to the larger pleasure.
Dhammapada, v. 290

Realizing the significance of this, the wise and righteous man should even quickly clear the path leading to release.
Dhammapada, v. 289

When a mortal here on earth has felt his own immortality, could he wish for a long life of pleasure, for the lust of deceitful beauty? There is the path of joy, and there is the path of pleasure. Both attract the soul. Who follows the first comes to good; who follows pleasure reaches not the End. The two paths lie in front of man. Pondering on them, the wise man takes the path of joy; the fool takes the path of pleasure.
Katha Upanishad, I.29; II.1.2

For, no other way has been found to raise men to sustained righteous action, to establish civilizations and cultures. The Buddha, better than all others and like His peers—the Founders of the other great Faiths—knew this only too well. How He described that ineffable state; what attributes He attached to *the Uncreated, the Unoriginated;* His definition of *the Eternal,* these, as we shall see in the following chapters, will require our analysis within the context of the Buddha's origins, if their meaning is to be clear to us. That He did acknowledge *the Eternal* and once again cleared the path to It, by sweeping away the overlain growth of centuries of blind beliefs and rituals, so that human beings with clearer vision and renewed vitality may approach 'It' to gain an assurance of immortality for their souls—of this, there can be no doubt, since the good that His Message and disciples wrought over most of Asia for a thousand years is sufficient testimony of their Faith to membership among that most wonderful of historical phenomena—a major Religion.

But, just as men cannot be motivated to sustained righteousness without assuring them of a higher good (immortality for themselves) in exchange for renouncing the mundane pleasures, so also Religion can lay no claim to men's allegiance and total dedication unless it proclaims its Message to be endowed with the authority of *the Eternal, the Unoriginated, the Causeless Cause,* God, however it may define the indefinable. And so it was with the

Buddha, to understand Whose meaning and message our imagination must return to that time and place when He dwelt on earth.

As no true lover will be content with a second-hand description of his beloved, but instead will hasten to attain her presence himself, so we, too, if we are sincere seekers of the way of the Buddha, must return to that early India which was the cradle not only of the physical and mental personality of the Buddha, but also for the tremendous spiritual message of His doctrine—a doctrine eventually destined to go beyond the confines of its homeland and ultimately become the basis of a humane civilization for the major part of Asia and a praxis of life for all sentient beings in their quest for immortality.

History shows us that every nation has its genius of greatness. Just as the genius of ancient Greece was Beauty and that of Rome was Law, so the genius of ancient India, hemmed in by mountains and cut off by oceans which isolated it from other cultures, was to seek within itself and find the Soul.[1] Its passion became the passion of the fragment for the whole—a passion to liberate itself from its finite existence and become one with the Infinite. Unrivalled among the religious thoughts of its day, the spirit of Indian religion addressing us from a past when time was congealing from legend into history, conveys in this verse of the Upanishads[2] an ageless message of Man's eternal aspirations:

> From delusion lead me to Truth
> From darkness lead me to Light
> From death lead me to Immortality.

Indian religion was the first to assert as its fundamental basis the belief in something above and beyond mankind's eternal round of petty cares, something far higher than a preoccupation with worldly activities. To the perplexity of life mired in the here-and-now of daily existence, it audaciously envisioned a path pregnant with the infinite possibilities of man's true potential—a reality, before which all his mundane experience becomes an illusion; darkness instead of light; death instead of life. To the Indian, religion revealed the arduous ascent requiring the renunciation of his limited self and all its trappings and a striving for oneness with the transcendental Reality, the divine source of all truth and goodness. For him, religion became a vehicle for finding and entering a new dimension of human potential—the dimension of the soul.

Unlike the purely intellectual criterion employed by the much later Platonic school of thought, the Indian theologians, while acknowledging the need for intellectual insight, nevertheless recognized that the ultimate

---

[1] *Katha Upanishad,* 4.1.
[2] *Brihadaranyaka Upanishad,* 1.3, 28.

attainment to this cosmic union was not merely an intellectual step, but required the complete change of one's character, an act of being born again, through long and difficult discipline. They reasoned, therefore, that, since life on this physical plane was really death, the task lay in escaping from it to the eternal abode, which is man's divine destiny. However, the pristine purity of Indian religious thought soon gave way to the emphasis on rituals and forms which every society eventually creates to protect its own 'pecking order'; and, in the ancient Indian religion, this emphasis moved increasingly towards the establishment of a rigid caste system which made the struggle to rise above one's stratum in society and gain a larger share of life's blessings more difficult, if not impossible.

Though little is known of the religious and political history of India in the centuries immediately preceding the birth of Gautama, enough is known to make it certain that this period was full of movement, both inside and outside Brahminical Hinduism. Outside, the ideas and beliefs of Hinduism were being modified by a widespread urge on the part of the intelligentsia, as well as the masses, towards simplicity of doctrine and practice of its intricate rituals—a desire for salvation shorn of the complicated conditions created by centuries of Brahminical rites with meaningless recitations in dead tongues. Inside Brahminical Hinduism, the desire for reform was equally strong in the light of the almost universal deterioration of morals within the very fibre of that religious system. Religious inquiry was being choked by atrophied traditions which increasingly forced the blind acceptance of the Vedas as infallible dogma. The correct performance of rituals and ceremonies became all important and was a constant source of contention and strife between different religious teachers, each claiming truth for his theory or practice and frequently embroiling the civil and political authorities of his region in military action against those in 'error'! This was the broad picture for nearly two centuries prior to the Buddha's arrival on the scene. Purity of religion was progressively deteriorating in the melting pot of mass movement and territorial conquest, and a strong tendency was growing on the part of the religious leaders in the direction of re-examination of the concepts concerning the origin and destiny of man—a deepening religious need was being felt again, leading towards a sweeping transformation of society. It was time once more for a renewal of religion, or a new religion, in order to redirect the essential message of salvation to the persistent and real need of humanity of that time. This need of the times became the task of the Buddha, who directed His message to sweep away the cobwebs of repetitious rites and meaningless dogma in which religion had become entangled, and by so doing to renew the central theme of religion to enable mankind, not only in His native India but also in the world, to attain a truer happiness and fulfil its ultimate potential. This was to be the saving message of His Faith and, in order to more clearly emphasize its separation from the past, He preached it in Maghada Prakrit,[3] the language of the common people of the area, instead of in Sanskrit, the language of the Brahmins. For Him, the ancient dogmas could no longer dominate the imagination, addressing themselves in a dead language to situations and issues that no longer existed: *Better than chanting a thousand words in a dead language is one soothing word spoken in the vernacular.*[4] The shape of life had changed. For Him, the questions of the times had assumed new terms, and He saw too clearly that only if religion engaged in the basic ills of society by helping the world fulfil itself would it once again rise to merit the allegiance of men. To Him, Hindu religion, which, by then, had become steeped in self-interest, class prestige and ecclesiastical niceties, seemed completely hollow. However, notwithstanding the Buddha's resolve to cleanse and revivify the pristine purity of religion, the discerning student of Buddhism, in order to gain a proper perspective of the Buddha's station and a comprehensive appreciation of His teachings, must constantly keep in mind the fact that the Buddha[5] came out of Hindu India—a land impregnated with the thought of the Vedas, Upanishads, Brahmanas and the best known and most beautiful of them all, the *Bhagavad Gita*[6] of Sri Krishna.[7] We must, therefore, expect much more than a passing similarity between the most important concepts underlying the gospel of the Buddha and the thoughts embedded in the Hindu scriptures, especially the *Bhagavad Gita* of Krishna, who preceded the Buddha by nearly five hundred years. It is this subject of conceptual and doctrinal identity between these two great religions of the Indian sub-continent, as a result of their common heritage, that must serve as the best instrument, or a 'Rosetta Stone,' for understanding the Buddha's

---

[3]From Maghada, the country of South Bihar. The Buddha used Prakrit since it was the popular language of the area where he lived, although He must have known Sanskrit, since Prakrit was a derivative of Sanskrit. From this Prakrit was developed the Pali language of the early Buddhist scriptures, especially those scriptures widely accepted by the Theravadin Buddhists. It is almost certain, therefore, that the Buddha himself did not speak Pali. *(See Glossary.)*

[4]*Dhammapada,* v. 100.

[5]As some have succinctly claimed: "Gautama was born, and brought up, and lived, and died a Hindu—He was the greatest, and wisest and best of the Hindus." He was naturally steeped in Hindu lore and is also regarded as the knower of the Vedas *(Samyutta,* i.168: *Sutta-nipata,* 463). See also *Bhagavad Gita,* XV.15. "It is I who am the author of the Vedanta as well as the Knower of the Vedas."

[6]Song (Gita) of the Lord (Bhagavad). Perhaps the most famous religious writings of Hinduism. Recognized as an orthodox scripture of the Hindu religion and possessing equal authority with the Vedas, Upanishads and the Brahma Sutra, forming the triple canon (Prasthana-traya) of Hinduism.

[7]Krishna, the eighth manifestation (avatar) of Vishnu, the most widely revered and most beloved figure in the Hindu pantheon, and author of the *Bhagavad Gita.* By 6th Century B.C. He was elevated to Godhood. Krishna worship is also mentioned in earliest Pali Canon in the Buddhist work *Niddesa (see* Glossary for details).

concept of the Supreme Creator, and the meaning and purpose of His Message (the Dharma). Otherwise, barring this all-consuming emphasis on 'living-the-life' according to His Message, and the Buddha's total insistence that one's deeds should proclaim one's beliefs, there is not much in His doctrine which cannot be found in the earlier Hindu religion and its scriptures extant in His time.

Hence, as with everything else, so too with the gospel of the Buddha, which, to understand, we must retrace our steps to its origins, not only to the place of its birth, but, even more important, to its beginnings in Time. For the hand of Time erases human memory with far greater ease than it effects the physical objects of man's handiwork, and the meaning of a teacher's words are soon altered by the student's understanding and the unconscious, or even deliberate, attempts to suit them to an ever-evolving society. Thus, we see that the original teachings of all the prophets, philosophers and social scientists, unless recorded by their authors, have undergone this fate at the hand of Time. Lacking a system of infallible interpretation of the founder's original teachings, a mechanism established by the founder himself and accepted by his followers as infallible, divisions and differences inevitably occur in every organization involving human understanding. Buddhism was no exception to this tragedy which befalls every Faith. In the absence of any authentically verifiable writings of the Buddha Himself and also of an infallible mechanism to interpret such teachings, His religion, like the Faiths gone before and others yet to come, was cleft with schisms soon after His passing.

Contemporary records of those times tell us that, during the Buddha's life-time, His Faith spread to the Indo-Gangetic plain, although not much is known of its further geographical expansion for some centuries following His death. Its history during the first three centuries of the Buddhist era is occupied mainly by that of the First and Second Buddhist Councils. The First Council[8] was held at Rajgriha within a few weeks (100 days) after the Buddha's death, with a view to collecting his precepts. It was presided over by the venerable Mahakasyapa and attended by five hundred monks including Ananda. However, with the lapse of time, differences arose over the interpretation of the rules for monastic life and within one hundred years after the Buddha's passing, the Second Council was held at Vaisali to condemn the ten extra legal indulgences enjoyed by the local monks. But, these Vaisali monks, not content with the decisions of the Council, rebelled and held a separate meeting, thus creating the Mahasanghika sect which was the precursor of Mahayana.

By the close of its first century, Buddhism had unfortunately already become divided into fourteen different schools of thought as to the original

---

[8]*See* Glossary for further details.

meaning and purpose of the Master's teachings and others soon crystallized. It was also very greatly influenced by the accretions of the sterile Hindu practices and rituals of those times, which surrounded the Buddha's nascent Faith as the desert surrounds the oasis, and like barren desert, those forms and practices of a Hinduism which was then in a period of spiritual stagnation continued to steadily encroach upon the pristine purity of the Buddha's teachings, finally stifling that simplicity of belief and conduct from which early Buddhism derived its life and vigour.

Thus, Buddhism's early history was a constant struggle to preserve its integrity from the inroads of a greatly incrusted Hinduism, from whose body the new Faith had arisen. Its author, the young Gautama, Himself a Hindu, had sought and preached a simple and pure doctrine dedicated to freeing men from their bonds, not the least of these being the meaningless rituals and the rigid caste system of Hinduism in His time. As this constant struggle of Buddhism to remain unpolluted continued on to an inevitable defeat (human nature being what it is), the revulsion by the early Buddhists at Hinduism's more blatant in-roads into their Faith would periodically become crystallized into organized mass effort dedicated to the re-discovery of, and a return to, the original simplicity of the Buddha's teachings, however vague and fragmentary the memory of those teachings or the authenticity of their source. Often, such Buddhist efforts against the too glaring practices of Hinduism took the easiest psychological path of revolt, namely, to oppose that which was the most offensively conspicuous within Hinduism. The focus of early Buddhistic efforts to extricate their young Faith from the coils of the rituals and beliefs of Hinduism was, above all else, directed against the widespread acceptance of a multitude of gods, big and small, personalized and semi-human, which by then had become the central preoccupation of the Hindus, themselves far removed in time from their own pure doctrinal sources. In order to avoid becoming a part of the controversies of His day, the Buddha refrained from giving any names at all, either Brahma, Vishnu, Narayana, Indra etc., to the Supreme. However, fully cognizant of Hinduism's overwhelming preoccupation with these deities he simply relegated them to the empirical order within His world-view and acknowledged the existence of those popularly accepted gods, with Brahma and Indra as their chiefs. By describing them as angels or spirit-beings within the empirical order of His doctrine, He rejected the concept then prevalent that salvation could be reached by supplications and sacrifices to those gods, many of which, according to Him, themselves stood in need of His Dharma (doctrine) to effect their own liberation and were thus envious of, and spiritually inferior to, that true mendicant in the way of the Buddha.

Nor will we find in Buddhism the standard anthropomorphic concepts of God that we have become familiar with, e.g., God the 'Creator', or 'Guide', or 'Friend', or 'Father', or 'Lover', for these are intimate and known symbols, created by the mind of man for itself, and we must agree that by its very nature the 'Unknown' and *the Absolute* cannot be familiar. However, this impossibility of comprehending the utter alieness of *the Absolute* was also well known to the Hindus, and the Buddha's aim was to assert and substantiate this concept of the Supreme, beyond definition, while at the same time eradicating the familiar idols of men's fancies which had become substituted as centers of worship and supplication and which the imagination of men had endowed with attributes of omnipotence.

While one may contend, and correctly so, that the Buddha merely replaced one concept (Brahma) by another (Nirvana), neither of which is really subject to definition or analysis by the Buddha or anyone else, yet His having relegated Brahma and the gods into a corner of His world-view became the chief factor in providing His early followers with a bastion upon which they periodically marshaled their arguments to withstand the encroachment of Hinduism and reinvigorate the central belief of their Faith, that righteous action, and not supplication to gods, would lead them to eternal bliss (Nirvana). However, to a tragically fatal degree this battle against the belief in the powers of the gods of Hinduism became the dominant passion of those early champions of Buddhism, and in their zeal to proclaim and emphasize the efficacy of the Dharma for the attainment of Nirvana, to the total exclusion of anything else, especially those gods and rituals discredited by the Buddha, the early Buddhist theologians found it beyond the scope of their simplistic cosmogony to form a true understanding or even an appreciation of the allusions by the Buddha concerning a *Causeless Cause,* or an *Un-Create,*[9] devoid of shape or size, and instead those Buddhist 'fundamentalists' felt it safer to predicate their philosophy on an adherence to a set of rules, leading to an unimaginable condition of bliss, the attainment of which was determined by a limited causality of discernible and explainable causes and effects, forever turning human actions into their resultant effects *ad-infinitum,* but without a clue to the real origin of this causality (Karma) and, therefore, devoid of the intrinsic meaning of its purpose. It was this tragic attitude which finally congealed into the fallacious doctrine to ignore and eventually deny the belief in an all-pervading, omniscient and omnipotent Cause for the whole scheme-of-things, physical and metaphysical—a fallacy in which the Buddha, as we shall see from His life and teachings, could have had no part. And, while one has no proof as to the time this rejection of a supreme and absolute Reality congealed within early Buddhism, or when it became transformed into a belief in a nebulous state of bliss, Nirvana, which itself was never acknowledged by the Buddha as the ground of all things, since such words of the Buddha as have come down to us concerning an underlying Reality refer to an Entity, *Unoriginated, Unborn,* and not to the

---

[9]*Udana,* 80-81.

state of bliss, *Nirvana,* or non-craving *(there is O monks a state where . . . there is the end of sorrow),* yet, it is well within the realm of possibility that those most interested in giving prominence to and even conceiving this Buddhist credo of non-belief in *the Absolute* might have been the Brahmins themselves, who, seeing the simplicity of the Buddha's doctrine and its dynamic appeal to the masses, by then fatigued and disenchanted with Hinduism's merry-go-round of complicated rituals, realized only too well the danger to their own priestly authority and recognized the 'advantage' of attaching to the Buddha's nascent doctrine that one label, the categorical denial of the existence of God, which would ensure its rejection by the large mass of people. Tragically, that is precisely the fate Buddhism experienced in the land of its birth. Hence, it should be no surprise to note that the denial of the existence of the Supreme or *the Absolute*—God—is, together with the rejection of the Soul, the main aspects of Buddhism to have been 'clearly understood' by the Brahmins!

This fallacious concept that the Buddha did not believe in an all-pervading, all-creating *Causeless Cause* is further aggravated in recent times by many a so-called authority on Buddhism, especially among western writers, jumping into the arena of expounding the Buddha's teachings, oblivious of that all-but-total identity of the Buddha's psyche with the concepts embedded in the philosophy and religion of Hindu India. Prisoners of their own Judaeo-Christian concepts of an anthropomorphic God, these western scholars rush in to analyze, dissect and describe what they conceive to be the meaning of the Buddha's doctrine, in an almost clinical atmosphere of isolation, where the phenomenon of the Buddha and His teachings appear as some detached and alien event, severed from its frame of reference and uprooted from the soil of its physical as well as psychological birth. Such analyses and expositions of the Buddha's teachings, by most if not all western scholars, and many Theravadin writers, has resulted in the production of a deformity. Instead of gaining a clearer understanding of the spiritual, as well as the practical, application of the great religions of the East, each and all predicated upon the belief in the existence of an *Unoriginated* and incomprehensible *Causeless Cause,* periodically manifesting 'Itself' to the world of creation for imparting a progressively wider boost to the evolutionary process of the sentient being or rational soul, such attempts at showing Buddhism as a uniquely different phenomenon, devoid of an underlying Reality, have resulted in the creation of an incongruity within the whole fabric of Religion, wholly contrary to the nature of Buddhism as well as of all Religion.

The whole process of logic contradicts a method of analysis which severs the personality or pronouncements of the founder of a movement—religious or otherwise—from the totality of its surroundings and the ground of its origin. Such a process of fragmentation and isolation, if pursued with reference to Buddhism, would arrive not to the authority of the Buddha's teachings for treading the noble eightfold path, but, instead, the license to follow one's empirical acceptance of an infinite variety of paths, terminating not in any order or organization but in confusion and chaos, thus obviating the need for a Buddha at all! Hence, while such views of the Buddha as a denier of the Supreme (however remote and incomprehensible the nature of that 'Entity') or of Buddhism as an atheistic religion may amuse their authors, with the excitement of a new discovery, a freak occurrence, within the panorama of Religion, yet, to the truth of the Buddha they have no bearing.

Given the very evident limits to man's senses of awareness, including the mind, for conceiving entities outside his own three dimensional world (since he cannot even yet visualize a four dimensional object although he concocts mathematical expressions for it), we can only relegate any cynicism and flippancy concerning this all-important issue (existence of the Supreme), typified by the oft-encountered but patently absurd question: 'if there is a God, who made God', to the category of the equally childish analogy in the 'flat-top' (two-dimensional) world where a painting might similarly ask 'if there is an artist who made the artist?' The painting is obviously incapable of knowing, seeing, or understanding the full reality of the artist. Only we, who are on the plane above and beyond the painting's world of two dimensions, know that the artist surely exists and that this artist, the real cause of the painting, is not the physical human, nor the artist's hand, or the paint, or the brush—the real cause is not in the next higher dimension than the painting, it is not even in the fourth or the fifth dimension etc. It is in a plane beyond dimensions as we conceive. It is in the mind of the artist, 'a vision,' and hence beyond the farthest possibilities of the painting to analyze its cause.

The very nature of the mind is to probe and bring forth, and yet, its existence, to the dimensions and planes of existence below it, can only be discerned through its effects, its creations, its attributes—so must it be with the 'Creator' of the mind. For there, as the writer of the Upanishad states, "words and thoughts cannot reach and the mind turns back on itself. It is known only by its attributes," and as the Buddha confirms, *how can the truth which is inexpressible be taught and heard? It is through Its attributes that it is taught and heard.*

1

GAUTAMA THE BUDDHA

BIRTH AND BACKGROUND

What would be our joy were we able to traverse back in time and separate the legend from the actual historical details of the Buddha's birth and life.

The earliest chroniclers of His life were removed from His time by at least 250 years. Hence, alas, we can never relate with sober fact the salient features of His life with any great confidence.

His given name was Siddharta and family name Gautama. But, whether we call Him Gautama or Sakyamuni,[10] to the centuries that followed and for most of the human race He has become known as Buddha—the Enlightened One.

Siddharta was born a prince of the Sakyas, probably in the year 563[11] before Christ. His father, Suddhodana, was a petty chieftain at Kapilavastu,[12] on the Nepalese border, one hundred miles north of Benares. Lumbini, where Buddha was born, has been identified with the site of Rummindei in the Nepalese Terai. The Sakyas formed one of the many little tribal prin-

---

[10]The Sage of the Sakyas. He is also known as the Tathagata, i.e. he who has fully arrived, meaning one who has attained Nirvana or self-realization.

[11]According to well-nigh unanimous tradition, Siddhartha died in his eightieth year in the year 483 B.C.

[12]The location of Siddharta's birth was later marked by the emperor Asoka with a stone pillar which still stands. The inscription on this column reads: "When King Devanampriya Priyadarsin (Asoka's title in inscriptions) had been anointed twenty years, he came himself and worshipped this spot, because Buddha Sakyamuni was born here . . . . He caused a stone pillar to be set up to show that the Blessed One was born here" (Hultzsch, *Inscriptions of Asoka*, p. 164).

1

cipalities, afterwards swept away in the advancing tide of empire which soon absorbed all the smaller states of Northern India. In due course, Siddharta married His cousin, Yasodhara, who bore Him a son, Rahula. Siddharta's youth and early manhood were surrounded by luxury and the trappings of sensual delight but, notwithstanding the very considerable lengths to which His father, Suddhodana, went to shelter Him from the travails and frustrations of mortal life, some time in his early twenties, He became cognizant of the tragedies of life, such as disease, old age and death, and thus, for the first time, experienced those deep miseries of a world in which physical decay and annihilation are merely the other side of the coin of life and growth. This experience moved Siddharta to puzzle and reflect on the mystery of existence and of its purpose and meaning for human destiny. Siddharta's reflections on His experience and His resolve to unravel its riddle had energized Him. It would now be left to an even deeper experience to bestow on Him the correct direction and define the goal.

ENLIGHTENMENT

It should be of interest to note the similarity between the claims of the Founders of other great Faiths, such as Christ, Moses, Zoroaster, Mohammed, Baha'u'llah, concerning their own enlightenment and awareness of their Prophetic mission through a dawning on their senses of a great spiritual inspiration or vision, taking various forms such as an angel, or a dove, or in the case of Christ, a holy spirit, and the vision that appeared to the Buddha to enlighten and confirm Him on his own Prophetic destiny—that vision of a holy man who had passed away, literally, a holy spirit! Such phenomena, or visions, in the life of the Founders of the great religions seem to be a kind of divine law, similar to the rays of the sun in the physical plane which must be allowed to fall on the moon (in this case the Prophet), before the moon can become a source of light for humanity in the night of the soul.

Here we quote in some detail the episode in the *Jataka Tales* (accepted by all schools of Buddhist thought) of the Buddha's vision and confirmation of his own Prophetic mission:[13]

While the Prince was meditating on the questions of evil, he beheld with his mind's eye under the jambu-tree a majestic and venerable figure. "Who art thou, and from whence thou comest?" asked the prince. The vision replied: "Oh, Bull among men, I am a samana. Troubled at the thought of

---

[13]*Jataka Tales* (Buddha's Birth Stories translated from Pali by Rhys Davids and from the *Fo-Sho-Hing-Tran-King,* a life of Buddha by Ashvaghosha, translated from Sanskrit into Chinese by Dharmarakhsha, A.D. 420, and from Chinese into English by Samuel Beal).

old age, disease, and death[14] I have left my home to seek the path of salvation. All things hasten to decay; only the truth abideth forever. Everything changes, and there is no permanency; yet the words of the Buddhas are immutable. I long for the happiness that does not decay; the treasure that will never perish; the life that knows of no beginning and no end. Therefore, I have destroyed all worldly thought. I have retired into an unfrequented dell to live in solitude; and, begging for food, I devote myself to the one thing needful."

Siddharta asked, "Can peace be gained in this world of unrest? I am struck with the emptiness of pleasure and have become disgusted with lust. All oppresses me, and existence itself seems intolerable."

The samana replied, "Where heat is, there is also a possibility of cold; creatures subject to pain possess the faculty of pleasure; the origin of evil indicates that good can be developed. For these things are correlatives. Thus, where there is much suffering, there will be much bliss, if thou but open thine eyes to behold it. Just as a man who has fallen into a heap of filth ought to seek the great pond of water covered with lotuses, which is nearby; even so seek thou for the great deathless lake of Nirvana to wash off the defilement of wrong. If the lake is not sought, it is not the fault of the lake. Even so when there is a blessed road leading the man held fast by wrong to the salvation of Nirvana, if the road is not walked upon, it is not the fault of the road, but of the person. And when a man who is oppressed with sickness, there being a physician who can heal him, does not avail himself of the physician's help, that is not the fault of the physician. Even so when a man oppressed by the malady of wrong-doing does not seek the spiritual guide of enlightenment, that is no fault of the evil-destroying guide."

The prince listened to the noble words of his visitor and said, "Thou bringest good tidings, for now I know that my purpose will be accomplished. My father advises me to enjoy life and to undertake worldly duties, such as will bring honor to me and to our house. He tells me that I am too young still, that my pulse beats too full to lead a religious life."

The venerable figure shook his head and replied "Thou shouldst know that no time can be inopportune for seeking a religious life.

A thrill of joy passed through Siddharta's heart. "Now is the time to seek religion," he said, "now is the time to sever all ties that would prevent me from attaining perfect enlightenment; now is the time to wander into

---

[14]It should be remembered that these were the very three aspects of life: old age, disease and death concerning which the seers had warned Siddharta's father Suddhodana never to permit his son to know, if Suddhodana wished his son to become an earthly ruler. Otherwise, his son, having knowledge of these failings of earthly existence, would go off to seek the remedy and become a Buddha.

homelessness and, leading a mendicant's life, to find the path of deliverance."

The celestial messenger heard the resolution of Siddharta with approval. "Now, indeed," he added, "is the time to seek religion. Go, Siddharta, and accomplish thy purpose. For thou art Bodhisattva, the Buddha-elect; thou art destined to enlighten the world."

"Thou art the Tathagata, the great master, for thou wilt fulfill all righteousness and be Dharmaraja, the king of truth. Thou art Bhagavad,[15] the Blessed One, for thou art called upon to become the savior and redeemer of the world."

"Fulfill thou the perfection of truth. Though the thunderbolt descend upon thy head, yield thou never to the allurements that beguile men from the path of truth. As the sun at all seasons pursues his own course, nor ever goes on another, even so, if thou forsake not the straight path of righteousness, thou shalt become a Buddha."

"Persevere in thy quest and thou shalt find what thou seekest. Pursue thy aim unswervingly and thou shalt gain the prize. Struggle earnestly and thou shalt conquer. The benediction of all deities, of all saints, of all that seek light is upon thee, and heavenly wisdom guides thy steps. Thou shalt be the Buddha, our Master, and our Lord; thou shalt enlighten the world and save mankind from perdition."[16]

Having thus spoken, the vision vanished, and Siddharta's heart was filled with peace. He said to himself, "I have awakened to the truth and I am resolved to accomplish my purpose. I will sever all the ties that bind me to the world, and I will go out from my home to seek the way of salvation."

"The Buddhas are beings whose words cannot fail; there is no departure from truth in their speech."

"For as the fall of the stone thrown into the air, as the death of a mortal, as the sunrise at dawn, as the lion's roar when he leaves his lair, as the delivery of a woman with child, as all these things are sure and certain—even so the word of the Buddhas is sure and cannot fail."

"Verily, I shall become a Buddha."[17]

Similarly, another version of this same great experience can also be found in *Ashvaghosha Buddhacarita:*[18]

He saw a man glide towards him, who remained invisible to other men,

---

[15] The Life of Buddha by Ashvaghosha in Sanskrit (see also *Sutta nipata*). This title of Bhagavad or Bhagavan meaning the Blessed Lord was also used for Krishna (see *Bhagavad Gita.* V.2; VI.1; etc.).

[16] *Dhammapada,* v. 190.

[17] *Vajraccedika,* also *Jataka Tales.*

[18] *Ashvaghosha Buddhacarita,* vv. 16-21, pp. 66-68.

and who appeared in the guise of a religious, a mendicant. The king's son said to him, "Tell me who you are" and the answer was, "Oh Bull among men, I am a recluse who, terrified by birth and death, have adopted a homeless life to win salvation. Since all that lives is to extinction doomed, salvation from this world is what I wish, and so I search for that most blessed state in which extinction is unknown. Kinsmen and strangers mean the same to me, and greed and hate for all this world of sense have ceased to be. Wherever I may be, that is my home—the root of a tree, a deserted sanctuary, a hill or wood. Possessions I have none, no expectations either. Intent on the supreme goal, I wander about, accepting any alms I may receive." Before the prince's very eyes, he then flew up into the sky. For he was a denizen of the heavens who had seen other Buddhas in the past, and who had come to him in this form so as to remind him of the task before him. When that being had risen like a bird into the sky, the best of men was elated and amazed.

In order to appreciate the Buddha's next step, it is necessary for the reader to understand here that sorrow, tribulation, tragedy and perserverence in perfecting one's self for treading the path of righteousness have been a part of the Hindu view of life even before the time of Rama, the legendary hero of the Ramayana epic. Rama's own privations, misfortunes and exile for fourteen years in the forest served as a constant example to every pious Hindu of those times. It was general practice for most Hindu boys to be taken from their parents at an early age to live the hard life of a novice, under a teacher, for twelve years or longer, before returning to assume the responsibilities of a householder. The Buddha, too, acknowledges and elaborates this same condition and goal:

Let the wise man leave the way of darkness and follow the way of light. After going from his home to a homeless state, that retirement so hard to love, let him there look for enjoyment. Putting away all pleasures, calling nothing his own, let the wise man cleanse himself from all the impurities of the heart.
Dhammapada, vv. 87, 88

But those who in purity and faith live in the solitude of the forest, who have wisdom and peace and long not for earthly possessions, those in radiant purity pass through the gates of the sun to the dwelling-place supreme where the Spirit is in Eternity.
Mundaka Upanishad, 2.11

Therefore, do not take a liking to anything; loss of the loved object is evil. There are no bonds for him who has neither likes nor dislikes.
Dhammapada, v. 211

Dispassion towards the objects of senses, and absence of egoism, constant revolving in mind of the pain and evil inherent in birth, death, old-age and disease.
Bhagavad Gita, XIII.8

Wise people do not say that the fetter is strong which is made of iron, wood, or fibre, but the attachment to earrings made of precious stones, to sons, and wives is passionately impassioned.
Dhammapada, v. 345

Absence of attachment, absence of self-identification with son, wife, home, etc., constant balance of mind both in favourable and unfavorable circumstances.
Bhagavad Gita, XIII.9

5

Wise people call strong this fetter which drags down, yields, and is difficult to unfasten. After having cut this, people renounce the world, free from longings and forsaking the pleasures of sense.

Dhammapada, v. 346

When the wise rests his mind in contemplation on our God beyond time, who invisibly dwells in the mystery of things and in the heart of man, then he rises above pleasures and sorrow.

Katha Upanishad, 2.13

Having tasted the sweetness of solitude and the sweetness of tranquility he becomes free from fear and free from sin, while he drinks the sweetness of the joy of the law.

Dhammapada, v. 205

Unflinching devotion to Me through exclusive attachment of mind, living in secluded and sacred places, absence of pleasure in the company of men.

Bhagavad Gita, XIII.10

He in whom a desire for the Ineffable has arisen, who is replete with mind, whose thought is freed from desires, he is called one who ascends the stream.

Dhammapada, v. 218

When the desires that are in his heart cease then at once the mortal becomes immortal and obtains here in this world Brahman.

Katha Upanishad, IV.10

Thus, history tells us that, after His tremendous experience with the holy man, Siddharta made plans to leave the palace for the homeless life. And upon returning to His palace, He decided to escape during the night. That very night, at midnight, He despatched Channa, his charioteer, to fetch His horse and then went into His bed-chamber to gaze for the last time upon the slumbering forms of His wife and infant boy. There, by the light from the flickering lamp, He beheld Yasodhara sound asleep with her arm over their child. Realizing that His wish to embrace His son for the last time could not be fulfilled for fear of awakening both mother and child, He tore himself away. Leaving behind His wife and only son, His power and riches, and with Channa as his only companion, He departed from His palace to become a homeless ascetic.[19]

After riding a long distance that night, beyond the domain of His wife's father, Gautama dismounted on the bank of the river Anoma beyond the Koliyan territory and, divesting himself of His ornaments, He gave those and His horse to Channa. Ignoring Channa's plea to be allowed to remain with Gautama to serve Him, He ordered Channa to return with them to Kapilavastu to tell His father and relatives what had transpired. When Channa had departed, Gautama cut off His flowing locks and, exchanging His princely clothes with a poor passer-by, continued on towards Rajagriha,[20] the capital of Magadha, ruled by King Bimbisara, the most powerful prince of the eastern Gangetic plain, there to pursue His quest for that ineffable peace of mind impervious to the twists and turns of life. Rajagriha was

---

[19]This is the circumstance which later came to be known as the Sutra of the Great Renunciation. *Mahabhinishkramana Sutra* (Sanskrit original).

[20]For a detailed description of the ruins at Rajagriha (modern Rajgir), see General Cunningham's *Ancient Geography of India—Buddhist Period*, pp. 462-468. The ruins of the walls of the new citadel built by Bimbisara are still traceable.

pleasantly situated in a valley surrounded by five hills which formed the northernmost limb of the Vindhya mountain range. The many caves of the hills surrounding Rajagriha had become the abodes of several ascetics and, noting the proximity of the town for conveniently procuring the simple wants while being far enough removed from the town to provide the solitude of nature for contemplating upon the mysteries of life, the young Siddharta, too, decided to settle there in one of the caves and at first became the student of a Brahmin ascetic named Alara Kalama and then later of another Brahmin named Udraka Ramaputra, absorbing from them their own philosophy and all the doctrine (dharma) and discipline (vinaya) about this world or the next contained in Hinduism. Gautama, too, like other leaders of thought, was to a great extent the product of His world and, hence, the search for relationship between Buddhism and the different systems of Hindu philosophy is far more interesting than any difficulties involved in its deciphering. Well before the time of Gautama, the Brahmins had delved into the most abstruse questions of religion and metaphysics and, although divided in their concepts, those different Brahminical schools of thought formed the considerable core from which Gautama Himself was to develop His own doctrine. His genius in this field did not consist so much in the origination of hitherto unknown concepts of metaphysics or ethics as on the total emphasis placed in His doctrine on moral behaviour and right action, through a reasoned enunciation of those very precepts already found embedded in the thought of the Upanishads and the *Bhagavad Gita.*

Unsatisfied with the teachings and discipline imparted to Him by His Brahmin teachers, Alara and Udraka, Gautama resolved to detach Himself from them, and with the words of His 'vision' perhaps still ringing in His ears, He forsook His abode in the hills around Rajagriha and withdrew into the forests of Uruvela[21] and there, for six years, together with five[22] disciples, undertook the severest penances and self-mortification which to the Hindu ascetics of His day seemed to provide the surest means for achieving those powers and capacity that rival the gods. While the news of His self-mortification and penances enabled His fame to spread around "like the sound of a great bell hung in the canopy of the skies"[23] and excited the esteem and envy of lesser men, Gautama Himself obtained no abiding sense of peace from His rigours. The more He drove and examined Himself, the greater grew His anguish born of doubt[24] in the efficacy of the methods He had embarked upon. And He began to fear that all his efforts would be to no avail

---

[21]Near the temple of Buddha Gaya. See Beal's *Travels of Fa Hian,* p. 120.

[22]These Five were: Kondanna, Bhaddhiya, Vappa, Mahanama, Assaji.

[23]Bigandet, p. 49 (first edition); compare *Jataka,* pp. 67, 27.

[24]Gautama's doubts and disquietudes at this juncture are again represented as temptations of the visible Tempter, the Arch-enemy, Mara. (Alabaster, *Wheel of the Law,* p. 140.)

and that He might die before achieving that ineffable certitude. If only He could attain to that peace of mind for which He longed, all His suffering through self-mortification and even death itself would have been worth the cost. But this was not to be. At least not then and not by the method He visualized.

At last, the rigours of His penances inflicted their toll on His physical body and one day, when walking together with His disciples, lost in meditation, He swooned and collapsed and His companions thought that He had expired. But, upon reviving and recognizing the futility of such rigours, He discarded this method of self-humiliation as the road to enlightenment and began to take proper nourishment again. Then, when He stood in greatest need of solace and encouragement, His disciples deserted Him and left for Benares. Their faith in the doctrine of self-mortification was too strong to countenance what to them appeared as a renunciation on Gautama's part of this cherished principle of theirs. Thus, abandoned and unfulfilled, He despaired of ever achieving His goal.

Gautama had forsaken all that men prized and sought so that He might achieve peace of mind. To gain His goal He had become a novice to others and undergone all the disciplines of meditation and penances that they had to impart. Unsatisfied, He had practised the severest self-denial and self-mortification, but His goal had eluded Him. His quest appeared to be in vain. And, at last, when His unshakeable resolve and faith had ultimately collapsed, He received the final blow—His so-called friends and disciples deserting and going off to Benares. But fate was to take a different turn. That very day, when His friends and followers had departed, He wandered out towards the river Nairanjara, accepting His morning meal from Sujata, the daughter of a villager close by, and sat down to eat under the shade of a large fig tree.[25] He probably had no inkling at this time of darkest despair that He was about to reach His goal and so remained throughout the day mulling over His next course of action. For He no longer had any confidence in the discipline and penance He had practiced so long, since all those rigours had brought Him no nearer to the peace of mind, and now the delightful memories of His previous life, in the comfort of the palace amidst His wife

---

[25](Ficus religiosa). From that time on it came to be known as the "tree of enlightenment." It became to the followers of the Buddha what the cross is to the Christians. It was actually worshipped and a shoot from it is still growing on the spot where the Buddhist pilgrims found it, and where it is believed the original tree had grown in the ancient temple at Bodh-Gaya, near Rajagriha, built by Amara Sinha around 540 A.D. Soon after the arrival of the first Buddhist mission to Ceylon under Mahinda, the son of Ashoka, following the Council of Patna, we read that Mahinda's sister Sanghamitta arrived to join Mahinda and brought with her a branch of the original sacred Bo tree and this was planted at Anuradhapura, a little to the south of the Ruwanwaeli Dogaba, where it still grows. The best estimates put it at 2217 years since it was planted in 245 B.C. There is a prophecy concerning it when it was planted, that it would live and grow forever.

and family, had begun once again to torture Him. However, He shirked off such thoughts, knowing that in the end this life of the flesh and its pleasures would only reach its inevitable bitter fruit of sorrow and pain. He continued on His meditation, passing from stage to stage, of the ephemeral joys of life and their pitfalls, and at last, as the sun was setting to plunge the land into the darkness of the night, that realization of the truth concerning life and its purpose and all else that is dawned on Him, endowing Him with that supreme secret in the blazing glory of which all darkness of doubt evaporated, and in its light Siddharta knew Himself. He was Buddha. [26]   The spiritual sun-burst had occurred while the physical sun had set.

The commentary on the *Brahmajala Sutta* tells us that, at the moment of enlightment, the Buddha with intense elation proclaimed His tremendous victory by the following verses:

I have run through a course of many births looking for the maker of this dwelling and finding him not; painful is birth again and again. Now you are seen, O builder of the house, you will not build the house again. All your rafters are broken, your ridge-pole is destroyed, the mind, set on the attainment of nirvana, has attained the extinction of desires.
Dhammapada, vv. 153, 154

The Essentially unmanifestable moveth within, the Lord of Generation vividly manifesteth Himself repeatedly; the steadfast behold from all sides the abode of the Original Cause; in that abide the worlds of the universe.
Yajur Veda, XXXI.19

Having reached that place supreme, the seers find joy in wisdom, their souls have fulfillment, their passions gone, they have peace. Filled with devotion, they have found the Spirit in all and go into the All.
Mundaka Upanishad, 3.2, 5

DIVINE STATION

It may be argued by some, and perhaps correctly so, that in the light of what He was to claim, i.e. the uniqueness of His kind, it was not only discipline or dharma that had led Him to Buddhahood but an *exaltation from the Absolute,* and that He only went through the gamut of penances and vigils in order to demonstrate to His disciples and friends that the ascetics and savants of His day were howling up the wrong tree and that Buddhahood was a world apart, a destined event. Early Buddhist legends recount that before His advent in this world Gautama Buddha was a Bhodisattva or Buddha potential in the Tusita heaven. It was at the request of the Tusita gods that he agreed to descend to earth to preach the Dharma for the salvation of mankind. He considered the time, continent, country and family in which he would choose to be born for the last time and decided that his mother should be queen

---

[26] *Mahavagga,* 1.5.

THE GOD OF BUDDHA

Maya and his father Suddhodana, the Chief of the Sakya clan of Kapilavastu in Jambudvipa (India):

The gods approached the Future Buddha in the heaven of delight (Tusita) and prayed to Him: "O Blessed One, you did not attain the ten perfections from the desire for the glories of Indra or Mara or Brahma or of a mighty emperor but you fulfilled them for achieving Omniscience so that mankind can be saved. Now has the moment come, O Blessed One, for thy Buddhahood; now has the time, O Blessed One, arrived."
, *Nidana-Katha*, p. 62
(Bombay University edition, 1953)

Arjuna, My birth and activities are divine. He who knows this in reality does not take birth again on leaving his body, but attains Me.
Bhagavad Gita, IV.9

This narrative shows some clear contradictions, unless one views it as an allegory within the context of the already accepted Hindu thought of the day that the Buddha was the recurring manifestation of the Omniscient and Almighty throughout recorded history. Otherwise, it would show that the gods in the Tusita heaven knew something that the Buddha, despite His omniscience, did not know, namely, that *it was time for Him to go down to earth for the salvation of mankind!* This also alludes to the existence of that law declared by Krishna in the Gita, "I am born from age to age,"[27] in conformity with which these high beings, the Divine Teachers, periodically appear for fulfilling, according to the Buddha's words, *the task set me.* And also that the privations endured by the Buddha for six years in the forest, in imitation of the Hindu ascetics of His day, were merely to prove that those practices which he had himself tested were futile in achieving the goal of transcendental enlightment and for *turning the wheel of Dharma.* This view is further substantiated by the episode of His first vision of that 'holy being' and Gautama's assertion of certain success: *Verily I shall become the Buddha.* Nevertheless, whatever the case may be, from that day on He not only claimed no merit on the performance of such penances and vigils but at every opportunity discredited such disciplines, stating that no merit could be derived from them.

However, as the efficacy of sacrifices and penances seemed to Him to fade into nothingness before the simplicity and power of the Truth that He had so dramatically beheld and which He now desired to preach to the world, the greater became the intensity of His feeling at the immense chasm separating His new found system and the worn-out beliefs of those about Him. Yet, despite the unbridgeable gap between the utter simplicity of His doctrine and

---

[27]*Bhagavad Gita*, IV. 7, 8.

the paraphernalia of multitudinous rites, charms, priestly powers, spirits and gods, which men of those days had come to trust and adore, He decided to go into this blinded world and proclaim His message of enlightenment and salvation, if for no other cause than in conformity with His innate love and pity for the mass of deluded humanity blindly groping for enlightenment and flight from this bramble-bush of existence. Gautama, like Krishna before Him and Jesus and Mohammed who followed, had an intense belief in Himself, and any sense of apprehension He may have had dissolved in the unbounded belief in His mission. As the story goes, Gautama at first decided to present His old teachers, Alara and Udraka, with the news of His great discovery but, learning that they were no longer alive, He resolved to go to Benares to proclaim His message to His former disciples. However, on the road to Benares, He met a young Brahmin acquaintance named Upaka and from him received His first rebuff. The account of the conversation is only preserved for us in one of the less known biographies,[28] but it is nevertheless worth relating as it once again indicates the unique nature of the Buddhas: "The Brahmin, surprised at Gautama's expression and carriage, says to him, 'The senses of others are restless like horses, but yours have been tamed. Other beings are passionate, but your passions have ceased. Your form shines like the moon in the night sky, and you appear to be refreshed by the sweet savour of a wisdom newly tested. Your features shine with intellectual power, you have become master over your senses, and you have the eyes of a mighty bull. No doubt that you have achieved your aim. Who then is your teacher, who has taught you this supreme felicity? Whence comes it that thy form is so perfect, thy countenance so lovely, thy appearance so peaceful? What system of religion is it that imparts to thee such joy and such peace?'"

To this question, Gautama replies, in verse, that He has overcome all worldly influences, ignorance, sin, and desire.

Then the Brahmin asks whither He is going, and on hearing He was going to Benares, asks Him for what purpose. To this, the Buddha replies by the following verse:

I now desire to turn the wheel of the excellent law. For this purpose I am going to that city of Benares to give light to those enshrouded in darkness, and to open the gate of Immortality to men.
Majjhima-nikaya, v. 26

I stretch bow for the howling in order to kill the tyrant and also enemies of the Great God; I create all happiness for the people, I enter, prevailed in Heaven and earth, clad in the attire of Manifestation.
Atharva Veda, IV. 30-5

He then informs Upaka that, having completely conquered all sin, and forever rid of every vestige of self, He desires, by the light of his religious system, to enlighten all, even as the moon enlightens all, that He is now on his

---

[28] *Mahavagga,* I.6, 7-9. See also *Majjhima-nikaya,* 26.

way to Varanasi, for the salvation of humanity still groping blindly and there to beat the eternal Dharma's drum, to set men free. Upaka, however, is unable to entertain what to him seem high-flown pretensions on Gautama's part and saying, "Venerable Gautama, your way lies yonder," himself turns away in the opposite direction, although repeatedly looking back with envy and wonder at the receding form of the Buddha.

Unfortunately, we do not have this episode in Pali, the Jataka commentary merely states that Gautama, on His way to Benares, met Upaka and announced to him His having become a Buddha.[29]

Ignoring this affront by Upaka, the new Prophet proceeded to Benares and, as dusk was falling, arrived at the deer park some three miles north of the city where He knew His former disciples to be then living. His arrival is noticed by the five who agree not to acknowledge Him as their teacher, since in their eyes he had failed in His attempts at mastery over His body and therefore forfeited every claim to any allegiance from them. However, one of them, Kondanna, refused to show any disrespect, but Gautama noticed the change of manner in the others and told them they were wrong in calling Him "Venerable Gautama," that they were still blind and ignorant and would continue in the cycle of births and deaths, whereas He had discovered the long hidden path to liberation and, having attained enlightenment (Buddhahood), He could also show them the way to rise above the sins and sorrows of existence.

Do not call the Tathagata by His name nor address Him as 'friend,' for He is the Buddha, the Holy One. The Buddha looks with a kind heart equally on all living beings, and they therefore call Him 'Father.' To disrespect a father is wrong; to despise him is wicked.
Mahavagga, I.6

Ignorant of this greatness of Yours, and thinking You only to be a friend, the way in which I have wantonly addressed You, either through heedlessness or even affection, as 'Krishna,' 'Yadava,' 'Friend' and so on, and the way in which You have been slighted by me in jest while playing, reposing in bed, sitting or dining, either alone or in the presence of others—I crave forgiveness for all that from You, who are infinite, O infallible Lord. Therefore, Lord, laying my body at Your feet and bowing low, I seek to propitiate You, the ruler of all and worthy of all praise. It behoves You to condone my fault even as a father condones the fault of his son, a friend that of his friend and the loving husband that of his beloved consort.
Bhagavad Gita, XI.41, 42, 44

However, their belief in Hindu asceticism was too deeply ingrained for them not to protest that Gautama, Who had failed before when He had His body under control, was hardly the one Who should be preaching to them now that

---

[29]*Jataka Tales* (Fausboll's translation, pp. 24, 63, 81).

He so freely catered to His physical needs. Gautama responded to their scorn and cynicism of Him and His system by setting forth the basic precepts of His religion. This account is preserved for us in the *Dhammacakkappavattana Sutta* (the Sutra of the Foundation of the Kingdom of Righteousness).

Now, while it is easy to see that we could not have any 'Buddhism' unless a Buddha had revealed it, we must, nevertheless, bear in mind that 'Buddha' is not the name of a person but designates a type. 'Buddha' in Sanskrit means someone who is 'fully enlightened' about the nature and meaning of life. Numerous 'Buddhas' appear successively at suitable intervals, and one of the most important facets of our premise, that the Buddha, like Krishna, Christ, and the other Prophets, was also inspired and endowed with His own mission by the Supreme Creator, rests on the fact that Buddhism clearly does not consider itself to be the record of the sayings of one man who lived in northern India about 500 B.C., but His teachings are represented as the uniform result of an oft-repeated manifestation of spiritual reality into this world.

In Pali and Sanskrit texts, the word 'Buddha' is always used as a title, not as a name. The historical Buddha, i.e. Gautama, is represented to have taught that He was only one of a long succession of Buddhas who appear at intervals in the world and who all teach the same religion. After the death of each Buddha, his religion (dharma) flourishes for a time, and then decays, till it is at last completely forgotten. The world is then steadily enveloped in wickedness. At last, a new Buddha appears, who again preaches the lost doctrine (dharma) of truth and gradually succeeds in improving the world and freeing humanity from sin, and so on *ad infinitum*. The names of twenty-four of these Buddhas who appeared previous to Gautama have been handed down to us, and in a period of 5,000 years, when the true message of Gautama is forgotten, and people will have strayed far from the path of salvation, a new Buddha will arise to again open the door of Nirvana to humanity. He will be called 'Maitrya Buddha,' which means the Buddha whose name is 'Kindness'.

Hence, it seems that the correct perspective from which to view the Buddha and His doctrine would be, according to His own words, as one of the *fully enlightened beings*, continuously manifesting themselves for the guidance and salvation of humanity—*the fully omniscient teachers of mankind*. This is the same role described half a millenium earlier by Krishna in his dialogue with Arjuna, namely, His own act of "bodying forth," time and time again for the triumph of the good and the "re-establishment of religion on a firm basis."[30] Thus, a continuity of Avatars (Manifestations), or Buddhas, or divine Messengers, or by whatever name the reader may wish to identify these great spiritual suns, becomes clearly recognizable in the annals of the slow but

---

[30]*Bhagavad Gita*, IV.7, 8. Also *Yajur Veda*, XXXI.19.

steady progress of humanity towards a higher state of ethical, social and scientific achievement, and the phenomenon called civilization, whether oriental or occidental, Roman or Persian, Indian or Chinese, Arab or European, when traced to its ultimate source is seen to be predicated on the ethical and social teachings of one or the other of these great divine Founders of religions.

These great spiritual luminaries, the divine teachers, the Buddhas, are no more different from each other than the sun of today is from the sun of yesterday or the sun of tomorrow. There are no yesterdays, todays and tomorrows on the sun. Only we who live on its satellites (the planets) experience these differences of days and nights due to the rotations of these planets during their revolutions around the solar orb. Hence, while it appears to us as rising and setting and rising again, sometimes from slightly different spots, the sun neither rises nor sets. The conditions of our world obscure only our view of the sun, they can neither touch nor effect its reality and power, for the sun is ever shining. Likewise, notwithstanding the desires and the ego that cloud the minds of men from experiencing spiritual light and understanding the essential oneness of the divine suns, the Buddhas, *there is no distinction between any of the Buddhas . . . for all the Buddhas are exactly the same as regards Buddha-dhammas.*[31]

Thus, Gautama, while affirming His identity with the Buddhas of the past, with equal forthrightness asserts what He is not, namely, that He is not human nor one of the petty gods or demons that the people of His time imagined and believed in:

I am not a Brahmin, rajah's son or merchant; nor am I any what; I fare in the world a sage, of no-thing, homeless, self-completely gone out—it is inept to ask me of my lineage.
Sutta-nipata, vv. 455-56 (condensed)

Neither gods nor the great sages know the secret of My birth; for I am the prime cause in all respects of gods as well as of the great seers.
Bhagavad Gita, X.2

This is further elaborated in the *Anguttara-nikaya.*[32]

At one time the Lord was journeying along the high-road between Ukkattha and Setabbya; so also was the Brahmin Dona. Dona approached the Lord and said: "Is your reverence a deva?" "No indeed, Brahmin, I am not a deva." "Then a gandharva?" 'No indeed, Brahmin." "A yaksha then?" "No indeed, Brahmin, I am not a yaksha." "Then is your reverence a human being?" "No indeed, Brahmin, I am not a human being." "You answer No to all my questions. Who then is

---

[31] *Milindapanha,* p. 285.

[32] *Anguttara-nikaya,* 11, 37-39. Also *Dhammapada,* vv. 58, 59.

your reverence?" "Brahmin, those outflows whereby, if they had not been extinguished, I might have been a deva, gandharva, yaksha or a human being—those outflows are extinguished in me, cut off at the root, made like a palm tree stump that can come to no further existence in the future. Just as a blue, red or white lotus, although born in the water, grown up in the water, when it reaches the surface stands there unsoiled by the water—just so, Brahmin, although born in the world, grown up in the world, having overcome the world, I abide unsoiled by the world. Take it that I am Buddha, Brahmin. As a lotus, fair and lovely, by the water is not soiled, by the world am I not soiled. Therefore, Brahmin, am I Buddha."

The Lord of Generations, the One greater than Whom none else is begotten, the One in the attire of Manifestation (Avatar), entered, inhabiting the worldly abodes, bestowing the richest bliss, He is the Bearer of the threefold splendor.

Yajur Veda, XIII.36

I am the source of all creation. Everything in the world moves because of Me, knowing thus the wise, full of devotion, worship Me.

Bhagavad Gita, X.8

And, again, to show that Buddhas are a race apart, when King Suddhodana invites his son Gautama to visit Kapilavastu, His birthplace, and meet His old father, and His wife, Yasodhara, and His now grown-up son, Rahula, the Buddha arrives with a begging bowl and garbed in an ascetic's robe. When Suddhodana asks Gautama why the ascetic's robe and beggar's bowl, the Buddha informs him that this is the manner of His race. When asked "what race"? by a surprised Suddhodana, the Buddha replies:

The Buddhas who have been and who shall be; Of these am I and what they did, I do, And this, which now befalls, so fell before, that at his gate a king in warrior mail should meet his son, a prince in hermit weeds.

And it is I who am installed in the hearts of all; from Me are memory and knowledge as well as their loss. I am indeed He who is to be known by all the Vedas. I indeed am the author of the Vedanta and I too the knower of the Vedas.

Bhagavad Gita, XV.15

It is a very moving moment when the brave old king states, in mistaken concept of his son's status, that he and his lineage are descended from an illustrious race of warriors who had never been known to beg, only to learn that his son was of a different breed and more than mortal—a divine teacher of humanity, a Buddha. It is on this occasion that the Buddha, informing His father of having found that hidden treasure (Dharma), states that it is His duty to first present His father with that precious jewel, and thus takes this opportunity to reveal two verses of the *Dhammapada:*[33]

Get up (rouse yourself), do not be thoughtless. Follow the law of virtue. He who practices virtue lives happily in this world as well as in the world beyond. Follow the law of virtue, do not follow the law of sin. He who practises virtue lives happily in this world as well as in the world beyond.

Divine virtues are regarded as conducive to liberation and demoniacal properties as conducive to bondage. Grieve not, Arjuna, for you are born with divine virtues.

Bhagavad Gita, XVI.5

---

[33]*Dhammapada*, vv. 168, 169.

THE GOD OF BUDDHA

To show that the appearance of a Buddha is rare but, nevertheless, a destined occurrence—a law in itself—the Buddha, in relation to his own predecessors as well as His successor who was yet to come, related this verse:

In this auspicious aeon three leaders have there been. Kakasandha, Konagamana[34] and the leader Kassapa too. I am now the perfect Buddha; And there will be Metteyya too before this same auspicious aeon runs to the end of its years.
Anagata-Vamsa, p. 34

Sri Bhagavan said: "I taught this imperishable Yoga to Vivasvan; Vivasvan told it to Manu and Manu spoke it to Ikshvaku."[35]
Bhagavad Gita, IV.1

And, again, Sariputta, a Tathagata remembers a variety of former habitations. . . . Thus does he remember diverse former habitations in all their mode and detail.
Majjhima-nikaya, 1.69-71

Arjuna said: "You are of recent origin, while the birth of Vivaswan dates back to remote antiquity. How, then, am I to understand that you taught at the beginning of creation!"
Bhagavad Gita, IV.4

[36]*At that time Ananda was the king and I myself was the golden peacock.*
Jataka, II.33-38

Sri Bhagavan replied: "Arjuna, you and I have passed through many births. I know them all, while you do not, O chastiser of foes."
Bhagavad Gita, IV.5

The Lord is speaking: "He, Vasettha, whose faith in the Tathagata is settled, rooted, established, firm, a faith not to be shaken by a recluse or Brahmin or deva or by Mara or Brahma or by anyone in the world—he may say: 'I am the Lord's own son, born of his mouth, born of Dhamma, formed by Dhamma, heir to Dhamma.' What is the reason for this? This, Vasettha, is a synonym for the Tathagata; Dhamma-body and again Brahma-body, and again Dhamma-become and again Brahma-become."
Digha-nikaya, III.84

He, who is happy within himself, enjoys within himself the delight of the soul, and even so is illumined by the inner light, such a Yogi identified with Brahma attains Brahma, who is all Peace.
Bhagavad Gita, V.24

Rama, Krishna and Buddha were all princes who taught the highest wisdom. These great teachers arose to renew Religion for humanity in their times. They were not only spiritually related as divine Messengers, but, and this is surprising, also geneologically. To gain some understanding of the close

---

[34]Pali-names of Krakacchanda, Kanakamuni, Kasyapa, and Maitrya. See also *Manorathaparani*, 87-90.

[35]Sanskrit Ikshvaku of Pali—Okkaka (Rulers of the ancient Solar dynasty). Vivasvan is also known as the Sun-god and Manu is his son while Ikshvaku is supposed to be the son of Manu. However, this 'sonship' of Manu to Vivasvan and Ikshvaku to Manu is not to be taken in the literal sense, since each of them were separated in time by hundreds of years, but should be understood as spiritual sonship just as indicated by the Buddha in the above quote: "I am the Lord's own son, born of His mouth, born of Dhamma . . ."

[36]In *Saddharmapundarika*, XV.1. The Buddha also claimed to have been the teacher of countless Bodhisattvas in bygone ages. Such statements, mean not any re-incarnation of the individual personality, either physical or mental, but, merely refer to the recurring principle of the Divine manifesting Itself throughout the ages and Its consequences in bringing to light the principal molds of human character, e.g. 'faithfulness' as portrayed by an Arjuna (or an Ananda) and the opposite as manifested by a Devadatta. The Manifestation being all-knowing knows of this recurring theme, but, His disciples do not.

geneological relationship, it should be noted that the Ikshvaku mentioned in the afore-referred verse (IV.1) of the *Bhagavad Gita* was the Ikshvaku of the Solar dynasty, who is none other than Rama, the hero of the Ramayana and regarded as the seventh incarnation of Vishnu by the Hindus, who also regard Krishna and Buddha as respectively the eighth and ninth incarnations of Vishnu. Moreover, this same lineage of Rama (Ikshvaku or Okkaka in Pali) continued throughout the centuries that followed, to acknowledge and encourage the promulgation of the Teachings of Rama, Krishna and the Buddha. Adequate testimony of such patronization by the kings of the Ikshvaku dynasty and their people is the abundance of Buddhist stupas and monasteries in the Krishna valley from the third century B.C. to the third century A.D. Some of their cities such as Amaravati, Goli and Nagar-junakonda, which grew into prosperous cosmopolitan centres of Buddhist activities, clearly contain inscriptions attesting to the munificence of the princesses of the ruling Ikshvaku family. A remarkable example of continuity and acknowledgement of not only a spiritual kinship between Rama, Krishna and the Buddha, but more especially, in the India of those days, where family relationship was considered of paramount importance, a striking indication of physical kinship between the Ikshvaku (Okkaka) and the Sakyas from whom the Gautama Buddha was descended and concerning which the following discourse from *Digha-nikaya*[37] is quite specific:

Long ago ... King Okkaka,[38] *wanting to divert the succession in favour of the son of his favourite queen, banished his elder children. ... And being thus banished they took up their dwelling on the slopes of the Himalayas on the borders of a lake where a mighty oak plantation grew. Okkaka the king burst forth in admiration: "Hearts of Oak (Sakya) are those young fellows! Right well they hold their own!" "That is the reason ... why they are known as Sakyas. Verily he is the progenitor of Sakyas."*

Of the Adityas, I am Visnu...
Bhagavad Gita, X.21

Among purifiers, I am the wind; among wielders of weapon, I am Rama.
Bhagavad Gita, X.31

Thus, the Buddha claims, that His clan, the Sakya, is descended from the elder children of the Okkaka[39] king. In order to appreciate the very intimate relationship in the Buddha's kinship with Rama, it should be noted that, in the first paragraph of the above quotation from the *Digha-nikaya*, the Okkaka (or Ikshvaku) king is Dasa-Ratha (mentioned in the Ramayana as

---

[37] *Digha-nikaya*, Part I, pp. 103-104, Bombay University ed., 1942.

[38] Okkaka (Pali): identical to Ikshvaku in Sanskrit.

[39] Suddhodana Gautama, father of Siddharta, claimed descent from the Okkaka kings of the Solar dynasty.

17

the ruler of Ayodhya) who, at the instigation of his favorite younger queen, Kaikeyi, diverted the succession to her son, Bharat, instead of his eldest son, Rama, and sent Rama off to a fourteen year exile in the oak forest girdling the slopes of the nearby Himalayas. Rama was accompanied on his exile by his wife, Sita (the heroine of Ramayana), and by his other two younger brothers, Lachman and his twin Satrughna. Secondly, the *Digha-nikaya* points out that Dasa-Ratha, the Okkaka king, called his sons (Rama, Lachman and Satrughna) Sakyas (meaning, men with hearts of oak), and that these, and by extension their father, are the progenitors of the Sakyas. Further investigation shows that Rama and his brothers, and more specifically Rama himself, were the progenitors of the Sakyas, for the Sakyas are the descendents of Lava, the elder of the two sons of Rama. Lava founded and ruled Sravasti, which in the time of the Buddha was the capital of Ayodhya (Oudh). Sravasti, known as the 'city of wonders' and a holy city, is just a short distance northwest of Kapilavastu (the Buddha's birthplace), close to which is also the other sacred city of ancient times, Ramagrama (Deokati), supposedly founded by Rama. The Ramayana tells us that Rama's second son, Kusa, founded and ruled Kusavati at the foot of the Vindhya mountains. Of Rama's other brothers, Lachman had two sons, Angada and Chandraketu. The former founded the kingdom of Karupada, and the latter founded the city of Chandrakanti in the Malwa country. Satrughna had two sons, Suvahu and Satrughati. The former became king of Mathura, later to become renowned and considered a sacred city because of its association with Krishna. The other son, Satrughati of Satrughna, founded Vridisha. Bharat had two sons, Taksha and Pushkala. The former founded Taksha-sila, to the east of the Indus, and known to Alexander and the Greeks as Taxila. The latter founded Pushkala-vati, to the west of the Indus, and known to the Greeks as Peukelaotis. Thus the sons of Bharat are said to have founded kingdoms which flourished on either side of the Indus river. As we see from the above, the lineage of Bharat, Lachman, and Satrughna was rather removed from the locality of the Sakya homeland and only Rama's sons Lava and Kusa, and more especially Lava, were the progenitors of the Sakya clans.

So that we may not confuse the uniqueness of Rama, Krishna and the Buddhas and their rare appearances at intervals of hundreds of years with the claims and views of those many naive people who think that they, too, have achieved Buddhahood by some course of exercises, or a formula, or some discipline of study, or privations, we list below some excerpts which hopefully, will serve to disabuse us of such notions and clearly demonstrate that between mortals and those unique divine personages—the holy Prophets and Messengers—there is not only a difference of degree, immeasurable though that may be, but also a difference of kind. They are a different creation—destined events, akin to sunrise:[40]

Subhuti, what do you think? When the Tathagata was with Dipankara[41] Buddha, was there any dharma (formula)[42] for the attainment of the Consummation of Incomparable Enlightenment? 'No, World-honored One, as I understand the Buddha's meaning, there was no dharma by which the Tathagata attained the Consummation of Incomparable Enlightenment.' 'Buddha, said: You are right, Subhuti! Verily there was no dharma by which the Tathagata attained the Consummation of Incomparable Enlightenment. Subhuti, had there been any such dharma, Dipankara Buddha would not have predicted concerning me: 'In the ages of the future you will come to be a Buddha called Sakyamuni'; but Dipankara Buddha made that prediction concerning me because there is actually no dharma for the attainment of the Consummation of Incomparable Enlightenment. The reason herein is that Tathagata is a signification implying all dharmas. In case anyone says that the Tathagata attained the Consummation of Incomparable Enlightenment, I tell you truly, Subhuti, that there is no dharma by which the Buddha attained it. Subhuti, the basis of the Tathagatha's attainment of the Consummation of Incomparable Enlightenment is wholly beyond; it is neither Sat (reality) nor Asat (non-Reality).

Vajra-Sattva, XVII (No one attains Transcendental Wisdom.) Also Nidana-Katha, I

Discrimination, true wisdom, sanity, forgiveness, truth, control over the senses and the mind, joy and sorrow, evolution and dissolution, fear and fearlessness, nonviolence, equanimity, contentment, austerity, charity, fame and disrepute—these diverse feelings of creatures emanate from Me alone.

Bhagavad Gita, X.4.5

Arjuna, I radiate heat as the sun, and hold back as well as send forth showers. I am immortality as well as death: I am being and non-being both.

Bhagavad Gita, IX.19

O noble soul, why should they not bow to You, who are the progenitor of Brahma himself and the greatest of the great? O infinite Lord of celestials, Abode of the universe, You are that which is existent (Sat) and that which is non-existent (Asat), and also that which is beyond both, viz. the indestructible Brahma. You are the prime Deity, the most ancient Person, You are the ultimate resort of this universe. You are both the knower and the knowable, and the highest abode. It is You who pervades the universe, assuming endless forms.

Bhagavad Gita, XI.37.38

Now I shall speak to you at length about that which ought to be known, and knowing which one attains immortality; that beginningless supreme Brahma is said to be neither Sat (Reality) nor Asat (non-Reality).

Bhagavad Gita, XIII.12

---

[40]Rama, Krishna and Buddha all claimed their clan's descent from the Sun—obviously a spiritual connotation signifying Light, Knowledge, Life, to the peoples of their times and to most of us even to this day.

[41]A former Buddha, Gautama's twenty-fourth predecessor.

[42]Dharma also denotes Formula.

THE GOD OF BUDDHA

Otherwise, anyone could by assiduously applying himself to religious study and by practising some formula for spiritual progress attain to Buddhahood. The reference to Buddha Dipankara's prediction about the future Buddha implies that this phenomenon (Buddha-rising) is an act of grace from *a wholly beyond; neither real nor unreal,* the 'Norm' or the 'Mean' entirely outside the scope of dualistic opposites and co-relatives. The reader may also wish to see the similarity of prophetic prediction by the Buddha Sakyamani to his favorite disciple, Ananda, concerning the future advent of the Buddha to be—Maitrya,[43] in the *Mahaparinibbana Sutanta.* Concerning His own attainment to Buddhahood, He goes on to add:

This dharma, which the Tathagata has fully known or demonstrated—it cannot be grasped, it cannot be talked about, it is neither a dharma, nor a non-dharma. And why? Because an Absolute exalts the Holy Persons.
Vajracchedika, 176, 11a

Not only by disciplined conduct and vows, not only by much learning, nor moreover by the attainment of meditative calm nor by sleeping solitary, do I reach the happiness of release which no worldling can attain. O mendicant, do not be confident so long as you have not reached the extinction of impurities.
Dhammapada, vv. 271, 272

Beholding the worlds of creation, let the lover of God attain renunciation; what is above creation cannot be attained by action. In his longing for divine wisdom, let him go with reverence to a Teacher, in whom live the sacred words and whose soul has peace in Brahman. To a pupil who comes with mind and senses in peace the Teacher gives the vision of Brahman, of the Spirit of truth and eternity.
Mundaka Upanishad, 2.12.13

Neither by study of Vedas, nor by penance, nor by charity, nor by ritual can I be seen in this form as you have seen me.
Bhagavad Gita, XI.53

The above is further proof that, in reality, it is not a course of study, or proficiency in religion (dharma), which makes Buddhas, but a bestowal of grace from the 'Unconditioned'—an *exaltation from the Absolute upon the Holy Persons.* This passage not only throws greater light on the mechanism of inspiration from *the Absolute* to the Buddhas (Prophets), like the sun through its rays lights up the moon to the eyes of the denizens of earth, but also affirms the existence of *the Absolute* to be the 'exalter of the Buddhas.' Hence, notwithstanding what wishful conclusions have been drawn by Buddhists or foreign scholars implying that Buddhism is a religion which admits of no supernatural revelations, the facts concerning even His very first enlightenment towards His mission of Buddhahood, as recounted by the *Jataka Tales (see* note 13, page 2), should be sufficient to dispel this fallacy and prove that the enlightenment experienced by the Buddha was in the same category as that experienced by Christ, Mohammed, Moses or Baha'u'llah, and every other 'Avatar', namely, a divine revelation. And then, again, He gives further proof of this uniqueness of His kind (the race of Buddhas).

---

[43]Also referred to on p. 16 *(Anagata-Vamsa,* p. 34).

Of those beings who live in ignorance, shut up and confused, as it were, in an egg, I have first broken the egg-shell of ignorance and alone in the universe obtained the most exalted, universal Buddhahood. Thus, O disciples, I am the eldest, the noblest of beings.

Parajika Suttavibhanga, I, pp. 1.4

I am the sustainer and the ruler of this universe, its father, mother, and grandfather, the knowable, the purifier, the sacred syllable OM, and the Vedas.

Bhagavad Gita, IX.17

While a few others before Gautama had attained Buddhahood and broken the shell of ignorance, yet each was unique and the noblest of beings, supreme in his own cycle, and a very rare and great occurrence in the life of the world. According to the old Buddhist teaching there cannot appear more than one Buddha at one time.[44] The *Milindapanha* states that this is because *the virtues of the Buddha are so great that the world cannot at one time support or produce more than one such being, . . . the simultaneous appearance of two Buddhas at the same time may lead to confusion.* This point concerning the rarity of the manifestation of Tathagatas, propounded by the Buddha, even in the context of His native India, which by His own time, had already known of other Buddhas as well as Rama and Krishna, is most significant for our understanding that these Manifestations, Avatars and Buddhas are of a higher order of being and certainly beyond our comprehension.

Rarely, O monks, do Tathagatas appear in the world. To the extent that they understand the rarity of a Tathagata's appearance, to that extent they will wonder at His appearance, and sorrow at His disappearance, and when they do not see the Tathagata, they will long for the sight of Him.

Saddharmapundarika, XV vv. 268-72

Those who know God in His manifestation through a human being know the One who dwells in the Most Great Abode: He who knoweth the One Who dwelleth in the Most Great Abode and Who knoweth the Lord of Generations is the Great Knower of God, those who know Him, Follow Him, know the Pillar[45] very well.

Atharva Veda, X.7-17

Buddhahood is a station *no worldling can attain or fully understand,*[46] and in the *Mahapadana Suttanta,* the divinity of the Buddha is unequivocally asserted. The same theme is also repeated by Krishna as well as in the Upanishads and the Vedas. Their powers are from a *wholly beyond.* In this same context, we can now better appreciate His warning to Sariputta about those that deny His 'supra-human' *(further-men)* station by erroneously regarding Him as merely another wise man who had devised his own system of salvation through a method of trial-and-error:

[44]*Abhidharmakosha,* p. 172; *Milindapanha,* p. 237; *Brahmajala Sutta;* Ashvaghosha's *Life of Buddha;* and the *Sutta of 42 Sections.*

[45]Pillar meaning Dharma (Religion), also the support of divine protection over humanity. See also *Atharva Veda,* X.7-7.

[46]*Dhammapada,* vv. 271, 272.

THE GOD OF BUDDHA

Whoever, Sariputta, knowing that it is so of me, seeing that it is so, should speak thus: "There are no states of further-men (beyond man), no excellent cognition and insight befitting the Ariyans (noble men) in the recluse Gautama; the recluse Gautama teaches Dhamma on (a system of) his own devising beaten out by reasoning and based on investigation"—if he does not retract that speech, Sariputta, if he does not retract that thought, if he does not cast out that view, he is verily consigned to Niraya Hell for this sin. Even if it were a monk, Sariputta endowed with moral habit, concentration and wisdom, who should here and now arrive at gnosis (all knowledge) I (still) say that this results thus: If he does not retract that speech and that thought, if he does not cast out that view, he is verily consigned to Niraya Hell."
Majjhima-nikaya, I, 71-72

Among thousands of men scarcely one strives for perfection and of those who strive and succeed, scarcely one knows Me in truth.
Bhagavad Gita, VII.3

Not only does He claim here that His own state is beyond man *(further-men)* but also that the Dharma itself has no relationship to any system derived by human logic or investigation, once again confirming that this unique phenomenon of the Manifestation (Avatar), the Buddha and His Message (the Dharma) is from the realm of the *wholly beyond—an exaltation from the Absolute.* No matter what heights of spirituality or knowledge a disciple may attain, if he misjudges this all important aspect of the phenomenon of Buddhahood, then, *he is verily consigned to Niraya Hell.*

The Buddhas are the *trackless travelers* who cross over from the farther side to *work the weal of the world.*

He whose conquest is not conquered again, into whose conquest no one in this world enters, by what track can you lead him, the awakened, of infinite perception, the trackless? He whom no desire net-like or poisonous can lead astray, by what track can you lead him, the awakened, of infinite perception, the trackless? Difficult is it to obtain birth as a human being; difficult is the life of mortals; difficult is the hearing of the true law, difficult is the rise of buddhahood.
Dhammapada, vv. 179, 180, 182

Strong is Thy friendship. O Lord of Strength may we have no fear, we sing hymns of praise to thee again and again, O never conquered Conqueror.
Rig Veda, I

He who knows Me in reality as without birth and without beginning, and as the supreme Lord of the universe, he, undeluded among men, is purged of all sins.
Bhagavad Gita, X.3

For the protection of the virtuous, for the destruction of evil-doers, and for establishing Dharma (righteousness) on a firm footing, I am born from age to age.
Bhagavad Gita, IV.8

Upon attaining Abhisambodhi (Consummation of Incomparable Enlightenment), the Buddha even more emphatically (in the *Majjhima-nikaya*) proclaims the unique greatness of this divine phenomenon—a Buddha, an Avatar, a Prophet. While, on other occasions, the Buddha states that He is only a preacher,[47] yet, in the following verse, the Buddha claims that He is omniscient.

Subdued have I all, all knowing am I now.
Unattached to all things, and abandoning all.
Finally freed on the destruction of all craving.
Knowing it myself, whom else should I credit?
There is no teacher of mine, nor is one like me;
There is none to rival me[48] *in the world of men*
and gods; Truly entitled to honour am I, a
teacher unexcelled. Alone am I a Supreme
Buddha, placid and tranquil, To found the
kingdom of righteousness, I proceed to Kasi's
capital, Beating the drum of immortality in
the world enveloped by darkness.

 Ariyaparyesana Sutta.
 (Majjhima-nikaya)

The path of the ship across the sea, A soaring eagle's flight He knows, The course of every wind that blows, and all that was and is to be.
      Rig Veda, 25.1

I have drunk the nectar of life, I have become immortal. I have attained enlightenment (Buddhahood), I have realized the ideal. What harm can the energy do to me now?
      Yajur Veda, 8

Arjuna, I am even that which is the seed of all beings. For there is no creature, animate or inanimate, which exists without Me.
      Bhagavad Gita, X.39

He again stresses His unique station (Buddhahood) and repeats that He has already entered Nirvana in this life. Having severed all bonds He has gone beyond all *becoming* and passed into the realm of *the Eternal*, outside the scope of any empirical analysis.

Those only who do not believe, call me Gotama, but you call me the Buddha, the Blessed One, the Teacher. And this is right, for I have in this life entered Nirvana, while the life of Gotama has been extinguished. Self has disappeared and the truth has taken its abode in me. This body of mine is Gotama's body and it will be dissolved in due time, and after its dissolution no one, neither god (deva) nor man, will see Gotama again.[49] *But the truth remains. The Buddha will not die; the Buddha will continue to live in the holy body of the law. The extinction of the Blessed One will be by that passing away in which nothing remains that could tend to the formation of another self.*

Thus spoke Yajnavalka: "As when a lump of salt is thrown into water and therein being dissolved it cannot be grasped again, but wherever the water is taken it is found salt, in the same way, O Maitreyi, the supreme Spirit is an ocean of pure consciousness boundless and infinite. Arising out of the elements, into them it returns again: there is no consciousness after death."

Thereupon Maitreyi said: "I am amazed, O my Lord, to hear that after death there is no consciousness."

To this Yajnavalka replied: "I am not speaking words of amazement; but sufficient for wisdom is what I say. For where there seems to be a duality, there one sees another,

---

[47]*Dhammapada*, v. 275 (. . .This path was preached by me when I became aware of the removal of the thorns.) See also *Dhammapada*, v. 276 (You yourself must strive. The Blessed Ones are [only] preachers). Also *Dhammapada*, vv. 179, 180.

[48]See also *Dhammapada*, v. 353.

[49]*Digha-nikaya*, 1.46.

one hears another, one feels another's perfume, one thinks of another, one knows another. But when all has become Spirit, one's own Self, how and whom could one see? How and whom could one hear? How and of whom could one feel the perfume? How and to whom could one speak? How and whom could one know? How can one know him who knows all? How can the Knower be known?'

Brihadaranyaka Upanishad, 2.4

Even as water becomes one with water, fire with fire, and air with air, so the mind becomes one with the Infinite Mind and thus attains final freedom.

Maitri Upanishad, 6.24

Some writers have mistakenly claimed that this passage from the *Digha-nikaya—no one, neither god (deva) nor man, will see Gotama again*—means that the Buddha is referring to His total annihilation. Nothing could be further from the truth, as one can easily see by reference to *Dhammapada*[50]—*Him I call a Brahmin whose path the gods do not know, nor spirits, nor men, whose taints are extinct and who has attained sainthood*—that this means not extinction but sainthood. Otherwise, the whole meaning of the Buddha's doctrine for righteous striving would terminate in an absurdity, where saint and sinner, seer and fool, would be equated in a mindless nothingness.

Instead, as we continue to read these same passages from the *Digha-nikaya*, and the Upanishad we see that the essential reality of the Tathagata and the 'seeker' of the Upanishad becomes one with *the Absolute*.

Nor will it be possible to, point out the Blessed One as being here or there. But it will be like a flame in a great body of blazing fire. That flame has ceased; it has vanished; and it cannot be said that it is here or there. In the body of the Dharma, however, the Blessed One can be pointed out; for the Dharma has been preached by The Blessed One. Ye are my children, I am your father,[51] *through me have ye been released from your sufferings. I myself having reached the other shore, help others to cross the stream; I myself having attained salvation, am a saviour of others; being comforted, I comfort others and lead them to the*

Abandoning all duties, come to Me alone for shelter. Be not grieved, for I shall release thee from all evils.

Bhagavad Gita, XVIII.66

---

[50] *Dhammapada*, v. 420. See also *Dhammapada*, v. 421.

[51] In Mahayana Buddhism, also, the Buddha is regarded as the Father and Transcendental Wisdom (Prajna) as the Mother of the Universe. (See also *Bhagavad Gita*, XIV.4. ("Of all the bodies that take birth from different wombs, the Primordial Matter is the Mother; and I am the procreating Father, O Arjuna.")

place of refuge. I shall fill with joy all the beings whose limbs languish; I shall give happiness to those who are dying from distress; I shall extend to them succor and deliverance. I was born into the world as the king of truth for the salvation of the world. The subject on which I meditate is truth. The practice to which I devote myself is Truth. The topic of my conversation is Truth. My thoughts are always in the Truth. For lo! my self has become the Truth. Whosoever comprehendeth the Truth will see the Blessed One, for the Truth has been preached by the Blessed One. And, again, Sariputta, a Tathagata with his purified deva-like vision surpassing that of men, sees beings as they are deceasing and uprising . . . and he comprehends that beings are mean, excellent, comely, ugly, in a good bourn, in a bad bourn according to the consequence of karma. And again, Sariputta, a Tathagata, by the extinction of the outflows, having realized here and now the freedom of mind and the freedom through wisdom that have no outflows, entering thereon abides therein. That a Tathagata does this. Sariputta is a Tathagata's power of a Tathagata owing to which he claims the leader's place, roars a lion's roar in assemblies, and sets rolling the Brahma-wheel. These, Sariputta, are a Tathagata's ten powers of a Tathagata endowed with which a Tathagata claims the leader's place, roars a lion's roar in assemblies, and sets rolling the Brahma-wheel.[52]

I am the goal, the upholder, the lord, the witness, the abode, the refuge and the friend. I am the origin and the dissolution, the ground, the resting place and the imperishable seed.

Bhagavad Gita, IX.18

On Me fix thy mind; to Me be devoted; worship Me: revere Me, thus having disciplined thyself, with Me as thy goal, to Me shalt thou come.

Bhagavad Gita, IX.34

It is Atman (pure Spirit) whose love is truth, whose thoughts are Truth. Even as here on earth the attendants of a king obey the king and are with him wherever he is and go with him wherever he goes, so all love which is Truth and all thoughts of Truth obey the Atman, the Spirit.

Chandogya Upanishad, 8.1

He who knows Brahman who is Truth, consciousness and infinite joy, hidden in the inmost of our soul and in the highest heaven, enjoys all things he desires in Communion with the all-knowing Brahman.

Taittirya Upanishad, I.1.2

The seers whose sins have been washed away, whose doubts have been dispelled by knowledge, whose mind is firmly established in God and who are actively engaged in promoting the welfare of all beings, attain Brahma, who is all Peace.

Bhagavad Gita, V.25

These, Sariputta are the four confidences of a Tathagata, endowed with which confidences the Tathagata claims the leader's place, roars a lion's roar in assemblies and sets rolling the Brahma-wheel.

Majjhima-nikaya, I.72-73

He who does not, in this world, help to turn the wheel thus set in motion, is evil in his nature, sensual in his delight, and he, O'Partha (Arjuna), lives in vain.

Bhagavad Gita, III.16

---

[52]The Brahma wheel essentially means the wheel of Divine Law (Dharma or Religion) set in motion for the salvation of humanity.

THE GOD OF BUDDHA

We are cautioned from falling into the trap of relating Him to any objective reality. The lesser can never truly define or understand the greater and it is futile to think of the Buddha in terms of man-conceived dimensions or attributes.

In the world with its devas, Maras and Brahmas, amid living beings with recluses and Brahmins, devas and mankind, the Tathagata is the victor unvanquished, the absolute seer, self-controlled. Therefore is he called Tathagata.

Digha-nikaya, III.135

You are the Father, also, the greatest teacher of this animate and inanimate creation and supremely adorable. O possessor of incomparable glory, in all the three worlds there is no one else equal to You; how can anyone be superior?

Bhagavad Gita, XI.43

Since a Tathagata, even when actually present, is incomprehensible, it is inept to say of him—the Uttermost Person, The Supernal Person, the Attainer of the Supernal—that after dying the Tathagata is, or is not, or both is and is not, or neither is nor is not.

Samyutta-nikaya, III.118

The Supreme Person is distinct from both, who, inter-penetrating the three worlds, sustains all, and is designated as the Universal Soul and the imperishable Lord. Since I am beyond perishable Matter and superior to the imperishable Soul, hence it is that I am known in the world as well as in the Vedas as the Supreme Person. Arjuna, the undeluded person, who thus knows Me in reality as the Supreme Person, he, knowing all, worships Me with his whole being.

Bhagavad Gita, XV.17, 18, 19

Nor is there any separation permitted between the recognition of the Buddha, the supremely enlightened teacher, and the complete acceptance of, and whole-hearted, active participation in, His teachings, i.e. the Dharma. For, as we shall see in the following chapter, the Dharma is all that we shall ever be able to grasp of the reality of the Buddha.

2

DOCTRINE

RENEWAL OF RELIGION

In the study of the whole panorama of religious revelation, we will see that religious truth—essentially, the fundamental golden rule, in one form or another—underlies the gospel of each and every divine Messenger without exception. It can be said in essence that there is but one religion and all the divine Messengers have taught it. It is therefore more correct to state that whenever a new Prophet or a Buddha appears it is not so much to found a new religion as it is to renew the fundamental golden rule and proclaim its unchanging truth as the standard to which everyone must revert, in order to conduct one's individual life as well as one's relationship to society. The appearance of the divine Teacher, the Prophet, from time to time is for accomplishing this renewal of religion and through it to impart once again the vital spiritual motivation for propelling humanity onward and upwards from the mere mundane life into the realm of ineffable glory.

Every divine Teacher has affirmed that he is but restating and clarifying the ancient truths, the eternal verities, the final Norm by which all actions and ideas of the human race must be tested. So clear and persistent is this pronouncement on the part of the Founders of the Aryan religions as well as the Founders of the other great Faiths, that it appears almost as a condition and a proof of their claim to the station of divine Manifestation. And the Buddha, too, like those peerless beings, the Avatars (divine Manifestations) gone before, clearly acknowledges that His Dharma is not something new but that is is an ancient[53] way, taught in bygone times for ages past by other Buddhas, whose essential reality was identical to His, and that He was now re-opening once again the way to that same Dharma, which had been lost and forgotten:

There is no distinction between any of the Buddhas in physical beauty, moral habit, concentration, wisdom, freedom, cognition and insight of freedom, the four confidences, the ten powers of the Tathagata, the six special cognitions, the fourteen cognitions of Buddhas, the eighteen Buddha-dhammas, in a word in all the dhammas of the Buddhas, for all Buddhas are exactly the same as regards Buddha-dhammas.[54]

Thus handed down from one to another the royal sages (Rajasris) knew it till that Yoga was lost to the world through long lapse of time, O Arjuna. The same ancient Yoga has this day been imparted to you by Me, because you are My devotee and friend, and also because this is a supreme secret.

Bhagavad Gita, IV.2,3

Blessed is the birth of the awakened; blessed is the teaching of the true law; blessed is concord in the Order; blessed is the austerity of those who live in concord.
Dhammapada v. 194

Arjuna, howsoever men approach Me, even so do I seek them; for all men follow My path from all sides.

Bhagavad Gita, IV.11

He adds, moreover, that the reality of the Buddha cannot be conceived from His body or His physical appearance, because Buddhahood is a unique spiritual phenomenon, which no 'worldling'[55] (human) can know, and the only way He can be known at all is through His Dharma (Religion).

Equally foolish are all these who adhere to the Tathagata through form and sound, and who in consequence imagine the coming or going of a Tathagata. For a Tathagata cannot be seen from his form-body. The Dharma-bodies are the Tathagatas.
Dhammadgata Ashtasahasrika XXXI, 512-13
Also Parajika Suttavibhanga, 1

Fools, not knowing My supreme nature, think low of Me, the Lord of creation, who has put on the human body. (That is, they take Me, who has appeared in human garb through My Yogamaya for the deliverance of the world, to be an ordinary mortal.)

Bhagavad Gita, IX.11

What is there, Vakkali, in seeing this vile body? Whosoever sees Dhamma sees me; whosoever sees me sees Dhamma. Seeing Dhamma, Vakkali, he sees me; seeing me, he sees Dhamma.
Samyutta-nikaya, 22,87,13 III, p. 120

Just as the extensive and all-pervading air (which is born of ether) always remains in ether, likewise know that all beings (sprung as they are from My thought) abide in Me.

Bhagavad Gita, IX.6

---

[53]*Milindapanha*, p. 218. See also *Mahaprajnaparamita-Shastra*, I, p. 157. He calls His dharma purana (ancient)—and likens it to the discovery of an everlasting city which had been buried and forgotten (*Nagara Sutta*).

[54]Enumerated in *Mahavastu*, i-160. See also *Milindapanha*, p. 285.

[55]See also *Dhammapada*, vv. 271, 272.

He who sees Me sees Dhamma.
Majjhima-nikaya Also *Itivuttaka*, p. 97

That which is Dharma, is the truth.
Brihadaranyaka Upanishad, i.4,14

Those who see me in any form or think of me in words, their way of thinking is false, they do not see me at all. The Beneficient Ones are to be seen in the Law (Dharma), theirs is a Law-body; the Buddha is rightly to be understood as being of one nature of the Law. He cannot be understood by any other means.
Vajracchedika Sutra, p. 38, XXVI

I abide not in heaven nor in the hearts of Yogis; I dwell where My devotees sing My glory.
Narada Sutra, 16-18

However, it is necessary for us to recognize that the authorities on the teachings of the Buddha are no more reliable than those sources we have concerning His life. None of the three Pitakas[56] can at present be satisfactorily dated before the Council of Ashoka held at Patna about 250 B.C., more than two centuries after the passing of Gautama. Hence, we do not have sufficient proof to assert that the doctrine of the Buddha as now represented did exist in the time of Gautama, or that it formed a part of His actual teaching concerning the most important and original aspects of His Message of Salvation. Nor is there enough evidence to state that it arose after the Buddha's passing. We have no way of attributing a more precise time to this question than the date for the Council of Ashoka. It is, nevertheless, clear that immediately after Gautama's passing a strong reaction did set in against the high standard of the Buddha's ethical teachings, and this opposition was further reinforced by the growth of the legends which sprang up rapidly regarding His life. Many of these latter changes are sufficiently evident from the books of the Pitakas themselves; but it is very difficult, if not impossible, at present to come to any definite conclusion as to what change took place in Buddhist doctrine, apart from the beliefs regarding the person of the Buddha, prior to the transcribing of the Pitakas in their present form. Hence, the question will always remain whether the Pali texts of the Singhalese Theravadins represent the oldest traditions which approach the actual teachings of the Buddha, or do we have to look to the scriptures of the other old schools and also of the Mahayana for a more correct and comprehensive picture of the Buddha and His Message. The assumption that only the Pali scriptures can give us an adequate idea is untenable, since the Pali Canon is merely the work of one sect, besides which many others existed at the time. However, the assiduous student can still find the stamp of authenticity on the fundamentals of His early doctrine, the salient events of His life, and the conditions prevailing in the India of His day, because of the essential accord on these aspects, evident from a comparative study of the Pali Canon, the Sanskrit works and the Ceylon Chronicles.

---

[56]Collections, as the canonical books of the southern Buddhists are called.

DHARMA

The old, all inclusive term for religion in India was Aryadharma (Noble-way), derived from 'Arya' meaning noble, and 'dharma', which is from the root 'dhar', meaning to sustain or carry. Dharma really implies Religion, Law and Truth, all rolled into one. Thus, it is essentially a system of man's conduct predicated on an ethical concept, including right action, right living, as well as the whole panorama of man's duties. Aryadharma therefore includes all the faiths of the Aryan people (Vedic and non-Vedic), Hinduism, Buddhism and Jainism, which were originated in India, as well as Zorastrianism, which was born in Iran. The Buddha also called His way of salvation the 'Aryan Path.'[57] The origin of the idea of Dharma goes back to ancient Iranian and Vedic-Aryan concepts. In both of these it is known by a similar word signifying order, e.g. arta (old Iranian), or asha (in Avestan) and rita in Vedic. The concept of rita encompasses the whole range of order, the physical order of things, the mental or metaphysical and, finally, the moral laws as well, related to the whole scheme-of-things. It is not conceived to be the handiwork of the Vedic gods, but rather itself endowed with the aura of divinity and above and beyond the gods of the Vedic pantheon; more precisely, an emanation from the source of divinity, the Supreme Itself. In a sense rita, and also Dharma, is the path leading to *the Eternal,* just like the rays of the sun, if one could travel on them, would lead us to the sun. In the *Vinaya-pitaka* we read that *Dharma is a door to the eternal.*[58]

It is clear that, whereas the Upanishads laid greater stress on the belief in *the Absolute* as the only intrinsic reality and identified Dharma as the emanation from It, just like the sun's rays emanate from the sun, the Buddha emphasized concentration on the Dharma itself as the standard for conduct in the actual world rather than dwelling on the totally incomprehensible 'Absolute Reality', which was *wholly beyond,* just as a wise teacher would direct the student to analyze the life-giving as well as death-dealing powers of the rays from the sun which envelope the student and his world, in order to fruitfully and wisely exist by those powers, rather than have the student aspiring to gaze at the unseeable solar orb directly or to approach its proximity. Thus, Dharma was considered to be the all in all in the actual world, for it *portrayed* and was the *image* of absolute truth, infallible justice and righteousness. It was as close as one could hope to approach that *Unoriginated* and *Uncaused* Reality. The Buddha called Dharma *the King of Kings,*[59] and taught that reverence and homage were to be directed towards Dharma, and He himself,

---

[57]See *Dhammapada,* vv. 22, 79.

[58]*Vinaya-pitaka,* i.5.

[59]*Anguttara,* iii.

after the attainment of full enlightenment, vowed to live under Dharma, *honoring and respecting it.*[60]

In the *Samyutta-nikaya* we read that Dharma is the unwavering law of Causality (Karma) or *Conditioned Origination* and *the law of Karma is all-pervading,* and its recognition is the most precious jewel (ratna) of knowledge, while the *Anguttara-nikaya* says that Dharma is the underlying law, not dependent for its existence on the appearance of the Buddhas, whose mission is merely to reveal it (Dharma) to humanity.

Whether tathagatas have arisen or not, certain is this fundamental Law (dhatu, principle), this rule of law (dhammatthitata) this lawful necessity (dharmaniyamata): All conditioned factors of being are subject to suffering, all dhammas (i.e.; the conditioned Sankharas) and the unconditioned dhamma, (that is Nirvana) are "without self" (without permanent substance, annatta). This the tathagata perceives and knows; and after he had perceived and, recognized it, he teaches it, shows it, reveals it, lays it open, explains it, preaches it, comments on it, and proclaims it.
Anguttara-nikaya, 3, 134, I. p. 286

I will speak words of truth and the words of the divine law (Dharma) shall be on my lips.
Taittiriya Upanishad, I.1

There is nothing higher than Dharma.
Brihadaranyaka Upanishad, i.4, 13

The light of all lights, It is said to be beyond the darkness of Maya. It is Knowledge itself, as well as the object of Knowledge, and is also worth attaining through Knowledge, It is specially seated in the hearts of all.
Bhagavad Gita, XIII.17

On various occasions the Buddha equated Dharma with the Upanishad concept of Brahma and claimed that the *way of the Dharma is the way of the Brahma,* [61] or to *dwell in Dharma is to dwell in Brahma,* [62] even to the extent of saying that *the Tathagata has Dharma as His body, the Brahma as His body* and that He is *one with Dharma and one with Brahma.*[63] And He calls the eight-fold path both *dharmayana and brahmayana.*[64] While the Dharma, together with Nirvana and Infinity of Space, is regarded by Buddhist doctrine as independent (asamskrita)[65] of anything for its rising (creation), yet, neither it (Dharma) nor Nirvana nor Infinity of Space is acknowl-

[60]*Samyutta,* ii.138f; *Anguttara,* ii.20f. Also see *Samyutta,* 12, 20, 3, II. p. 25.

[61]*Samyutta-nikaya,* i.161.

[62]*Anguttara-nikaya,* i.207.

[63]*Digha-nikaya,* iii.84,81.

[64]*Digha-nikaya,* III.84,81.

[65]This becomes clear if we understand these entities (Nirvana, Dharma, etc.) as emanations of the Supreme and hence not 'caused' in time but co-existent with *the Absolute.*

edged as the absolute ground of being or as the quintessence of all creation. However, whether Dharma is the ground of being or not, it is the only path that must be trod by all to gain liberation, and in treading it we must teach it to others. We must drink deeply from its life-giving waters and then in our turn impart it to those thirsty souls in search of salvation.

I, monks, am freed from all snares, both those of devas (gods) and those of men. And you, monks, are freed from all snares, both those of devas (gods) and those of men. Walk, monks on tour for the blessing of the many, for the happiness of the many, out of compassion for the world, for the welfare, the blessing, the happiness of devas (gods) and men. Let not two of you go by the same way. Monks, teach Dharma that is lovely at the beginning, lovely in the middle and lovely at the ending. Explain with the spirit and the letter of the Brahma-faring competely fulfilled and utterly pure. There are Beings with little dust in their eyes who not hearing Dharma, are decaying, but if they are learners of Dharma they will grow. And I, monks, will go along to Uruvela, the Camp township, in order to teach Dharma.

Vinaya-pitaka, I.20-21

Sri Bhagavan said: "Arjuna, hear once again My supreme word, which I shall speak to you, who are so loving, out of solicitude for your welfare."

Bhagavad Gita, X.1

This sacred teaching should never be imparted to a man without austerity, nor to one without devotion; nor even to him who is unwilling to hear, nor again to him who finds fault with Me.

Bhagavad Gita, XVIII.67

And he who studies this sacred dialogue of ours, by him I would be worshipped through the sacrifice of knowledge, so I hold. And the man who listens to it with faith and without scoffing, even he, being liberated, shall attain to the happy worlds of the righteous.

Bhagavad Gita, XVIII.70,71

In the same way, headman, my monks and nuns are like the excellent field. It is to these that I teach Dharma that is lovely at the beginning, lovely in the middle and lovely at the ending, with spirit and the letter, and to whom I make known the Brahma-faring completely fulfilled, utterly pure. And why? It is these that dwell with me for light, me for shelter, me for stronghold, me for refuge.

Samyutta-nikaya, IV.314-16

O son of Kunti (Arjuna) Know thou for certain that My devotee perishes never.

Bhagavad Gita, IX.31

With their mind fixed on Me, with their lives surrendered to Me, enlightening one another about My greatness and speaking of Me, they ever remain contented and take delight in Me.

Bhagavad Gita, X.9

Having in his person attained the Deathless element (cause) which has no 'basis', by making real the casting out of 'basis', The Perfect Buddha, of no outflows, Teaches the griefless, stainless state.

Itivuttaka, p. 62

Men of no understanding think of Me, the unmanifest, as having manifestation, not knowing My higher nature, changeless and supreme. Veiled by My creative power I am not revealed to all. This bewildered world knows Me not, the unborn, the unchanging. I know the beings that are past, that are present, O Arjuna, and that are yet to come but no one knows Me. Those who take refuge in Me and strive for deliverance from old age and death, they know the Brahman (Absolute) entire (they know) the Self and all about action.

Bhagavad Gita, VII.24,25,26,29

This is the age-old message of every Avatar, and the claim is all the more interesting because the Buddha uses these words to show that His mission was to strain away the impurities of vain imaginings and ridiculous rituals which had polluted the pure Dharma, and, thus, once again, *utterly pure,* offer this life-giving elixir (Dharma) to the thirsty souls of men, so that their quest for the bliss of Nirvana could be *completely fulfilled.* The message of salvation, of love and righteousness proclaimed by these Divine Teachers—Rama, Krishna, Buddha and the others—is open to all, irrespective of one's station in life or one's color or creed. It is an all-inclusive and comprehensive message and not something narrow or restrictive or exclusive of one group or another. It is the all-encompassing haven—the only refuge for humanity:

Dhamma has been taught by me without making a distinction between esoteric and exoteric. For the Tathagata has not the closed fist of a teacher in respect of mental states.
Digha-nikaya, II.100

For those who take refuge in me, O Partha (Arjuna), though they are lowly born, women, Vaisyas, as well as Sudras, they also attain to the highest goal.
Bhagavad Gita, IX.32

Men driven by fear go to many a refuge, to mountains, and to forests, to sacred trees, and shrines. That verily, is not a safe refuge, that is not the best refuge. After having got to that refuge a man is not delivered from all pains. But he who takes refuge in the Buddha, the Law, and the Order, he perceives, in his clear wisdom, the four noble truths.

I have found the small path (Dharma) of old that stretches far away. By it the sages who know the Spirit arise to the regions of heaven and thence beyond to liberation. Let man find the path of the Spirit. Who has found this path becomes free from the bonds of evil. This is the Spirit of the universe, a refuge from all fear.
Brihadaranyaka Upanishad, 4,33

That, verily, is a safe refuge, that is the best refuge; after having got to that refuge a man is delivered from all pains.
Dhammapada, vv. 188,189,190,192

To him who seeks My protection even once and requests help of Me saying 'I am yours' I shall give him fearlessness from all beings. This is my resolve.
Ramayana

But the Dharma (Religion) is not something any person could concoct or create for himself out of a conglomeration of rituals and traditions; it is that straight and perfect eternal path, sharp as the razor's edge, to be trod only by the vigilant, who, completely shorn off their burden of worldly trappings, with a fully controlled and balanced mind, embark on this path, leaving behind the ephemeral and crossing over the chasm of *becomings,* to reach that deathless farther shore of immortality, experience that Supreme Bliss of Nirvana.

There is no path in the sky, there is no recluse outside, mankind delights in worldliness; the Buddhas are free from worldliness.
Dhammapada, v. 254

Those, however, who, finding fault with this doctrine (dharma) of Mine, do not follow it, know them to be deluded in the matter of all knowledge, senseless and lost.[66]
Bhagavad Gita, III.32

[66]See also *Bhagavad Gita,* XIII.7; IX.19; X.2,3.

This is the path; there is none other that leads to the purifying of insight. You follow this (path). This will be to confuse Mara (Death). Going on this path, you will end your suffering. This path was preached by me when I became aware of the removal of the thorns (in the flesh).

Dhammapada, vv. 274, 275

He cannot be taught by one who has not reached Him; and He cannot be reached by much thinking. The way to Him is through a Teacher who has seen Him. He is higher than the highest thoughts, in truth above all thought. This sacred knowledge is not attained by reasoning; but it can be given by a true Teacher.

Katha Upanishad, II.8,9

Know this, O man, that evil things befall the unrestrained. Let not greed and wrong-doing bring you to grief for a long time. There is no path in the sky, there is no recluse outside (of us). Nothing in the phenomenal world is eternal, there is no instability to the awakened.

Dhammapada, vv. 248, 255

Possessed of hypocrisy, conceit and arrogance and given to insatiable passion, and adopting false doctrines due to delusion, they take to action with impure vows.

Bhagavad Gita, XVI.10

However, before the traveller can find the path (Dharma), he must be able to recognize the true guide (the Buddha) and have complete faith in His guidance and direction. So salvation requires these three conditions: the Buddha, the Dharma, and complete faith in both.

FAITH

Through that inexplicable power of total faith in the Buddha, our Teacher, our Guide, and with our whole being (action and mind) merged in the Dharma, we ourselves begin to reflect the deathless light and become as beacons for other seeking souls, so that they, too, may emerge from the darkness of doubt to the light of faith.

Faith is the wealth here best for man—by faith the flood is crossed.

Suttampata, vv. 182, 184
Samyutta-nikaya, Milindapanha, 35-36

Arjuna, the faith of each is shaped to his own mental constitution. Faith constitutes the very being of man; therefore, whatever the nature of his faith, that verily he is.

Bhagavad Gita, XVII.3

By faith you shall be free and go beyond the realm of death.

Suttampata, v. 1146

Arjuna, sacrifice, gift and penance, and any other action done without faith, is declared as 'Asat' (non-existent). It is nought here or hereafter.

Bhagavad Gita, XVII.28

The universe, according to the Buddha, is certainly sensitive to our ethical endeavours and the Dharma itself manifesting in the world as the natural and spiritual law is the greatest instrument for manipulating and determining the operation of the universe and not just some metaphysical negation. He goes on to assure us that man can make the Dharma operate for achieving higher spiritual progress, even to attaining Nirvana, through the power of his faith. As He says, *if a good man full of faith were to fervently desire, upon having got rid of his vices, to pass from this present tainted world into the abode of sinlessness of heart and mind, he could certainly achieve this by his own transcendent knowledge.*[67]

The essence of faith consists of an unselfish appreciation of, and a kinship to, the workings of the Divine Mind in the whole of creation and is not related to the paraphernalia of religion, such as rituals, recitations, and blind obedience to dead traditions.

Not nakedness, not matted hair, not dirt, not fasting, not lying on the ground, not rubbing with ashes, not sitting motionless purify a mortal who is not free from doubt.
Dhammapada, v. 141

The man who listens to it full of faith and in an uncarping spirit, freed from evil, he shall gain the happy worlds of the virtuous.
Bhagavad Gita, XVIII.71

Man in truth is made of faith. As his faith is in this life, so he becomes in the beyond; with faith and vision let him work.
Chandogya Upanishad, 3.14

True faith is not to be equated with blind beliefs or thoughtless acts however noble the motive behind them. It is born of reason and must be sustained through wisdom. The great principles of existence are not so jumbled that they need to be accepted blindly. They can be clearly known only through reflection and reason by minds which are purified from the mists of prejudice, superstition and arrogance. The doubts and uncertainties of life and its meaning can only be dispelled by reasoned faith. Man is a rational soul and any proposition (religious or otherwise) that he accepts as being of some lasting worth must be grounded in reason. Only through discrimination and reflection can we sustain and even enhance our faith in the Dharma (Religion) and we in turn are sustained by it (our Faith) in time of our greatest need.

Happy is virtue lasting to old age; happy is faith firmly rooted; happy is the attainment of wisdom; happy is the avoidance of sins.
Dhammapada, v. 333

In the faith of 'He is' his existence must be perceived, in his essence. When he is perceived as 'He is' then shines forth the revelation of his essence.
Katha Upanishad, 6.14

These two wings, religion and reason, are not mutually incompatible, but are attached to the same bird—the spirit of man. And faith is that cohesive force

---

[67] *Majjhima-nikaya,* 41; Also *Digha-nikya,* i.125.

which makes them beat in unison to lift the questing soul on to ever greater heights. Soon after preaching His first sermon, the Buddha instructs His earliest group of disciples to spread His Dharma to the world: *Go now and wander for the gain of many, for the welfare of many, out of compassion for the world, for the good, for the gain, and for the welfare of gods and men. Let not two of you go the same way. Preach the doctrine, which is glorious in the beginning, glorious in the middle, and glorious in the end, in the spirit and in the letter proclaim a consummate, perfect and pure life of holiness.* Both Krishna and the Buddha tell us that our highest duty consists of teaching the Dharma to our fellow-men. It is then that we can gage our own faith in the Dharma, by learning through reasoned discussion with others whether our faith in our beliefs is grounded on reason or, if it is merely floating on our own emotions. By imparting real faith to others we also increase our own store of it.

Subhuti, if there be one who gives away in gifts of alms a mass of the seven[68] treasures equal in extent to as many Mount Sumerus as there would be in three thousand galaxies of worlds, and if there be another who selects even only four lines from this Discourse upon the Perfection of Transcendental Wisdom, receiving and retaining them, and clearly expounding them to others, the merit of the latter will be so far greater than that of the former that no conceivable comparison can be made between them.

Vajra Sattva, XXIV, (The Incomparable Merit of This Teaching)

He who teaches this supreme secret to My devotees, showing the highest devotion to Me, shall doubtless come to Me. There is none among men who does dearer service to Me than he; nor shall there be another dearer to Me in the world.

Bhagavad Gita, XVIII.68,69

Later on, during the course of His ministry, near the end of His life, the Buddha repeats this injuction about teaching the Dharma and makes it obligatory to every man and woman.

Subhuti, someone might fill inummerable worlds with the seven treasures and give all away in gifts of alms, but if any good man or any good woman awakens the thought of Enlightenment and takes even only four lines from this Discourse, reciting, using, receiving, retaining and spreading them abroad and explaining them for the benefit of others, it will be far more meritorious. Now in what manner may he explain them to others? By detachment from appearances—abiding in Real Truth—So I tell you—Thus shall ye

Arjuna said: "What are the marks of him who has risen above the three Gunas, and what his conduct? And how, Lord, does he rise above the three Gunas?"
Sri Bhagavan replies: "He who takes sorrow and joy alike, is established in the self, regards a clod of earth, a stone and a piece of gold as equal in value, receives both pleasant and unpleasant things in the same spirit, and views censure and praise alike."
"And he who constantly worships Me through the Yoga of exclusive devotion, trans-

---

[68]'The Seven Treasures' are gold, silver, lapis-lazuli, crystal, agate, red-pearl, and cornelian.

think of all this fleeting world: A star at dawn, a bubble in a stream; A flash of lightning in a summer cloud, a flickering lamp, a phantom and a dream.

Vajra Sattva, XXXII
(The Delusion of Appearances)

cending these three Gunas, he becomes eligible for attaining Brahma."

Bhagavad Gita, XIV.21,24,26

Look upon the world as a bubble: look upon it as a mirage. Him who looks thus upon the world the king of death does not see.

Dhammapada, v. 170

He, who regards well wishers, friends, foes, neutrals, mediators, the objects of hatred, relatives, the virtuous and the sinful alike, he stands supreme.

Bhagavad Gita, VI.9

However, the Dharma is not to be taught to others by mere intellectual arguments, but, instead, through an act of transformation of our whole personality. One must become the living embodiment of the Dharma in one's own being and thus demonstrate to others through righteousness of conduct the truth of the Dharma's claim to make men anew.

RENUNCIATION

In the Hindu as well as the Buddhist Faiths the renunciation of social life, family and home to go off to the homeless life, e.g. to become a sannyasin (a renouncer) is much admired as a final severing of the bonds that bind one to the things of this world. In the Hindu faith, the sannyasins literally die to the world.[69] Often times their departure into the homeless life is marked by the performance of actual funeral rites, so complete is the break from society, and, as we have seen from the previous chapter, the Buddha, too, was greatly attracted by the goal of the sannyasin and, ultimately renouncing his family, palaces and princely power, embarked on the road of the homeless ascetic:

The Buddha, most excellent in the three worlds, having abandoned wealth, child, wife and bodily existence for mankind, having fulfilled the thirty Paramis and attained the unparalleled constituents of Transcendental Knowledge, attaining pure intelligence, which bestows all virtues, he having put an end to suffering has rescued virtuous people from misery.

Jina ankara, p. 21

Unswerving devotion to Me with wholehearted discipline, resort to solitary places, dislike for a crowd of people. Fixity in Self-knowledge, observing everywhere the object of true Knowledge (God): all this is declared to be Knowledge (Wisdom); what is contrary to this is called ignorance.

Bhagavad Gita, XIII.10, 11

---

[69]In the *Brihadaranyaka Upanishad* we also read: "Knowing Him, the Atman, the Brahmins relinquish the desire for posterity, for possessions, for progeny and fame, and embark as mendicants."

THE GOD OF BUDDHA

But, as we saw from the Buddha's own experience, renunciation does not consist of isolating one's self from society and its problems. Since our real tests come in the form of our fellow men, we will not be able to meet these tests or achieve any degree of inner strength if we withdraw from society. Together with every other great religious faith, both Hinduism and Buddhism insist on self-mastery and conquest of desire and passion. An equanimity of mind should be achieved for accepting whatever comes our way, whether it be pain or pleasure, without excitement or revolt. Their teachings emphasize the control of both the body and the mind. Freedom from passion of the physical senses is not enough; one must also be liberated from mental desires. The chief instrument for attaining this liberation is Meditation:

Meditate, O mendicant, be not negligent. Let not your thought delight in sensual pleasures, that you may not for your negligence have to swallow the iron ball,[70] that you may not cry out when burning 'This is suffering!' There is no meditation for one who is without wisdom, no wisdom for one without meditation; he in whom there are meditation and wisdom, he indeed is close to nirvana.
Dhammapada, vv. 371,372

On those ever united through meditation with Me and worshipping Me with love, I confer that Yoga of wisdom through which they attain Me.
Bhagavad Gita, X.10

If men thought of God as much as they think of the world, who would not attain liberation (Nirvana).
Maitri Upanishad, 6.24

From meditation springs wisdom; from lack of meditation there is loss of wisdom. Knowing this two-fold path of progress and decline, a man should place himself in such a way that his wisdom increases.
Dhammapada, v. 282

Meditation is in truth higher than thought. The earth seems to rest in silent meditation; and the waters and the mountains and the sky and the heavens seem all to be in meditation. Whenever a man attains greatness on this earth, he has his reward according to his meditation.
Chandogya Upanishad, 7.6

And through meditation the darkness of ignorance is dispelled by the shining light of knowledge:

But he who is above good and evil and is chaste, who comforts himself in the world with knowledge, he, indeed, is called a mendicant.
Dhammapada, v. 267

Even if you are the most sinful of all sinners, you will cross over all sin by the raft of Knowledge. For, as the blazing fire reduces the fuel to ashes, Arjuna, even so the fire of Knowledge reduces all actions to ashes.
Bhagavad Gita, IV.36,37

But there is an impurity greater than all impurities. Ignorance is the greatest impurity. O mendicants, having cast away that impurity, be free from all impurities.
Dhammapada, v. 243

In this world, there is no purifier like knowledge: he, who has attained purity of heart through practice of Karmayoga, automatically realizes it in the self in course of time.
Bhagavad Gita, IV.38

---

[70]Recognized as a form of punishment in hell—swallowing red hot iron balls!

He who knows both knowledge and action,
with action overcomes death and with knowledge reaches immortality.

Isa Upanishad

The Buddha tells us that by retaining purity of mind one can achieve transmigration of life (Samsara) in one's own mind. For what a man thinks is what
he becomes. On the other hand, if we are overcome by lust and greed, we can
lose both memory and intelligence and fall into abysmal ruin.

*This mind of mine would wander formerly as
it liked, as it desired, as it pleased. I shall now
control it thoroughly even as the rider holding
the hook controls the elephant in a state of rut.
Be not thoughtless, guard your thoughts.
Extricate yourself out of the evil way as an elephant sunk in the mud.*

Dhammapada, vv. 326,327

Arjuna said: "Krishna, this Yoga in the form
of equanimity, which You have taught, owing
to restlessness of mind I do not perceive its
stability. For, Krishna, the mind is very unsteady, turbulent, tenacious and powerful;
therefore, I consider it as difficult to control as
the wind."

Bhagavad Gita, VI.34

*Give up what is before, give up what is behind,
give up what is in the middle, passing to the
farther shore of existence. When your mind is
wholly freed you will not again return to birth
and old age.*

Dhammapada, v. 348

Sri Bhagavan replied: "The mind is without
doubt unsteady and difficult to curb, Arjuna;
but it can be controlled through practice (of
meditation) and dispassion, O son of Kunti."

Bhagavad Gita, VI.35

In both the Hindu and the Buddhist texts the human psyche and the physical
body are likened to a chariot, the senses being the steeds, self-control, the
reins, and the teacher, or guide, or the Buddha (and Krishna), the charioteer.

*He who curbs his rising anger like a chariot
gone astray (over the plain), him I call a real
charioteer, others but hold the reins (and do
not deserve to be called charioteers).*

Dhammapada, v. 222

*Is there in the world any man so restrained by
modesty that he avoids censure as a well-
trained horse avoids the whip? Like a well-
trained horse when touched by a whip, be
strenuous and swift and you will, by faith, by
virtue, by energy, by meditation, by discern-
ment of the law, put aside this great sorrow (of
earthly existence), endowed with knowledge
and (good) behavior and mindfulness.*

Dhammapada, vv. 143,144

Know the Atman as Lord of a chariot; and the
body as the chariot itself. Know that reason is
the charioteer; and the mind indeed is the
reins. The horses, they say, are the senses; and
their paths are the objects of sense. When the
soul becomes one with the mind and the senses
he is called 'one who has joys and sorrows'. He
who has not right understanding and whose
mind is never steady is not the ruler of his life,
like a bad driver with wild horses. But he who
has right understanding and whose mind is
ever steady is the ruler of his life, like a good
driver with well-trained horses. He who has
not right understanding, is careless and never
pure, reaches not the End of the journey; but
wanders on from death to death. But he who
has understanding is careful and ever pure,
reaches the End of the journey, from which he
never returns.

Katha Upanishad, 3(3-8)

Hence one can and should act by holding the stallions of his senses in check by the reins of his mind. On His own success in achieving spiritual emancipation, the Enlightened One (Buddha) uttered the following:

Blessed is he who does no harm to his fellow beings. Blessed is he who overcomes wrong and is free from passion. To the highest bliss has he attained who has conquered all selfishness and vanity. He has become the Buddha, the Perfect One, the Blessed One, the Holy One.

The Karmayogi, who has fully conquered his mind and subdued his senses, whose heart is pure, and who has identified his self with the Self of all beings (viz. God) remains unaffected, even though performing action.
Bhagavad Gita, V.7

The things of the world and its inhabitants are subject to change. They are combinations of elements that existed before and all living creatures are what their past actions made them, for the law of Karma (Cause and Effect) is uniform and without exception.
Samyutta-nikaya, 12.20.30

Man is bound by shackles of Karma only when engaged in actions other than work performed for the sake of sacrifice. Therefore, Arjuna, do you efficiently perform your duty, free from attachment, for the sake of sacrifice alone.
Bhagavad Gita, III.9

Self-control is the mark of the awakened soul. Only when we renounce the treasures of the world can we possess the jewel of immortality.

Death carries off a man who is gathering (life's) flowers, whose mind is distracted, even as a flood carries off a sleeping village.
Dhammapada, v. 47
When the Brahmin has reached the other shore in both laws, to him who knows all bonds vanish.
Dhammapada, v. 384
Cut off the five, get rid of the five, master the five. A mendicant who has freed himself from the five fetters is called 'one who has crossed the flood' (of rebirth).*
Dhammapada, v. 370

A man whose mind wanders among desires, and is longing for objects of desire, goes to life and death according to his desires. But he who possesses the end of all longing, and whose self has found fulfillment, even in this life his desires will fade away.
Mundaka Upanishad, 3.2
The five subtle elements, the ego, the intellect, primordial matter, the ten organs, the mind and the five objects of sense.
Bhagavad Gita, XIII.5

The five factors which should be severed are doubt, egoism, lust, hatred and false asceticism. The five conditions to be eliminated are desire for existence of form, formless existence, self-assertion, pride and ignorance. The five stages to be mastered are faith, courage, cognizance, contemplation, and wisdom. The five fetters are avarice, hatred, folly, pride and false beliefs. When ignorance and desire are eliminated and wisdom and purity take their place, the mind achieves meditative calm and experiences the bliss of Nirvana. Its senses are stilled and it is in rapturous contemplation with its own reality and sees the life of the body and the material world as having no intrinsic worth. Such a detached mind has no hope for selfish or personal gain, and is without envy, or desire, or demands. It wants for nothing.

Sometimes also regarded as greed, anger, conceit, pride and ignorance (See also *Bhagavad Gita, XIII.6*).

DETACHMENT

Detachment in one's actions in life is emphasized as a requisite to attainment of purity. The human entity is viewed as the raft cast upon a sea of desires and the test lies in sailing the seas to the farther shore in serenity with fixity of purpose while avoiding the storms and turbulences of desire, lust and cravings. While in a negative sense this condition of detachment can be achieved by freeing one's mind from any cravings for the outcome of one's actions of sacrifice, or renunciation, the correct and positive method emphasized in both Hinduism and Buddhism for achieving freedom from life's turbulences and entrapments and attaining the *farther shore* (Brahmavihara or Nirvana) is through undeviating concentration on the goal, i.e. the Supreme, or in the case of Buddhism, the Buddha and the Dharma.

The craving of a thoughtless man grows like a creeper. Like a monkey wishing for fruit in a forest he bounds hither and thither (from one life to another). Whomsoever this fierce craving, full of poison, overcomes in the world, his sorrows increase like the abounding birana grass.

Dhammapada, vv. 334,335

Arjuna, in this blessed path the intellect is determinate and one-pointed; whereas the intellect of the undecided (ignorant men moved by desires) is scattered in many directions and endlessly diverse. Arjuna, those who are obsessed by desire and devoted to the letter of the Vedas, who look upon heaven as the supreme goal and argue that there is nothing beyond heaven, are unwise. They utter flowery speech recommending many acts of various kinds for the attainment of pleasure and prosperity with rebirths as their fruit. Those whose minds are carried away by such words, and who are deeply attached to pleasure and worldly prosperity, cannot attain the determinate intellect concentrated on God.

Bhagavad Gita, II.41,42,43,44

I declare to you this good (counsel). "Do ye, as many as are gathered here, dig up the root of craving as one digs up the birana grass to find the usira root, that Mara (Death) may not destroy you again and again even as the river destroys the reeds (on the bank). As a tree, even though it has been cut down, grows again if its root is firm and uninjured (i.e. safe), even so if the adherences of craving are not destroyed, this suffering returns to us again and again."

Dhammapada, vv.337,338

The branches of this tree, nourished by the three Gunas, and having sense-enjoyments for their tender leaves, extend both downwards and upwards; and its roots (in the shape of egoism and latent desires) which bind the soul according to his actions in this mortal world are also spread in all regions, higher as well as lower. Its nature, what it is stated to be, is not actually perceived here; for it has neither beginning nor end, nor even stability. So, cutting down this Peepul tree, whose roots are so deep-laid, by the formidable weapon of dispassion, one should deligently seek that Supreme State (God), having reached which one never returns.

Bhagavad Gita, XV.2,3,4

THE GOD OF BUDDHA

Him whose thirty-six[72] streams flowing towards pleasures of sense are strong, whose thoughts are set on passion, the waves carry away that misguided man. The streams flow everywhere; the creeper (of passion) keeps on springing up. If you see that creeper sprung up, cut its root by means of wisdom.
Dhammapada. vv. 339,340

Turbulent by nature, the senses even of a wise man, who is practicing self-control forcibly carry away his mind, Arjuna. Therefore having controlled them all and collecting his mind, one should sit for meditation devoting oneself heart and soul to Me. For he whose senses are mastered, his mind has become stable. For the uncontrolled, there is no intelligence; nor for the uncontrolled is there the power of concentration, and for him without concentration there is no peace and for the unpeaceful how can there be happiness?
Bhagavad Gita, II.60,61,66

To creatures happen pleasures and wide-ranging endearments. Hugging those pleasures they hanker after them. Those men indeed undergo birth and old age. Men driven on by craving run about like a hunted hare. Fast bound in its fetters, they undergo suffering for a long time, again and again.
Dhammapada, vv. 341,342

But unsafe are the boats of sacrifice to go to the farthest shore; unsafe are the eighteen books where the lower actions are explained. The unwise who praise them as the highest end go to old age and death again. Abiding in the midst of ignorance, but thinking themselves wise and learned, fools aimlessly go hither and thither, like blind led by the blind.
Mundaka Upanishad, II.7,8

Men driven on by craving run about like a hunted hare. Let, therefore, the medicant, wishing for himself freedom from passion, shake off craving.
Dhammapada, v. 343

When the mind runs after the roving senses, it carries away the understanding, even as a wind carries away a ship on the waters.
Bhagavad Gita, II.67

And the first step towards 'Detachment' is 'Restraint':

Restraint in the eye is good; good is restraint in the ear; in the nose restraint is good; good is restraint in the tongue. In the body restraint is good, good is restraint in speech; in thought restraint is good, good is restraint in all things. A mendicant who is restrained in all things is freed from all sorrow.
Dhammapada, vv. 360,361

But a man of disciplined mind, who moves along the objects of sense, with the senses under control and free from attachment and aversion, he attains purity of spirit. And in that purity of spirit, there is produced for him an end of all sorrow; the intelligence of such a man of pure spirit is soon established in the peace of the self.
Bhagavad Gita, II.64,65

He whose pleasance is the law, who delights in the law, meditates on the law, follows the law, that mendicant does not fall from the true law.
Dhammapada, v.364

Therefore, O Mighty-armed (Arjuna), he whose senses are all withdrawn from their objects his intelligence is firmly set.
Bhagavad Gita, II.68

---

[72]Thirty-six streams are the six organs of sense and the six objects of sense in relation to a desire for sensual pleasures (kama), a desire for existence (bhava), and a desire for prosperity (vibhava).

He who controls his hand, he who controls his feet, he who controls his speech, he who is well-controlled, he who delights inwardly, who is collected, who is alone and content, him they call a mendicant.

Dhammapada, v. 362

The man who is united with the Divine and knows the truth thinks 'I do nothing at all' for in seeing, hearing, touching, smelling, tasting, walking, sleeping, breathing; in speaking, emitting, grasping, opening and closing the eye he holds that only the senses are occupied with the objects of the senses.

Bhagavad Gita, V.8,9

The mendicant who controls his tongue, who speaks wisely, not with pride, who illuminates the meaning and the law, his utterance is sweet.

Dhammapada, v. 363

Unoffensive, truthful, agreeable and wholesome speech, and practice of study of the Vedas—these are called austerity of speech.

Bhagavad Gita, XVII.15

Like the Teachers of the other great Faiths, the Buddha, too, clearly asserts that we can become masters of Karma through detachment and faith in His Dharma and by so doing negate our Karmic formations right here on earth, in this world of *comings and goings*. In this very life we can become free in our deepest being. There is no implication here of overriding the natural order by any transcendental purpose, but the recognition that this same natural order comprises an even higher plain, the spiritual, where faith born of knowledge in the Dharma replaces mere action as the way to spiritual perfection.

He who is without craving, without appropriation, who is skillful in understanding words and their meanings, who knows the order of letters (which are before and which are after), he is called the great sage, the great person. This is his last body.

Dhammapada, v. 352

When your mind confused by hearing conflicting statements, will remain steadfast and firm in meditation you will then attain Union with God.

Bhagavad Gita, II.53

Weeds are the bane of fields and passion the bane of this mankind; therefore offerings made to those free from passion bring great reward. Weeds are the bane of fields and hatred is the bane of this mankind; therefore offerings made to those free from hatred bring great reward.

Dhammapada, vv. 356,357

When a man dwells in his mind on the objects of sense, attachment to them is produced. From attachment springs desire and from desire comes anger. From anger arises bewilderment, from bewilderment loss of memory; and from loss of memory, the destruction of intelligence and from the destruction of intelligence he perishes.

Bhagavad Gita, II.62,63

Him I call a Brahmin who has cut all the fetters, who never trembles, who has passed beyond attachments, who is separated.

Dhammapada, v. 397

He unto whom all desires enter as waters into the sea, which, though ever being filled is ever motionless, attains to peace and not he who hugs his desires.

Bhagavad Gita, II.70

Self-discipline is not so much a product of one's intelligence as of will power, and when our mind establishes a communion with *the Eternal*, self-discipline and detachment come naturally to us. We are told that by detaching our true self from the not-self our ego can become transformed into a vehicle for the manifestation of the deathless within us.

Craving increases more to a creature who is disturbed by thoughts, full of strong passions, yearning for what is pleasant; he indeed makes his fetters strong.
Dhammapada, v. 349

He whose mind is untroubled in the midst of sorrows and is free from eager desire amid pleasures, he from whom passion, fear, and rage have passed away, he is called a sage of settled intelligence. He who is without affection on any side, who does not rejoice or loathe as he obtains good or evil, his intelligence is firmly set (in wisdom).
Bhagavad Gita, II.56,57

He who delights in quieting his thoughts, always reflecting, dwells on what is not pleasant, he will certainly remove, nay, he will cut the bonds of death.
Dhammapada, v. 350

He who has reached the good, who is fearless, who is without craving and without sin, he has broken the thorns of existence, this body is his last.
Dhammapada, v. 351

The Yogi, however, who diligently takes up the practice, attaining perfection in this very life through the help of latencies of many births, and being thoroughly purged of sin, forthwith reaches the supreme state.
Bhagavad Gita, VI.45

And in the sailing of life's raft over the waters of the world, full of the objects of sense and their corrupting influences on the soul that needs to be vigilant, both Faiths give, as an example of detachment, the analogy of the Lotus leaf, which, though growing out of stagnant water, yet, does not permit any water to cling to it.

He who overcomes in this world this fierce craving, difficult to subdue, sorrows fall off from him like water drops from a lotus leaf.
Dhammapada, v. 336

He, who acts, offering all actions to God and shaking off attachment, remains untouched by sin, as the lotus-leaf by water.
Bhagavad Gita, V.10

Him I call a Brahmin who, like water on the leaf of a lotus or a mustard seed on the point of an awl, does not cling to pleasures.
Dhammapada, v. 401

The difference between the wise man and the fool is not so much appearance or outward behavior but plan and purpose. It is these elements that give meaning to life and our actions. Without a transcendental purpose, which only Religion can provide, man becomes mired in the meaningless. Left to his own devising, engrossed in self-love and vanity, he remains a fool, even though to all outward appearances he may go through the motions of playing the savant or the saint.

Let a fool month after month eat his food with the tip (of a blade) of kusa grass; nevertheless he is not worth the sixteenth part of those who have well understood the law.

Dhammapada, v. 70

All actions are being done by the modes of Prakriti. The fool, whose mind is deluded by egoism considers himself to be the doer.

Bhagavad Gita, III.27

Riches destroy the foolish, not those who seek the beyond (the other shore). By a craving for riches the foolish person destroys himself as he destroys others.

Dhammapada, v. 355

And that by which a misguided fool does not abandon sleep, fear, grief, despondency and also arrogance, that firmness is called Tamasic, Arjuna.

Bhagavad Gita, XVIII.35

Good people walk on whatever happens to them. Good people do not prattle, yearning for pleasures. The wise do not show variation (elation or depression), whether touched by happiness or else by sorrow.

Dhammapada, v. 83

Arjuna, whatever you do, whatever you eat, whatever you offer as oblation to the sacred fire, whatever you bestow as a gift; whatever you do by way of penance, offer it all to Me.

Bhagavad Gita, IX.27

The Buddha, despite being fully cognizant of the extreme difficulty of cultivating a serene and detached mind while living in society with its accompanying snares of pleasures of the senses, did not support asceticism *per se,* but instead taught that right attitude and correct conduct within the context of His Dharma would enable the person to regulate such joys of the senses and relegate them to their proper place in life. The essential was to follow the middle way in facing life and this could only be achieved, according to the Buddha, by understanding the Dharma.

SELFLESS ACTION

It has been argued that, while Hinduism, especially the *Bhagavad Gita,* has urged men on to righteous action as the chief means to perfection and attainment of that complete liberation of spirit, the Buddha has emphasized contemplation and non-action as the swiftest path to Nirvana. One can find both views upheld in the writings of both these great Faiths, and, as we shall see from the following, the Buddha, also, to a remarkable degree, upheld righteous and selfless action as the greatest good and highest duty open to humanity in this world. In fact, if one precept stands out in the whole life and doctrine of the Buddha it is the call for selfless action. Essentially, the highest good in the Buddha's message was attainable not merely by avoiding evil, but by performing correct actions through the cleansing of one's own inner being. One is taught not to renounce works of guiding and improving the world, but to strive for such things and to regard such works as an offering to the Dharma rather than for any thought of personal gain.

45

But he who lives a hundred years, wicked and unrestrained, a life of one day is better if a man is virtuous and reflecting.
Dhammapada, v. 110

Behold the universe in the glory of God; and all that lives and moves on earth. Leaving the transient, find joy in the Eternal; set not your heart on another's possession. Working thus, a man may wish for a life of a hundred years. Only actions done in God bind not the soul of man.
Isa Upanishad, I.1-5

And he who lives a hundred years, ignorant and unrestrained, a life of one day is better for one who is wise and reflecting.
Dhammapada, v. 111

Arjuna, he who works for my sake depends on Me, is devoted to Me, has no attachments and is free from malice towards all beings, reaches Me.
Bhagavad Gita, XI.55

And he who lives a hundred years, idle and weak, a life of one day is better if a man strenuously makes an effort.
Dhammapada, v. 112

Only doing work here, one should wish to live a hundred years. No way is here for thee but this. Only thus Karma (action) cleaveth not to man.
Yajur Veda, 2.40

Get up, do not be thoughtless. Follow the law of virtue. He who practises virtue lives happily in this world as well as in the world beyond.
Dhammapada, v. 168

Those, however, who, controlling all their senses, and even-minded towards all, and devoted to doing good to all creatures, constantly adore as their very self the unthinkable, all pervading, imperishable, ineffable, eternal, immobile, unmanifest and immutable Brahma, they too come to Me.
Bhagavad Gita, XII.3,4

The eschewing of all evil, the perfecting of good deeds, the purifying of one's mind, this is the teaching of the Buddhas.
Dhammapada, v. 183

Therefore, let the scripture be your authority in determining what ought to be done and what ought not to be done. Knowing this, you should do here only such action as is sanctioned by scriptural ordinance.
Bhagavad Gita, XVI.24

Those who discern evil as evil and what is not evil as not evil, such men, following the true doctrines, enter the good path.
Dhammapada, v. 319

When a man speaks words of truth he speaks words of greatness: know the nature of truth. When a man knows, he can speak truth. He who does not know cannot speak truth; know the nature of knowledge.
Chandogya Upanishad, 7.16

As we see, seven out of the eight aspects of the noble eightfold path fall into the category of active striving while the last one, right meditation, is considered as 'contemplation':

The eightfold path consists of: right views (sammadithi); right aspirations (sammasamkappa); right speech (sammavaca); right ac-

What is needful? Righteousness, and sacred learning and teaching. Truth, and sacred learning and teaching. Meditation, and sacred *tions (sammakammanto); right living (sammajivo); right exertion (sammavayamo); right recollection (sammasati); right meditation (sammasamadhi).*

learning and teaching. Self-control, and sacred learning and teaching. Peace, and sacred learning and teaching. Ritual, and sacred learning and teaching. Humanity, and sacred learning and teaching.

Taittirya Upanishad, I.5-6

However, the correct action that the Buddha enunciates is not the kind of action performed for the sake of merits or rewards. It is to be totally selfless and without desire for gain, either material or spiritual. Nor should one expect to reach 'liberation' through any hypocritical means. Only those actions done with a selfless and unattached mentality will not enmesh the soul in the coils of the ephemeral world.

He, who will wear the yellow robe without having cleansed himself from impurity, who is devoid of truth and self-control, is not deserving of the yellow robe.

Dhammapada, v. 9

Sri Bhagavan said: "He who does the work which he ought to do without seeking its fruit he is the sannyasin, he is the yogi, not he who does not light the sacred fire, and performs no rites."

Bhagavad Gita, VI.1

He who, for his own sake or for the sake of another, does not wish for a son, or wealth or a kingdom, if he does not wish for his own prosperity by unfair means he certainly is virtuous, wise, and religious.

Dhammapada, v. 84

What they call renunciation, that know to be disciplined activity, O Pandava, for no one becomes a yogi who has not renounced his selfish purpose.

Bhagavad Gita, VI.2

But he who puts away depravity, is well grounded in all virtues, and is possessed of self-restraint and truth is indeed worthy of the yellow robe.

Dhammapada, v. 10

Arjuna, perform your duties dwelling in Yoga, relinquishing attachment, and indifferent to success and failure; equanimity is called Yoga.

Bhagavad Gita, II.48

Many men who are clad in yellow robes are ill-behaved and unrestrained. Such evil-doers by their evil deeds go to hell.

Dhammapada, v. 307

For wise men endowed with equanimity, renouncing the fruit of actions and freed from the shackles of birth, attain the blissful superstate.

Bhagavad Gita, II.51

Subhuti, if one Bodhisatva bestows in charity sufficient of the seven treasures to fill as many worlds as there be sand grains in the river Ganges, and another, realizing that all things are egoless, attains perfection through patient forbearance, the merit of the latter will far exceed that of the former. Why is this Subhuti? It is because all Bodhisattvas are insentient as to the rewards of merit. Subhuti, Bodhisattvas who achieve merit should not be

Therefore, mentally surrendering all actions to Me and with myself as your sole object, have your mind constantly fixed on Me. resorting to the Yoga of equanimity. With your mind thus fixed on Me, you shall get over all difficulties by My grace. And if out of pride you will not listen to me, you will be utterly destroyed.

Bhagavad Gita, XVIII.57,58

47

THE GOD OF BUDDHA

fettered with desire for rewards. Thus it is said that the rewards of merit are not received.
Vajra-Sattva XXVIII
(Attachment to Rewards of Merit)

Your right is to work only, but never to the fruit thereof. Let not the fruit of action be your object, nor let your attachment be to inaction.
Bhagavad Gita, II.47

Arjuna, those actions, however, do not bind Me, unattached as I am to those actions and remain indifferent.
Bhagavad Gita, IX.9

The splendid chariots of kings wear away; the body also comes to old age but the virtue of the good never ages, thus the good teach to each other.
Dhammapada, v. 151
The swans go on the path of the sun, they go through the sky by means of their miraculous power. The wise are led out of this world, having conquered Mara (the tempter) and his hosts.
Dhammapada, v. 175

I know that treasures pass away and that the Eternal is not reached by the transient. I have thus laid the fire of sacrifice of Nachiketas, and by burning in it the transient I have reached the Eternal. Before your eyes have been spread, Nachiketas, the fulfillment of all desire, the dominion of the world, the eternal reward of ritual, the shore where there is no fear, the greatness of fame and boundless spaces. With strength and wisdom you have renounced them all.
Katha Upanishad, II.10,11

Hence, selfless and without any attachments to the results of one's acts, one's deeds begin to reflect the attributes of the 'Divine Doer.' This is the kind of action which supersedes all other acts, whether performed for penance, or as sacrifice, or charity for obtaining some merit, or for attainment of some higher goal. Because the truly liberated person has nothing to gain by action or non-action and hence perfectly content in the joy of having recognized the Supreme, *the Eternal,* he, without any desire or attachment, undertakes to act for the welfare of the world. The Buddha announces that activity for achieving the *weal of the world* is the duty of every person. Similarly, in the *Bhagavad Gita,* Krishna proclaims that one who merely devotes one's time to the worship of God, but is indifferent to the needs of one's fellow beings, obtains no merit and is actually a hypocrite, for even the Lord is constantly manifesting[73] Himself in action for the protection of the righteous and the order of the world. The Vedas, also, attest, in the strongest terms, to this duty to work for the welfare of humanity. Spiritual thoughts must be proved by selfless action—one without the other is not possible.

He, indeed, is called a mendicant who does not count as his own any name and form, who does not grieve from having nothing.
Dhammapada, v. 367

O man, if thou has power over the six passions (viz. lust, anger, greed, foolish attachment, envy and vanity) then do something constructive for the good of thy fellow-beings; otherwise, thou art good for nothing.
Ako Sam Veda 1

---

[73]*Bhagavad Gita,* III.24 ('. . . Arjuna, if I do not perform action these worlds will perish . . .'); Also see *Atharva Veda,* 5.

The mendicant who lives in friendliness and calm (has faith) in the doctrine of the Buddha, he will attain the tranquil, blessed place where (bodily) existence is at rest.
Dhammapada, v. 368

Completely rid of passion, fear and anger, wholly absorbed in Me, depending on Me, and purified by the penance of wisdom, many have become one with me even in the past.
Bhagavad Gita, IV.10

Empty the boat, O mendicant; when emptied it will go lightly. Having cut off passion and hatred then you will go to freedom.
Dhammapada, v. 369

Therefore, without attachment, perform always the work that has to be done, for man attains to the highest by doing work without attachment.
Bhagavad Gita, III.19

That mendicant is said to be calmed who has a calmed body, a calmed speech, and a calmed mind, who is well-established, who has rejected the baits of the world.
Dhammapada, v. 378

Similarly, in this world he has no interest whatever to gain by the actions that he has done and none to be gained by the actions that he had not done. He does not depend on all these beings for any interest of his.
Bhagavad Gita, III.18

The mendicant full of delight, calm (with faith) in the doctrine of the Buddha, will certainly reach the peaceful state, the cessation of natural existence and happiness.
Dhammapada, v. 381

Even among all Yogis, he who devoutly worships Me with his mind focused on Me is considered by Me to be the best Yogi.
Bhagavad Gita, VI.47

Even if he recites a large number of scriptural texts but being slothful, does not act accordingly, he is like a cowherd counting the cows of others, he has no share in religious life. Even if he recites only a small number, if he is one who acts rightly in accordance with the law, he having forsaken passion, hatred, and folly, being possessed of true knowledge and serenity of mind, being free from worldly desires both in this world and the next, has a share in the religious life.
Dhammapada, vv. 19,20

A Brahmin, who has obtained enlightenment, has the same use for all the Vedas as one has for a small pond in the midst of a place flooded with water on all sides.
Bhagavad Gita, II.46
Of what use is the Rig Veda to one who does not know the Spirit from Whom the Rig Veda comes, and in Whom all things abide? For only those who have found Him have found peace.
Svetasvatara Upanishad, 4.8

And, further, from the conversations with Kutadanta, the leader of the Brahmins, we see true wisdom as the fruit of practice:

Kutadanta said: "I have faith in the glory and excellency of thy doctrines. My eye cannot as yet endure the light; but I now understand that there is no self, and the truth dawns upon me. Sacrifices cannot save, and invocations are idle talk. But how shall I find the path to life everlasting? I know all the Vedas by heart and have not found the truth."[74]

The ships of Truth bear the righteous man across (the ocean of misery).
Rig Veda, 9

---

[74] *The Questions of King Milinda.*

THE GOD OF BUDDHA

Said the Buddha:[75] *"Learning is a good thing;
but it availeth not. True wisdom can be acquired by practice only. Practice the truth that
thy brother is the same as thou.*[76] *Walk in the
noble path of righteousness and thou wilt
understand that while there is death in self,
there is immortality in truth."*
*Said Kutadanta: "Let me take my refuge in
the Blessed One, in the Dharma, and in the
brotherhood. Accept me as thy disciple and let
me partake of the bliss of immortality."*

By light do thou quicken and advance Truth
for the sake of Truth; by Renunciation, by
Dharma (righteousness) do thou advance
Dharma.

Yajur Veda, 15

With the idea that everything belongs to Him
(TAT) the various acts of sacrifice, penance
and gifts are performed by the seekers of
liberation without desiring any fruit in return.
The Divine name 'Sat' is employed in the
sense of truth and goodness; even so, Arjuna,
the term 'Sat' is used in the sense of a praiseworthy act. Steadfastness in sacrifice, penance
and gift is also designated 'Sat'; and verily
action for the sake of Him (God) is termed
'Sat'.

Bhagavad Gita, XVII.25,26,27

The whole gamut of Buddha's teachings concerning our behaviour toward
our fellow beings is beautifully contained in the following, oft-quoted verses:

*Do not deceive, do not despise each other any-
where. Do not be angry, nor should ye secret
resentment bear, for as a mother risks her life
and watches over her child, so boundless be
your love to all, so tender, kind and mild.*
Metta Sutta, Sutta-nipata, v. 148

Freedom from hate I bring to you concord and
unanimity. Love one another as the cow her
newborn calf loves.

Athur Veda, 3.27

As a mother her child, protect us, O Life: give
us glory and give us wisdom.

Prasna Upanishad, 2.13

*Let a man overcome anger by non-anger, let
him overcome evil by good, let him overcome
the miser by liberality, let him overcome the
liar by truth.*
Dhammapada, v. 223

Conquer the anger of others by non-anger,
conquer evil doers by saintliness; conquer the
miser by gifts; conquer falsehood by truth.
Mahabharata (Udyogaparva, 38,73,74)

DOING ONE'S DUTY

The Buddha Himself leads the way in service to humanity. He teaches us to
live in the world and yet not be a part of its worldliness. To Him, our duty
consists of active participation in the task to lift mankind to its full human
potential, material as well as spiritual.

---

[75] *Udana.*
[76] *Dhammapada,* vv. 129,130.

Let no one neglect his own task for the sake of another's however great; let him, after he has discerned his own task, devote himself to his task.

Dhammapada, v. 166

One's own duty, though devoid of merit, is preferable to the duty of another well performed. Even death in the performance of one's own duty brings blessedness: another's duty is fraught with fear.

Bhagavad Gita, III.35

In further substantiation of the fact that the Buddhas do not appear in the world merely to proclaim some kind of passive and purely contemplative system of life, divorced from the everyday needs of society and indifferent to one's duties and responsibilities therein, the following conversation with the Jain general, Siha (who after this discourse with the Buddha became a firm convert to His Dharma), should serve to give a gist of the Buddha's teachings concerning 'living the life'.[78] We quote from the *Mahavagga* on Siha's 'Questions Concerning Annihilation.'

At that time many distinguished citizens were sitting together assembled in the town-hall and spoke in many ways in praise of the Buddha, of the Dharma, and of the Sangha. Siha, the general-in-chief, a disciple of the Niggantha sect, was sitting among them. And Siha thought: "Truly, the Blessed One must be the Buddha, the Holy One. I will go and visit him." Then Siha, the general, went to the place where the Niggantha chief, Nataputta, was; and having approached him, he said: "I wish, Lord, to visit the samana Gautama." Nataputta said: "Why should you, Siha, who believes in the result of actions according to their moral merit, go to visit the samana Gotama, who denies the result of actions? The samana Gautama, O Siha, denies the result of actions; he teaches the doctrine of non-action; and in this doctrine he trains his disciples." Then the desire to go and visit the Blessed One, which had arisen in Siha, the general, abated. Hearing again the praise of the Buddha, of the Dharma, and of the Sangha, Siha asked the Niggantha chief a second time; and again Nataputta persuaded him not to go. When a third time the general heard some men of distinction extol the merits of the Buddha, the Dharma, and the Sangha, the general thought: "Truly, the samana Gautama must be the Holy Buddha. What are the Nigganthas to me, whether they give their consent or not? I shall go without asking their permission to visit him, the Blessed One, the Holy

---

[77] It should be of interest here to note that this dictum had clearly proclaimed the principle of the dignity of labor milleniums before western society conceived and acted on it.

[78] *Mahavagga,* VI.31.

Buddha." And Siha, the general, said to the Blessed One: "I have heard, Lord, that the samana Gautama denies the result of actions; he teaches the doctrine of non-action, saying that the actions of sentient beings do not receive their reward, for he teaches annihilation and the contemptibleness of all things; and in this doctrine he trains his disciples. Teachest thou the doing away of the soul and the burning away of man's being? Pray tell me, Lord, do those who speak thus say the truth, or do they bear false witness against the Blessed One, passing off a spurious Dharma as thy Dharma?" The Blessed One said: "There is a way, Siha, in which one who says so is speaking truly of me; on the other hand, Siha, there is a way in which one who says the opposite is speaking truly of me, too."

"Listen, and I will tell thee: I teach, Siha, the not-doing of such actions as are unrighteous, either by deed, or by word, or by thought; I teach the non-bringing about of all those conditions of heart which are evil and not good. However, I teach, Siha, the doing of such actions as are righteous, by deed, by word, and by thought; I teach the bringing about of all those conditions of heart which are good and not evil. I teach, Siha, that all the conditions of heart which are evil and not good, unrighteous actions by deed, by word, and by thought, must be burnt away. He who has freed himself, Siha, from all those conditions of heart which are evil and not good, he who has destroyed them as a palm-tree which is rooted out, so that they cannot grow up again, such a man has accomplished the eradication of self."

He comes to the thought of those who know him beyond thought, not to those who imagine he can be attained by thought. He is unknown to the learned and known to the simple. He is known in the ecstasy of an awakening which opens the door of life eternal. For a man who has known him, the light of truth shines; for one who has not known, there is darkness.

Kena Upanishad, II.3

Man does not attain freedom from action without entering upon action; nor does he reach perfection merely by renunciation of action.

Bhagavad Gita, III.4

Even the wise are at a loss to know what is action and what is inaction. Therefore, I shall expound to you the truth about action, knowing which you will be freed from its evil effect (binding nature). The truth about action must be known; and the truth of prohibited action must also be known; even so, the truth about inaction must be known. For mysterious are the ways of action.

Bhagavad Gita, IV.16,17

Arjuna, as the unwise act with attachment, so should the wise man, seeking maintenance of the world order, act without attachment. A wise man established in Me should not unsettle the mind of the ignorant attached to action, but shall get them to perform all their duties, duly performing them himself.

Bhagavad Gita, III. 25,26

He, who sees inaction in action, and action in inaction, is wise among men; he is a Yogi, who has accomplished all action. He whose undertakings are all free from desire and thoughts of the world, and whose actions are burnt up by the fire of wisdom, him even the wise call a sage. He, who, having totally given up attachment to actions and their fruits, has got over the dependence on the world, and is ever satisfied, does nothing at all, though he may be ever engaged in action.

Bhagavad Gita, IV.18,19,20

He, whose attachment has gone, whose mind is established in Knowledge, and who works for the sake of sacrifice, all actions of that liberated man melt away.

Bhagavad Gita, IV.23

Arjuna, acquiring that Knowledge, you will no more be subject to delusion like this, and through it you will see all beings first in your own self, and then in Me.

Bhagavad Gita, IV.35

"I proclaim, Siha, the annihilation of egotism, of lust, of ill-will, of delusion. However, I do not proclaim the annhiliation of forbearance, of love, of charity, and of truth. I deem, Siha, unrighteous actions contemptible, whether they be performed by deed, or by word, or by thought; but I deem virtue and righteousness praiseworthy."

And Siha said: "One doubt still lurks in my mind concerning the doctrine of the Blessed One. Will the Blessed One consent to clear the cloud away so that I may understand the Dharma as the Blessed One teaches it?"

The Tathagata having given his consent, Siha continued:[79] *"I am a soldier, O Blessed One, and am appointed by the king to enforce his laws and to wage his wars. Does the Tathagata, who teaches kindness without end and compassion with all sufferers, permit the punishment of the criminal? and, further, does the Tathagata declare that it is wrong to go to war for the protection of our homes, our wives,our children, and our property? Does the Tathagata teach the doctrine of a complete self-surrender, so that I should suffer the evil-doer to do what he pleases and yield submissively to him who threatens to take by violence what is my own? Does the Tathagata maintain that all strife, including such warfare as is waged for a righteous cause, should be forbidden?"*

It is indeed impossible for any embodied being to abstain from action altogether. But he who gives up the fruit of action, he is said to be the relinquisher. Pleasant, unpleasant and mixed—threefold is the fruit of action accruing after death to those who have not relinquished, there is none whatever for those who have renounced. O Mighty-armed (Arjuna), learn from Me, these five factors, for the accomplishment of all actions, as stated in the Sankhya doctrine. The seat of action and likewise the agent, the instruments of various sorts, the many kinds of efforts and providence being the fifth.

Bhagavad Gita, XVIII.11,12,13,14,15

The Buddha replied: "He who deserves punishment must be punished, and he who is worthy of favor must be favored. Yet at the same time he teaches to do no injury to any living being but to be full of love and kindness. These injunctions are not contradictory, for whosoever must be punished for the crimes which he has committed, suffers his injury not

Yield not to unmanliness, Arjuna; ill does it become you. Shaking off this paltry faint-heartedness arise, O scorcher of your enemies.

Bhagavad Gita, II.3

Besides, considering your own duty you should not waver; for there is nothing more welcome

[79] Also in, *Questions of King Milinda,* pp. 254-257.

through the ill-will of the judge but on account of his evil-doing. His own acts have brought upon him the injury that the executer of the law inflicts. When a magistrate punishes, let him not harbor hatred in his breast, yet a murderer, when put to death, should consider that this is the fruit of his own act. As soon as he will understand that the punishment will purify his soul, he will no longer lament his fate, but rejoice at it."

for a man of the warrior class than a righteous war.

Bhagavad Gita, II.31

Just as boyhood, youth and old age are attributed to the soul through this body, even so it attains another body. The wise man does not get deluded about this. O son of Kunti, the contacts between the senses and their objects, which give rise to the feelings of heat and cold, pleasure and pain, etc., are transitory and fleeting; therefore, Arjuna, ignore them. Arjuna, the wise man to whom pain and pleasure are alike, and who is not tormented by these contacts, becomes eligible for immortality. This soul is unmanifest; it is unthinkable; and it is spoken of as immutable. Therefore, knowing this as such, you should not grieve.

Bhagavad Gita, II.13,14,15,25

And the Blessed One continued: "The Tathagata teaches that all warfare in which man tries to slay his brother is lamentable, but he does not teach that those who go to war in a righteous cause after having exhausted all means to preserve the peace are blameworthy. He must be blamed who is the cause of war."

Now, if you will not wage such a righteous war, then, abandoning your duty and losing your reputation, you will incur sin. Either slain in battle you will attain heaven, or gaining victory you will enjoy sovereignty of the earth; therefore, arise, Arjuna, determined to fight. Treating alike pleasure and pain, gain and loss, victory and defeat, get ready for the fight, then, fighting thus you will not incur sin.

Bhagavad Gita, II.33,37,38

"The Tathagata teaches a complete surrender of self, but does not teach a surrender of anything to those powers that are evil, be they men or gods or the elements of nature. Struggle must be, for all life is a struggle of some kind. But he that struggles should look to it lest he struggles in the interest of self against truth and righteousness."

Therefore, Arjuna, My considered and best opinion is that these acts of sacrifice, gift and penance, and all other duties, must be performed relinquishing attachment and fruit.

Bhagavad Gita, XVIII.6

He who forsakes his duty for fear of bodily discomfort, saying that all action is troublesome, practicing this Rajasic form of relinquishment, he does not get the fruit of relinquishment at all.

Bhagavad Gita, XVIII.8

"He who struggles in the interest of self, so that he himself may be great or powerful or rich or famous, will have no reward, but he who struggles for righteousness and truth will have great reward, for even his defeat will be a victory."

An action enjoined by the scriptures, which is done as a duty, giving up attachment and fruit, that alone is regarded as a Sattvic form of relinquishment.

Bhagavad Gita, XVIII.9

"Self is not a fit vessel to receive any great success; self is small and brittle and its contents will soon be spilt for the benefit, and perhaps also for the curse, of others."

"He who goeth to battle, O Siha, even though it be in a righteous cause, must be prepared to be slain by his enemies, for that is the destiny of warriors; and should his fate overtake him he has no reason for complaint."

He who neither hates action, which does not lead to happiness, nor is attached to action, which is conducive to good, that person, imbued with the quality of goodness, has attained freedom from doubts, he is wise and a man of true renunciation.

Bhagavad Gita, XVIII.10

"But he who is victorious should remember the instability of earthly things. His success may be great, but be it ever so great the wheel of fortune may turn again and bring him down into the dust."

Therefore, dedicating all actions to Me with your mind fixed on Me, the Self of all, freed from hope and the feeling of meum and cured of mental fever, fight.

Bhagavad Gita, III.30

"However, if he moderates himself and, extinguishing all hatred in his heart, lifts his downtrodden adversary up and says to him, 'Come now and make peace and let us be brothers,' he will gain a victory that is not a transient success, for its fruits will remain forever.

Krishna, I covet not victory, nor kingdom, nor pleasures. Govinda, of what use will kingdom, or luxuries, or even life be to us. Krishna, I do not want to kill them, though they may kill me, even for the sovereignty of the three worlds; how, then, for this earth.

Bhagavad Gita, I.32,35

"Great is a successful general, O Siha, but he who has conquered self is the greater victor." [xo]

"The doctrine of the conquest of self, O Siha, is not taught to destroy the souls [x1] of men, but to preserve them. He who has conquered self is more fit to live, to be successful, and to gain victories than he who is the slave of self.

Arjuna, this soul residing in the bodies of all can never be slain; therefore, it does not behove you to grieve for any being.

Bhagavad Gita, II.30

"He, whose mind is free from the illusion of self, will stand and not fall in the battle of life."

He, who has subdued his mind and body, has given up all objects of enjoyment and has no craving—performing sheer bodily action, such a person does not incur sin.

Bhagavad Gita, IV.21

[xo]See also *Dhammapada*, vv. 103, 104, 105

[x1]Note: It is of interest to note that the Buddha here specifically acknowledges the existence of the soul and also states that His doctrine is to ensure the immortality of the soul. See also previous page (54), about the murderer rejoicing for his soul when put to death, because, thereby, his soul is purified.

THE GOD OF BUDDHA

"He, whose intentions are righteousness and justice, will meet with no failure, but be successful in his enterprises and his success will endure. He who harbors in his heart love of truth will live and not die, for he has drunk the water of immortality."

He, who is contented with whatever is got unsought, is free from jealousy and has transcended all pairs of opposites (like joy and grief), and is balanced in success and failure—such a Karmayogi, though acting, is not bound.

Bhagavad Gita, IV.22

"Struggle then, O general, courageously; and fight thy battles vigorously, but be a soldier of truth and the Tathagata will bless thee."

When the Blessed One had spoken thus, Siha, the general said:[82] "Glorious Lord, glorious Lord! Thou hast revealed the truth. Great is the doctrine of the Blessed One. Thou, indeed, art the Buddha, the Tathagata, the Holy One. Thou art the teacher of mankind. Thou showest us the road of salvation, for this indeed is true deliverance. He who follows Thee will not miss the light to enlighten his path. He will find blessedness and peace. I take my refuge, Lord, in the Blessed One, and in His doctrine, and in His brotherhood. May the Blessed One receive me from this day forth while my life lasts as a disciple who has taken refuge in Him."

Therefore, do you perform your alloted duty; for action is superior to inaction. Desisting from action you cannot even maintain your body. Arjuna, he who does not follow the wheel of creation thus set going in this world (i.e. does not perform his duties), sinful and sensual, he lives in vain. Therefore, always efficiently do your duty without attachment. Doing work without attachment, man attains the Supreme.

Bhagavad Gita, III.8,16,19

Having known thus, action was performed even by the ancient seekers of salvation; therefore, do you also perform such actions as were performed by the ancients in the former times.

Bhagavad Gita, IV.15

And the Blessed One said: "Consider first, Siha, what thou doest. It is becoming that persons of rank like thyself should do nothing without due consideration."

Siha's faith in the Blessed One increased. He replied: "Had other teachers, Lord, succeeded in making me their disciple, they would carry around their banners through the whole city of Vesali, shouting: Siha, the general has become our disciple! For the second time, Lord, I take my refuge in the Blessed One, and in the Dharma, and in the Sangha; may the Blessed One receive me from this day forth while my life lasts as a disciple who has taken his refuge in Him."

Said the Blessed One: "For a long time, Siha, offerings have been given to the Nigganthas in thy house. Thou shouldst therefore deem it right also in the future to give them food when they come to thee on their alms-pilgrimage."

Acts of sacrifice, gift and penance should not be relinquished; they must be performed at all events. For sacrifice, gift and penance performed by wise men purify the heart.

Bhagavad Gita, XVIII.5

---

[82]*Mahavagga,* VI.31.

And Siha's heart was filled with joy. He said: "I have been told, Lord, that the samana Gautama says: 'To me alone and to nobody else should gifts be given. My pupils alone and the pupils of no one else should receive offerings.' But the Blessed One exhorts me to give also to the Nigganthas. Well, Lord, we shall see what is seasonable. For the third time, Lord, I take my refuge in the Blessed One, and in His Dharma, and in His fraternity."

And, finally, the Buddha, in His inimitable manner, brings even this performance of one's duty in a righteous war into the framework of that wider and age-old message of all Religion, the message of love and unity.

Not at any time are enmities appeased here through enmity but they are appeased through non-enmity. This is the eternal law.
Dhammapada, v. 5

Victory breeds hatred; the conquered dwells in sorrow. He who has given up (thoughts of both) victory and defeat, he is calm and lives happily.
Dhammapada, v. 201

Fie on the Kshaitrya's Code of Conduct, fie on might and valour, fie on wrath, since through these such a calamity hath overtaken us. Neither have we gained our objective, nor they. We have not vanquished them, nor have they vanquished us.
Mahabharata, (Santiparva, VII.5,24)

The Buddha's advice on co-existence even with our enemies is the product of a higher wisdom that sees beyond the limits of 'me and mine'. He teaches us to destroy those primitive emotions which breed intolerance and conflict and shows us a new and higher level of human relationship based on mutual confidence and universal love.

Just as with her own life a mother shields from hurt her own, her only, child, let all embracing thoughts for all that live be thine—an all-embracing love for all the universe in all its heights and depths and breadth, unstinted love, unmarred by hate within, not rousing enmity.
Sutta-nipata, vv. 149-150

Like the enlightened ones of the past who used to acquire their share in unity, live ye all in harmony with one another, consort in loving sweetness with all, be one in thought and in knowledge. Let the mind-protecting Divine Commandment be equal to all, let there be equal comingling of ye all, let all their minds be as one mind, their attentions be in one accord. I command ye all to be equal under One Holy Command, I bring ye up all alike offering Myself as a sacrifice. Be united in your purpose, let your hearts be as one heart, minds of all as one mind, so that your affairs may be co-operatively well organized.
Rig Veda, VIII.7

MODERATION CONCERNING FOOD

According to the Buddha, all the Tathagatas proclaimed the middle path, not pointing to austerities and penances as the way to salvation, nor to self-indulgence in the world of pleasures. He asked His disciples to avoid either of the extremes of life, to keep from self-indulgence in worldly things, which would ultimately lead to hell, or self-mortification, which would bring them only painful delusion, useless and unprofitable, but, instead, to choose the middle way, the road of moderation and reason. As he states: *Neither abstinence from fish or flesh . . . will cleanse a man who is not free from delusions.* Hence, in matters of food, as in all other aspects of living-the-life, the Buddhas have always preached moderation, unless some practice was to prove definitely harmful to the health of humanity and, hence, required to be forbidden. Thus, we see from the following that the Buddha, just like the Hindus before him, did not specifically lay down prohibitions against the eating of meat, beef, fish or fowl. The *Mahabharata,* also, refers to eating of beef or veal and all other kinds of animals which were usually offered to honored guests.

Not reviling, not injuring, restraint according to the law, moderation in eating, dwelling in solitude, diligence in higher thought, this is the teaching of the awakened.
Dhammapada, v. 185

Arjuna, this Yoga is not for him who eats too much, nor for him who does not eat at all, nor for him who is given to too much sleep, nor for him who is ceaselessly awake. Yoga, which rids one of woes, is accomplished only by him who is regulated in diet and recreations, regulated in performing actions, and regulated in sleeping and waking.
Bhagavad Gita, VI.16,17

And we read from the Vinaya-pitaka:

Then the Lord talked on various things to General Siha. And when he had seen, attained, known Dhamma and plunged into it, had crossed over doubt, put away uncertainty, and had attained without another's help to full confidence in the Teacher's instruction, he invited the Lord to a meal with him on the morrow together with the Order of monks. And the Lord consented by becoming silent. So General Siha asked a man to go and find out if there was meat to hand and during the night had sumptuous solid and soft food prepared. In the morning he told Gautama that the meal was ready, and together with the Order of monks he went to Siha's dwelling and sat down on the appointed seat.

Now at that time many Jains, waving their arms, were moaning from carriage-road to carriage-road, from cross-road to cross-road in Vesali: "Today a fat beast, killed by General Siha, has been made into a meal for the

Birds and beasts were immolated for the sacrificial food. Then before the sacred charger,

recluse Gautama and he had made use of this meat, knowing that it was killed on purpose for him, that the deed was done for his sake."
A certain man whispered these reports into General Siha's ear. "Enough," he replied. "For a long time now these venerable ones have been desiring dispraise of the Buddha, Dhamma and the Order. But, vain, bad, lying as they are, they do not harm this Lord because they are misrepresenting him with what is not fact. Why, even we, for the sake of our livelihood, would not intentionally deprive a living thing of life."

Then General Siha, having with his own hand served and satisfied the Order of monks with the Buddha at its head, sat down at a respectful distance after the Lord had eaten and had withdrawn his hand from the bowl. And when the Lord had roused, rejoiced, gladdened, delighted General Siha with talk on Dhamma, he departed. Having given reasoned talk on this occasion, he then addressed the monks, saying:
'Monks, one should not knowingly make use of meat killed on purpose for one. Whoever should make use of it, there is an offence of wrong-doing. I allow you, monks, fish and meat that are quite pure[83] in these three respects: if they have not been seen, heard or suspected (to have been killed on purpose for a monk).'

Vinaya-pitaka, I. 236-38
(Teaching of the Elders)

priests in rank and order stood. And by rules of Veda guided slew the horse of noble breed, Placed Draupadi, Queen of yajna, by the slain and lifeless steed, Priests adept in sacred duty cooked the steed with pious rite, And the steam of welcome fragrance sanctified the sacred site.
Mahabharata, XII (Aswa-Medha, VI.1,2,4)

Beasts whose flesh is pure and wholesome, dwellers of the lake or sky, Priests assigned each varied offering to each heavenly power on high, Bulls of various breed and colour, steeds of mettle true and tried, Other creatures, full three hundred, to the many stakes were tied.
Mahabharata, XII(Aswa-Medha, III.19,20)

Countless creatures of the wide earth, fishes from the lake and flood, Buffaloes and bulls from pasture, beasts of prey from jungle wood, Birds and every egg-born creature, insects that from moisture spring, Denizens of cave and mountain for the sacrifice they bring. Noble chiefs and mighty monarchs gaze in wonder on the site, Filled with every living object, corn and cattle for the rite, Curd and cake and sweet confection are for feasting Brahmans spread, And a hundred thousand people are with sumptuous viands fed!
Mahabharata, XII
(Aswa-Medha, II.6,7,8,9)

The taboos against beef eating were established in comparatively recent time. Certainly, in the Buddha's time, the kings, at the behest of the Brahmins, sacrificed bullocks and ate of their flesh, and in His conversation with Kutadanta, the head of the Brahmins in the village of Danamati, the Buddha acknowledges this: *Greater than the immolation of bullocks is the sacrifice of self. He who offers to the gods his evil desires will see the uselessness of slaughtering animals at the altar. Blood has no cleansing power, but the eradication of lust will make the heart pure. Better than worshipping gods is obedience to the laws of righteousness.*[84] Further, in the 'Parable of the Mus-

---

[83]The term for this in Pali is 'Pavattamamsa' (Sanskrit: 'Pavitramahs'). See also *Dhammapada,* v. 92.

[84]*Questions of King Milinda.*

tard Seed,"[85] the Buddha, expounding to Kisa Gotami, who had lost her child, consoles her about the transitory nature of life and again refers to the slaughter of bullocks: *Mark! While relatives are looking on and lamenting deeply, one by one mortals are carried off, like oxen that are led to slaughter*—thus again affirming that cattle were certainly slaughtered and eaten even in his day.

The *Majjhima-nikaya* is also quite specific about beef eating by the Hindus of Buddha's day: *And again, monks, a monk reflects on this body according to how it is placed or disposed in respect of the elements, thinking: "In this body are elements of earth, water, heat and wind. It is like a skilled cattle-butcher or his apprentice who, having slaughtered a cow, might sit displaying its carcase at cross-roads. For even so does a monk reflect precisely on this body itself according to how it is placed or disposed. . . ."*[86] In the *Sutta-nipata*, we read that every kind of killing, even human sacrifice, was being practised in His time and in His own kingdom by the Okkaka (Sakya) king.

They asked but rice, beds, garments, ghee, and oil; and with such gifts they made their offerings;—no cows were slaughter'd for their sacrifice. Then came corruption. Bit by bit, they saw the monarch's splendour, women richly dight.

You with your heart full of compassion condemned that part of the Vedas which deals with the sacrifices ordaining the slaughter of animals, O you Kesava, who assumed the body of the Buddha, victory to you, Hari, lord of the world.

Gitagovinda, I.9

Thereon, they (the Brahmins) framed these verses and they sought Okkaka (Sakya): "King," said they, "abounding wealth is thine and substance; offer sacrifice! great store, great wealth hast thou; make sacrifice."

Theron the king, that doughty charioteer, won o'er by Brahmins, offered sacrifice of horses, human victims, and the rest; and, at the close, to Brahmins largesse gave.
Sutta-nipata, vv. 295-299,302,303

"This poor offering of cows that are too old to give milk and too weak to eat grass or drink water must lead to a world of sorrow." And Nachiketas thought of offering himself, and said to his father: "Father, to whom will you give me?" He asked once, and twice, and three times; and then his father answered in anger: "I will give you to Death."

Katha Upanishad, I.1,3

And, finally, as we read in the *Mahaparinibbana Suttanta* (the Book of the Great Decease), the Buddha's last meal itself consisted of rice-cakes and dried flesh of the boar.

---

[85] *Anguttara-nikaya*. (Kisa Gotami was a cousin of the Gautama Buddha.)
[86] *Majjhima-nikaya*, I, 55-63.

THE MEANING OF BRAHMIN

While the Buddha Himself was born into the Kshaitrya class, many of His chief disciples as well as the most distinguished members of His order were Brahmins, and He considered them, together with the Buddhist Mendicants, as deserving of veneration, and used the term Brahmin as a term of honor for the Buddhist Saints or Arahats. Some have even misguidedly called Buddhism a reformed Brahmanism because of the repeated honorofic use made by the Buddha of the title of Brahmin, but such a view cannot be predicated on reality if one views the whole panorama of the Buddha's life and teaching. For, to the Buddha, Brahmin had ceased to mean an individual born in a certain class, or preoccupied in the performance of the rituals, etc., as accepted by the Hindus of His day; instead, it meant a mode of high-minded and righteous life which could be led by any person, irrespective of the class or background he derived from:

Just as, O monks, the great rivers such as the Ganga, the Vamuna, Aciravati, Sarabhu, and Mahi, when they fall into the ocean, lose their former names and clans and are known as the ocean even so do the four castes of Brahmin, Kshatriya, Vaisya and Sudra, when they have gone forth in the Doctrine and Discipline taught by the Tathagata, from a home to a homeless life, lose their former names and class (namagotra) and are known as ascetics.[87]

Just as the flowing rivers disappear in the ocean casting off name and shape, even so the knower, freed from name and shape, attains to the divine person, higher than the high.
Mundaka Upsanishad, 3.2,8

Brahminhood, therefore, to the Buddha, was not a matter of birth but of temperament, and it is because of this that He makes no difference between the titles of Brahmin, or Samana (ascetic), or Bikku (friar).

He who though adorned fosters the serene mind, is calm, controlled, is established (in the Dharma), is chaste, and has ceased to injure all other beings, he indeed is a Brahmin, an ascetic, a Friar.
Dhammapada, v. 142

I consider as a Brahmana that Sudra who is ever endowed with self-restraint, truthfulness and righteousness. A man becomes a Brahmana by his conduct.
Mahabharata (Aranyakaparva, 206.12)

Not by birth does one become an outcast, not by birth does one become a Brahmin; by deeds one becomes an outcast, by deeds one becomes a Brahmin.
Vasala Sutta, 21.27

If these characteristics be observable in a Sudra, and if they be not found in a Brahmana, then such a Sudra is no Sudra and such a Brahmana is no Brahmana.
Mahabharata, (Santiparva, 182.8)

---

[87] *Udana, v. 5.* See also *Bhagavad Gita, Ch.* VI, 7, 8, 9, 10 and Chapter XXVI, (177-187). "Brahmanavaggo" of the *Dhammapada.* Also *Prasna Upanishad, vi.5.*

THE GOD OF BUDDHA

Do not ask about descent, but ask about conduct; from wood, it is true, fire is born; likewise a firm sage, although belonging to a low family, may become noble when restrained (from sinning) by humility.

Sundarikabharadvaja Sutta, 9

Not fish or flesh, not abstinence, not nakedness, shaven head, matted hair, dirt, or garments of hide, not observance of the fire sacrifice or many immortal penances in this world, charms and oblations, observance of the seasons by sacrifice, not these make clean the mortal who has not passed beyond doubt.

Amangandha Sutta, 7.II (Culla Vaga, 2)

Not by matted hair, not by lineage, not by caste does one become a Brahmin. He is a Brahmin in whom there are truth and righteousness. He is blessed. What is the use of matted hair, O fool, what of the raiment of goat skins? Thine inward nature is full of wickedness; the outside thou makest clean. I do not call him a Brahmin because of his origin or his mother. If he be with goods he is called bhovadi. Him I call a Brahmin who is free from goods and free from attachment.

Dhammapada, vv. 393,394,396

Him I call a Brahmin who is free from anger, who is careful of religious duties, observes the moral rules, pure, controlled, and wears his last body. Him I call a Brahmin who, even here, knows the end of his suffering, who has laid aside his burden, who is detached.

Dhammapada, vv. 400,402

Him I call a Brahmin who here has passed beyond the attachments of good and evil, who is free from grief, free from passion, free from impurity. Him I call a Brahmin who, casting off attachment to human things, rises above attachment to heavenly things, is separated from all attachments.

Dhammapada, vv. 412,417

Him I call a Brahmin who does not take, here in the world, what is not given him, be it long or short, small or large, good or bad. Him I call a Brahmin who in this world giving up all craving, wanders about without a home, in whom all craving for existence is extinguished.

Dhammapada, vv. 409,416

He who is clothed with anything, who is fed on any food, who lies down anywhere, him the gods call a Brahmin.

Mahabharata, (Santiparva, 245.12)

Serenity, self control, austerity, purity, forbearance and uprightness, wisdom, knowledge, and faith in religion, these are the duties of the Brahmin, born of his nature.

Bhagavad Gita, XVIII.42

Everything in this whole round of the universe is God-made, God-protected and God pervaded; enjoy what He gives thee, sharing it with thy fellow creatures and without attachment. For whose is all this wealth? It is God's and God's alone. Be not proud, be not greedy.

Yajur Veda, 40.1

He who craves for nothing, who is both internally and externally pure, who is clever and impartial, and has risen above all distractions, who renounces the feeling of doership in all undertakings, that devotee is dear to Me.

Bhagavad Gita, XII.16

He, who neither rejoices nor hates, nor grieves, nor desires, who renounces both good and evil and is full of devotion to Me, is dear to Me.

Bhagavad Gita, XII.17

He who takes praise and reproach alike, who is given to contemplation and content with whatever comes unasked for, without attachment to home, fixed in mind and full of devotion to Me, that man is dear to Me.

Bhagavad Gita, XII.19

Him I call a Brahmin who lays aside the rod with regard to creatures, moving or unmoving, and neither kills nor causes (their) death.

Dhammapada, v. 405

He who is not a source of annoyance to the world, and who never feels offended with the world, who is free from delight and anger, perturbation and fear, he is dear to Me.

Bhagavad Gita, XII.15

Him I call a Brahmin whose passion and hatred, pride and hypocrisy have fallen like a mustard seed from the point of an awl. Him I call a Brahmin who utters true speech, free from harshness, clearly understood, by which no one is offended. Him I call a Brahmin who has no desires for this world or for the next, who is free from desires and who is separated (from impurities). Him I call a Brahmin who knows everywhere the perishing of living things and their uprising, who is free from attachment, living aright, and who is awakened.

Dhammapada, vv. 407,408,410,419

He who is free from malice towards all beings, who is friendly as well as compassionate, who has no feeling of meum and is free from egoism, to whom pleasure and pain are alike and who is forgiving by nature, who is ever content and mentally united to Me, who has subdued his body, mind and senses and has a firm resolve, who has surrendered his mind and intellect to Me, that devotee of Mine is dear to Me.

Bhagavad Gita, XII.13,14

Do not deem, O Brahmin, that purity comes by merely laying sticks in fire, for it is external. Having therefore left that course, I kindle my fire only within, which burns for ever. Here in this sacrifice the tongue is the sacrificial spoon and the heart is the altar of the fire.

Samyutta-nikaya, i.168

Brood not over this mass of words, for it is a waste of breath.

Brihadaranyaka Upanishad, iv. 4,21

Sacrifices are frail boats across the ocean of samsara.

Mundaka Upanishad, i.2,7

Thus, the Buddha shows that he who would aspire to be a true Brahmin must become possessed of the moral and spiritual qualities, so as to become the embodiment of righteous conduct and the repository of true knowledge and wisdom. As we see from comparable quotes, this is also the view taken by the pristine teachings of the Hindu scriptures, notwithstanding the tragedy that by the Buddha's time a morass of rituals and caste dogma had congealed over those truths—truths not only dealing with rectitude of conduct and purity of thought, but those far more fundamental, concerning 'the reason for being good' and delving into the nature of man himself, his soul, his mind, his self.

SOUL-MIND AND SELF

The Sanskrit word 'atman'[88] which translates the 'self' of man has been used and understood in the Buddhist texts in a manner compatible with the Buddha's own concepts of 'self'. While the Buddha rejected the commonly

---

[88]'Atman' is derived from 'an'—'to breathe', i.e. the breath of life.

accepted concept of 'self' which was understood by His contemporaries as some kind of a soul monad, an inexplicable ego-being individuality residing in the human physique as a separate entity divorced from the mind and thoughts, He did not deny man's mentality, his spiritual constitution, his thoughts, his mind or manas, in brief, his soul. However, we must understand that there is no dualism involved here since, to the Buddha, man's soul does not consist of two things, an atman (self) and a manas (mind or thoughts), but of only one reality. Our thoughts are our self, our soul or atman, and hence it would be completely erroneous to assert that the Buddha denied the soul or self. This premise is also corroborated by Buddhist scholars of different schools and countries, including the Theravadin Buddhists, who claim for themselves greater precision and faithfulness concerning the Buddha's doctrine. We should also recognize here that the Budha, above all, was cognizant of the impossibility of attributing definitions and form to such inherently 'indefinables' as self, soul, mind etc. and, hence, once again took the middle course, between the two extremes. This middle way placed no demands on the Buddha to prove or disprove either of the contending concepts, both being by their very nature outside the realm of empirical verification. The way He chose provided Him with the flexibility of being able to contain both views, and also enabled Him to endow His own concept of the 'self' with just that correct measure of reality necessary to incorporate it into His message as the 'motive' for self-improvement and righteous living. The need for righteous effort and detached sacrifice in living-the-life would be pointless if there was no permanency to the 'self' and it simply vanished into utter nothingness at the end of physical existence. Hence, we see from the following that the Buddha rejects both extremes of positions concerning the self, namely, that the self is a permanently unchanging entity or that at death it is annihilated:

Those, Ananda, who affirm a self, fall into the extreme of belief in its eternal continuation; those who deny it fall into the extreme of belief in its eventual annihilation. *Vatsagotra Sutra*	Arjuna, the contacts between the senses and their objects, which give rise to feelings of heat and cold, pleasure and pain, etc., are transitory and fleeting; therefore, Arjuna, ignore them. The wise man to whom pain and pleasure are alike, and who is not tormented by these contacts, becomes eligible for immortality. *Bhagavad Gita*, II.14,15

The above provides a better perspective on the Buddha's oft-quoted, but greatly misunderstood, discourse in the *Samyutta-nikaya:*

Mendicants, in whatever way the different teachers (Samanas and Brahmanas) regard the soul, they think it is the five skandhas, or one of the five. Thus, mendicants the un-	He who draws away the senses from the objects of sense on every side as a tortoise draws in his limbs (into the shell), his intelligence is firmly set (in wisdom). The objects

learned, unconverted man—who does not associate either with the converted or the holy, or understand their law, or live according to it—such a man regards the soul either as identical with, or as possessing, or as containing, or as residing in the material properties (rupa) or as identical with, or as possessing, or as containing, or as residing in sensation (vedena), and so on of each of the other three skandhas (ideas, propensities, and mind). By regarding the soul in one of these twenty states he gets the idea 'I am'. Then there are the five organs of sense, and mind, and qualities, and ignorance. From sensation (produced by contact and ignorance), the sensual unlearned man derives the notions 'I am'. 'This I, exists,' 'I shall be,' 'I shall not be,' 'I shall or shall not have material qualities,' 'I shall or shall not have, or shall be neither with nor without, ideas.' But now, mendicants, the learned disciple of the converted, having the same five organs of sense, has got rid of ignorance and acquired wisdom; and therefore (by reason of the absence of ignorance, and the rise of wisdom) the ideas 'I am' do not occur to him.

Sutta-pitaka (Samyutta-nikaya, 5th Sutta Khandha-Vagga)

of sense turn away from the embodied soul who abstains from feeding on them but the taste for them remains. Even the taste turns away when the Supreme is seen.

Bhagavad Gita, II.58,59

The soul (Jivatma) in the body is an eternal portion of Myself; it draws with it the mind and the five senses that rest in Matter.

Bhagavad Gita, XV.7

Correctly understood, the Buddha is simply dissociating the ineffable soul (the real self) from the labels of various descriptions and attributes pinned to it in His day, and both He and the Hindu scriptures show the individual the road to differentiate and discern the true-self (the soul) as apart from the transitory non-self composed of sense perceptions of the object world. The Hindu concept points out that, when the mind is concentrated on the Supreme, the non-self disappears. The Buddha asserts the same view, but simply substitutes the 'Bodhi' (Wisdom or Enlightenment), instead of the Supreme. Obviously, if one is not to subscribe to the illogical claims of nihilism attributed to the Buddha's doctrine by certain so called scholars, but without any evidence from the Buddha's own words—unless they are deliberately misunderstood—then, such concepts as Sakkaya-ditthi (heresy of individuality) and Attavada (heresy of the doctrine of soul or self), regarded as fundamental tenets 'predicated on the Buddha's own teachings', should undergo a radical re-examination and be rejected, since their popular interpretations contradict the total picture of His doctrine. Nor should the claim that 'the Brahmins also understand this to be so in the Buddha's doctrine' be regarded as anything else than the perennial desire of the Brahmins to have the masses reject the Buddha's doctrine on these two most fundamental aspects—the existence of the Supreme and the existence of the soul—the two vital conditions, the negation of which would single-handedly ensure the defeat of any 'cause' concerned with the 'why' and 'how' of spiritual progress, the salvation of the soul.

SOUL-MIND

Our mind, which is our real self, is present and active in heaven, just as on earth, and its most precious asset is immortality.

The Blessed One proceeded to the village Nadika with a great company of brethren and there he stayed at the Brick Hall. And the venerable Ananda went to the Blessed One and mentioning to him the names of the brethren and sisters that had died, anxiously inquired about their fate after death, whether they had been reborn in animals or in hell, or as ghosts, or in any place of woe.

Krishna, what is Adhiyajna (Indestructible) here and how does it dwell in the body? And how are You to be realized at the time of death by those of steadfast mind?

Bhagavad Gita, VIII.2

And the Blessed One replied to Ananda and said: "Those who have died after the complete destruction of the three bonds of lust, of covetousness and of egotistical cleaving to existence, need not fear the state after death. They will not be reborn in a state of suffering; their minds will not continue as a karma of evil deeds or sin, but are assured of final salvation.[89] When they die, nothing will remain of them but their good thoughts, their righteous acts, and the bliss that proceeds from truth and righteousness. As rivers must at last reach the distant main, so their minds will be reborn in higher states of existence and continue to be pressing on to their ultimate goal which is the ocean of truth, the eternal place of Nirvana."

All perishable objects are Adhibhuta . . . and, Arjuna, in this body I myself, dwelling as the inner witness, am Adhiyajna.

Bhagavad Gita, VIII.4

They who have taken refuge in Me . . . and they who, possessed of a steadfast mind, know Me even at the hour of death, they also know Me.

Bhagavad Gita, VII.29,30

Here we are clearly told that the mind clothed in its *good thoughts, righteous acts, and the bliss that proceeds from truth and righteousness* will be reborn in higher states of existence and continue on from stage to stage till finally it reaches the perfection and bliss of Nirvanic existence. Likewise, it can be understood that those minds which are encrusted by the dross of low desires and ignorance will continue to wallow in the lower realms of consciousness until, through diligent effort, they are able to shirk off their bonds and wing their flight to freedom of spirit. For further clarification of this relationship, we quote the Buddha's interview with the Brahmin in the garden of Anathapindika at Jetavana:

---

[89]*Questions of King Milinda* (Mirror of Truth parable).

The Brahmin said, "Who is the most dangerous thief? What is the most precious treasure? Who is most successful in grasping, not only on earth, but also in heaven? What is the securest treasure-trove?" The Blessed One replied: "Evil thought is the most dangerous thief; virtue is the most precious treasure. The mind takes possession of everything not only on earth, but also in heaven, and immortality is its securest treasure-trove."

(Buddhist Catena)

Four types of virtuous men worship Me, Arjuna—the seeker of worldly objects, the sufferer, the seeker of knowledge, and the man of wisdom. But those men of virtuous deeds whose sins have come to an end, being freed from delusion in the shape of pairs of opposites, worship Me with a firm resolve in every way.

Bhagavad Gita, VII.16,28

This immortality is not an acquisition of the soul-mind but an inherent aspect of its very being, an intrinsic attribute of its own reality. Hence, whether in the state of Nirvanic bliss or in the torment of Niraya hell, the mind (soul) is not subject to annihilation. The Buddha affirms this in conversation (see *Milindapanha*) with one of the officers of General Siha and, while shunning the quasi-physical concept of the 'soul' as accepted by the Hindus of His day, simply substitutes the word mind for soul.

And there was an officer among the retinue of Siha who had heard of the discourses of the Blessed One, and there was some doubt left in his heart.

This man came to the Blessed One and said: "It is said, O Lord, that the samana Gotama denies the existence of the soul. Do they who say so speak the truth, or do they bear false witness against the Blessed One?"

Hardly anyone perceives this soul as marvellous, scarce another likewise speaks thereof as marvellous, and scarce another hears of it as marvellous; while there are some who know it not even on hearing of it.

Bhagavad Gita, II.29

And the Blessed One said: "There is a way in which those who say so are speaking truly of me; on the other hand, there is a way in which those who say so do not speak truly of me."

When your mind will cross the mire of delusion, you will then grow indifferent to what had been heard and what is yet to be heard about this world and the next.

Bhagavad Gita, II.52

"The Tathagata teaches that there is no self. He who says that the soul is his self and that the self is the thinker of our thoughts and the actor of our deeds teaches a wrong doctrine which leads to confusion and darkness."

When your mind confused by hearing conflicting statements, will remain steadfast and firm in meditation you will then attain union with God.

Bhagavad Gita, II.53

"On the other hand, the Tathagata teaches that there is mind. He who understands by soul mind, and says that mind exists, teaches the truth which leads to clearness and enlightenment."

. . . of senses, I am the mind and of beings, I am consciousness.

Bhagavad Gita, X.22

. . . Seen and unseen, heard and unheard, felt and not felt, the mind sees all since the mind is

THE GOD OF BUDDHA

all. But when the mind is overcome by its own radiance, then dreams are no longer seen: joy and peace come to the body.

Prasna Upanishad, IV.5.6

The officer said: "Does, then, the Tathagata maintain that two things exist—that which we perceive with our senses and that which is mental?"

Who sees the many and not the One, wanders on from death to death. Even by the mind this truth is to be learned: there are not many but only ONE. Who sees variety and not the unity wanders on from death to death.

Katha Upanishad, 4.11

Said the Blessed One: "Verily, I say unto thee, thy mind is spiritual, but neither is the sense-perceived void of spirituality. The Bodhi is eternal and it dominates all existence as the good law guiding all beings in their search for truth. It changes brute nature into mind, and there is no being that cannot be transformed into a vessel of truth."
Milindapanha (All Existence is Spiritual)

Arjuna said: "Krishna, what is the mark of a God-realized soul, stable of mind and established in wisdom? How should the man of settled intelligence speak, how should he sit, how should he walk?"
Sri Bhagavan replied: "Arjuna, when one thoroughly abandons all cravings of the mind, and is satisfied in the self through the self, then he is called stable in mind."

Bhagavad Gita, II.54,55

Since neither of the two words ('soul' and 'mind') is definable or knowable as to its essential nature, it is really immaterial for our purpose or understanding by what name the Buddha chose to call this entity. And the Buddha, moreover, used these words interchangeably on occasion just as, surprisingly, he did the words 'self' and 'truth'!

In the following quotation from the Buddha's conversation with Kutadanta, the head of the Brahmins in the village of Danamati, we obtain further elucidation of the Buddha's concept of the soul-mind. In response to Kutadanta's question—that if he is merely a compound of sensations and ideas and desires, where can he go at the dissolution of the body—the Buddha replies:[90]

Thy heart, O Brahmin, is cleaving still to self; thou art anxious about heaven but thou seekest the pleasures of self in heaven, and thus thou canst not see the bliss of truth and the immortality of truth.

Verily I say unto thee: The Blessed One has not come to teach death, but to teach life, and thou discernest not the nature of living and dying.

This body will be dissolved and no amount of sacrifice will save it. Therefore, seek thou the

Atman, the Spirit of vision, is never born and never dies. Before him there was nothing, and he is *one* for evermore. Never-born and eternal, beyond times gone or to come, he does not die when the body dies. If the slayer thinks that he kills, and if the slain thinks that he dies, neither knows the ways of truth. The Eternal in man cannot kill: the Eternal in man cannot die. Concealed in the heart of all beings is the Atman, the Spirit, the Self; smaller than the smallest atom, greater than the vast spaces. The man who surrenders his human will leaves sorrows behind, and beholds the

---

[90]*Questions of King Milinda.*

life that is of the mind. Where self is, truth cannot be: yet when truth comes, self will disappear. Therefore, let thy mind rest in the truth; propagate the truth, put thy whole will in it, and let it spread. In the truth thou shalt live forever.

glory of the Atman by the grace of the Creator (God). Resting, he wanders afar; sleeping, he goes everywhere. Who else but my Self can know that God of joy and of sorrows?

Katha Upanishad, 2(18-21)

The man whose chariot is driven by reason, who watches and holds the reins of his mind, reaches the End of the journey, the supreme everlasting Spirit. Beyond the senses are their objects, and beyond the objects is the mind. Beyond the mind is pure reason, and beyond reason is the Spirit in man.

Katha Upanishad, 3 (9-10)

When a man ceases to have any attachment either for the objects of senses or for actions and has renounced all thoughts of the world, he is said to have attained Yoga.

Bhagavad Gita, VI.4

In line with the above, the Buddha states that *all beings in the world . . . shall lay aside their complex form.*

TRUE SELF

To obtain a correct view of the meaning of 'self' as recognized by the Buddha, it is vital for us to understand the near identity of concept existing between Hinduism and Buddhism concerning the definition of 'self'.

This true self, the ego (jiva), is the soul-mind and it is not extinguished in the state of liberation. Furthermore, the *Anguttara* (iv. 36) states that, "the Buddha is the redeemed soul not subject to any bonds." Thus, aside from the use and even interchange of the words 'soul' with 'mind', the same concept is embedded in both words and we can appreciate, therefore, that the self talked of here is not the self composed of the fleeting imprints of joys and sorrows resulting from sense perceptions. The Buddha, of course, rightly denies the existence of such a combination which, if it had any permanency of its own, would, in essence, constitute a second person, a separate ego entity, resulting in a two-in-one split-mind absurdity. For those who think that the Buddha aimed at the extinction of the true self, the real 'we', it may be of interest to note the following remarkably explicit passage in contradiction of such fallacy:

"My disciples get rid of what is not yours. Get rid of them. If a man were to take away

The wise should surrender speech in mind, mind in the knowing self, the knowing self in *branches and leaves in this Jeta wood, would it occur to you to say, the man is taking us away, burning us or using us for his need?"*

"Certainly not Lord."

"And why not?"

"Because, Lord it is not ourself or anything belonging to our self."

"Just in the same way, my disciples, get rid of the constituents (Skandhas), the not-self."

Majjhima-nikaya, 22

the spirit of the universe, and the spirit of the universe in the spirit of peace. Awake, Arise! Strive for the Highest, and be in the Light! Sages say the path is narrow and difficult to tread, narrow as the razor's edge. The Atman is beyond sound and form, without touch and taste and perfume. It is eternal, unchangeable, and without beginning or end: indeed above reasoning. When consciousness of the Atman manifests itself, man becomes free from the jaws of death.

Katha Upanishad, III.13,14,15

This discourse of the Buddha's is further corroborated by the Buddhist formula, *This is not mine; I am not this; this is not myself,* the purpose of which is clearly the separation of the 'non-self' from the 'real-self'. The real spiritual self is not some abstraction, but is itself the absolute life. Its existence cannot be predicated on any knowledge of the self as an objective entity, for it is open only to itself.

The self is the lord of self; who else could be the lord? With self well subdued a man finds a lord who is difficult to obtain. The evil done by oneself, born of oneself, produced by oneself, crushes the fool even as a diamond breaks a precious stone.

Dhammapada, vv. 160,161

One's own self is the friend of that soul by whom the lower self has been conquered; on the other hand, the very self of him, who has not conquered his lower self, behaves inimically like one's own enemy.

Bhagavad Gita, VI.6

Rouse your self by your self, examine your self by your self. Thus guarded by your self and attentive you, mendicant, will live happy. For self is the lord of self; self is the refuge of self; therefore curb yourself even as a merchant curbs a fine horse.

Dhammapada, vv. 379,380

One should lift oneself up by one's own efforts and should not degrade oneself; for one's own self is one's friend, and one's own self is one's enemy.

Bhagavad Gita, VI.5

Moreover, as we read from *Dhammapada* (v. 379) above, the Buddha considers the 'reality' of self within us to be the chief instrument for awakening and protecting us from the illusion of the world of sense and for ensuring our happiness. And this real 'self' the Buddha equates with truth itself:

Be ye as those who have the self as their light. Be ye as those who have the self as their refuge. Betake yourselves to no external refuge. Hold fast to the truth as to a refuge.

Mahaparinibbana Sutta, vv. 33,35

The Supreme Spirit is firmly established in the knowledge of the self-controlled man whose mind is perfectly calm in the midst of pairs of opposites such as cold and heat, joy and sorrow, and honor and shame.

Bhagavad Gita, VI.7

It is the innermost aspect of ourselves (the soul), which one can discover only by destroying the reliance of the mind on external supports and sense perceptions. The Buddha nowhere objected to this concept. He also acknowledges that the mind or soul is not dependent on the physical for existence; that this real or intrinsic self, shorn of the paraphernalia of desire and ignorance, is the 'permanent' soul-mind. The individual is shown to recognize the true self as distinct from the ephemeral and objective cosmos and taught that the components of ego are in a constant flux, nothing fixed, or changeless, no eternal core.

From the arising of ignorance is the arising of the karma-formations; from the stopping of ignorance is the stopping of the karma-formations. This ariyan eightfold Way is itself the course leading to the stopping of the karma-formations, that is to say: right view, right thought, right speech, right action, right mode of livelihood, right endeavour, right mindfulness, right concentration.

When an ariyan disciple comprehends 'condition' thus, its arising, its stopping and the course leading to its stopping thus, he is called an ariyan disciple who is possessed of right view, of vision, one who has come into this true Dhamma, who sees this true Dhamma, who is endowed with the knowledge and lore of a learner, who has attained the stream of Dhamma, who is an Ariyan of penetrating wisdom, and who stands knocking at the door of the Deathless.

Samyutta-nikaya, II.43

The unreal has no existence, and the real never ceases to be; the reality of both has thus been perceived by the seers of truth. Know that to be imperishable by which all this is pervaded; for none can bring about the destruction of this indestructible substance. All these bodies pertaining to the imperishable, indefinable and eternal soul are spoken of as perishable; therefore, Arjuna, struggle. The soul is never born nor dies; nor having once come to be will it again cease to be. It is unborn, eternal, permanent and primeval; even though the body is slain, the soul is not.

Bhagavad Gita, II.16,17,18,20

"Is suffering wrought by oneself, good Gotama?"

"No, Kassapa."

"Then by another?"

"No."

"Then by both oneself and another?"

"No, Kassapa."

"Well then, has the suffering that has been wrought neither by myself nor by another come to me by chance?"

"No, Kassapa."

"Then, is there not suffering?"

"No, Kassapa, it is not that there is not suffering. For there is suffering."

"Well then, the good Gotama neither knows nor sees suffering."

"It is not that I do not know suffering, do not see it. I know it, I see it."

"To all my questions, good Gotama, you have answered 'No', and you have said that you know suffering and see it. Lord, let the Lord explain suffering to me, let him teach me suffering."

"Whoso says, 'He who does (a deed) is he

When a man is bound by the three powers of nature, he works for a selfish reward and in time he has his reward. His soul then becomes the many forms of the three powers, strays along the three paths, and wanders on through life and death.

The soul is like the sun in splendour. When it becomes one with the selfconscious 'I am' and its desires, it is a flame the size of a thumb; but when one with pure reason and the inner Spirit, it becomes in concentration as the point of a needle.

The soul can be thought as the part of a point of a hair which divided by a hundred were divided by a hundred again; and yet in this living soul there is the seed of Infinity.

The soul is not a man, nor a woman, nor what is neither a woman nor a man. When the soul takes the form of a body, by that same body the soul is bound.

The soul is born and unfolds in a body, with dreams and desires and the food of life. And then it is reborn in new bodies, in accordance with its former works.

71

who experiences (its result)', is thereby saying that from the being's beginning suffering was wrought by (the being) himself—this amounts to the Eternity-view. Whoso says, 'One does (a deed), and another experiences (the result)', is thereby saying that when a being is smitten by feeling the suffering was wrought by another—this amounts to the Annihilation-view.

"Avoiding both these dead-ends, Kassapa, the Tathagata teaches Dhamma by the mean: conditioned by ignorance are the karma-formations . . . and so on. Thus is the origin of this whole mass of suffering. By the utter stopping of that very ignorance is the stopping of the karma-formations . . . and so on. Thus is the stopping of this whole mass of suffering."

Samyutta-nikaya, II.19-21

The quality of the soul determines its future body: earthly or airy, heavy or light. Its thoughts and its actions can lead it to freedom, or lead it to bondage, in life after life.

But there is the God of forms infinite, and when a man knows God he is free from all bondage. He is the Creator of all, everliving in the mystery of his creation. He is beyond beginning and end, and in his glory all things are.

He is an incorporeal Spirit, but he can be seen by a heart which is pure. Being and non-being come from him and he is the Creator of all. He is God, the God of love, and when a man knows him then he leaves behind his bodies of transmigration.

Svetasvatara Upanishad, V. 7-14

By removing the veils of ignorance through understanding the Dharma, it is possible for us to rise above all personal factors and see our true self as one with *the eternal.* The Buddha's clear purpose in the preceding excerpts as well as in His sermon on the *Burden and the Bearer,* as recorded in *Samyutta-nikaya* (III.25) and His references to look to our *self* for guidance and *refuge* and to *regard nothing dearer than this knowledge of the self* (*Udana*-47), is not merely to assert the existence of this real self; it conforms to the identical dictum, 'know thyself', proclaimed by the Founders of all the great religions, and constituting in itself the greatest goal of Religion! Thus, from the various references in the *Anguttara-nikaya* (i.149, ii.211) and in *Majjhima* (i.344, ii.159), we see the Buddha equating Dharma itself with this real self and stating that the experience of this real self constitutes the most precious and the highest goal of each person. Nor can we fail to note from these references that there is a remarkable similarity of views between the Buddha and the Upanishads, and the 'real-self', as conceived by Him, is identical to the 'atman' in Hinduism. Moreover, Nagasena also asserts (*Madhyamika Karika,* XVIII.6) that "the Buddhas have taught that there is the self, that there is the not-self, as also that there is neither the self nor the not-self". Thus, the discerning mind finds no ground here for simplistic denials of the existence of this all-important entity called self, but rather a call to recognize and accept the true self as differentiated from the *not-self.*

As previously stated (pp. 24, 65), this should also serve to put in proper perspective the concept of Sakkaya-ditthi as well as Attavada. For, both these nebulous concepts are devoid of any separation or distinction between the true-self and the not-self. Consequently, the popular assertion that the Buddha did not believe in the soul or self is simply unfounded conjecture and Nagasena's dialogue with King Milinda should also be understood as his rejection of the *not-self* and not the real self. Likewise, Vasubandhu's discourse in *Abhidharma Kosho* (IX) is also a futile exercise in semantics, since there again the two protagonists are discussing aspects and conditions of what are, fundamentally, undefinable entities, e.g. 'soul' and 'self'. And we see, from *Milindapanha* (pp. 52, 55), that the Buddha not only enjoins the eradication of the 'false self', but He also explains this *eradication of self,* or, more correctly, the *not self,* by clearly separating in that same para the transitory self from the immortal soul, whose preservation the Buddha acknowledges is dependent upon the conquest of self. The soul is very much in evidence in the Buddha's discourses. And we read, in *Milindapanha* (p. 54), about the Buddha teaching Siha that when a murderer is put to death he should be happy, as the punishment will purify his soul. Now, if there was no soul and nothing to purify, then the murderer would hardly be expected to rejoice for being relegated to oblivion. Even after the bubbles of our desires, selfishness, and egotism, which cover and often obscure our real self, have burst, *their contents* (our real self) *will be preserved* and continue to lead an everlasting life in the truth:

Truth, however, is large enough to receive the yearnings and aspirations of all selves and, when the selves break like soap-bubbles, their contents will be preserved and in the truth they will lead a life everlasting. *Mahavagga* (Siha's Question Concerning Annihilation)	The foolish run after outward pleasures and fall into the snares of vast-embracing death. But the wise have found immortality, and do not seek the Eternal in things that pass away. *Katha Upanishad,* 4.2

The Buddha shows here that when the bubbles of our ignorance and cravings have burst, our real self will emerge to the vision of reality and partake of eternal life. Shorn of the desire for the ephemeral or the mundane, having completely quieted the stallions of the senses, that intrinsic spiritual essence in each of us attains to that ultimate wisdom which every one of us has the potential to experience—*knowing of your self by your self.*[91] Or, as the Upanishads have claimed, "the Creator made the senses outward-going, they go to the world of matter outside, not to the Spirit within. But a sage who sought immortality looked within himself and found his own Soul."[92] Thus, we must discover that splendrous world of our own soul and obtain joyous peace in the ineffable bliss of the true nature of the soul in perfect harmony with the Cosmos and the operation of its eternal plan.

---

[91] *Dhammapada,* v. 379, See also *Mahaparinibbana Sutta,* ii. 26, where the Buddha tells King Pasenadi: "When we traverse all regions with a thoughtful mind we will not reach anything dearer than the self (attana); so also is the common self of others (puthuatta) dear. Who seeks the self (attakama) will injure (himse) no one."

[92] *Katha Upanishad,* 4.1.

NON-EGO—ILLUSORY-SELF

On the other hand, if we do not let our minds rise above ignorance and if we permit the trappings of desire to make us prisoners of our senses, the lustre of our soul is dimmed, and it is no longer able to light the path towards freedom, to the world of Reality. Thus, "careless and devoid of purity we reach not the end of the journey but wander from death to death."[93] This, too, the Buddha tells us in terms of that 'perversion of self,' and its constituents: egotism, fanciful assertiveness, and of desires for the objects of sense—all products of the ignorance of our real self, our soul (mind). He shows that only by conscious and unwavering discipline of thought and conduct can we hope to shed these encrustations, which mire our soul in this swamp of *comings and goings,* and set it free to partake of everlasting life. The shedding of that false 'self' is certainly not to be construed as the annihilation of the intrinsic individual, but rather as the exposing of the truth in us, when those scabs of craving and egotism which obscure our soul are peeled off.

There is self[94] and there is truth. Where self is, truth is not. Where truth is, self is not. Self is the fleeting error of samsara; it is individual separateness and that egoism which begets envy and hatred. Self is the yearning for pleasure and the lust after vanity.

By meditation some perceive the Self in the self by the self; others by the path of knowledge; and still others by the path of works. For, as he sees the Lord present equally everywhere, he does not injure his true Self by the self and then he attains to the supreme goal.
Bhagavad Gita, XIII.24,28

Self is death and truth is life. The cleaving to self is a perpetual dying, while moving in the truth is partaking of Nirvana which is life everlasting.

Now consider the continuation of the personality, which is preserved in thy karma. Dost thou call it death and annihilation, or life and continued life?

"I call it life and continued life," rejoined Kutadanta, "for it is the continuation of my existence, but I do not care for that kind of continuation."

But for those in whom ignorance is destroyed by wisdom, for them wisdom lights up the Supreme Self like the sun. Thinking of That, directing their whole conscious being to That, making That their whole aim, with That as the sole object of their devotion, they reach a state from which there is no return, their sins washed away by wisdom.
Bhagavad Gita, V.16,17

The Tathagata continued: "It is by a process of evolution that sankharas come to be. There is no sankhara which has sprung into being without a gradual becoming. Thy sankharas are the product of thy deeds in former ex-

As a man puts on new clothes in this world, throwing away those which he formerly wore, even so the soul of man puts on new bodies which are in accordance with its acts in a former life.
Brihadaranyaka Upanishad
(Visnu Smrti, XX.50)

---

[93] *Katha Upanishad* 3.7.
[94] *Questions of King Milinda* (with the Brahmin Kutadanta).

istences, the combination of thy sankharas is thy self. Wheresoever they are impressed thither thy self migrates. In thy sankharas thou wilt continue to live and thou wilt reap in future existence the harvest sown now and in the past."

There is indeed the other soul composed of the elements of the body, the bhutatman, who is bound by the light or darkness which follow works and who, born again from good or evil rises or falls in its wanderings under the impulse of contrary powers.

Maitri Upanishad, 3.2

"Verily, O Lord," rejoined Kutadanta, "this is not a fair retribution. I cannot recognize the justice that others after me will reap what I am sowing now.

As a man discarding worn-out clothes, takes other new ones, likewise the embodied soul, casting off worn-out bodies, enters into others which are new.

Bhagavad Gita, II.22

"Verily, I say unto thee: Not in the heavens, not in the midst of the sea, not if thou hidest thyself away in the clefts of the mountains, wilt thou find a place where thou canst escape the fruit of thine evil actions."[95]

Notwithstanding that, he who, owing to impure reason, views the absolute Self as the doer, is of perverse understanding, and does not see at all.

Bhagavad Gita, XVIII.16

"At the same time thou art sure to receive the blessings of thy good actions. The man who has long been traveling and who returns home in safety, the welcome of kinfolk, friends, and acquaintances awaits. So, the fruits of his good works bid him welcome who has walked in the path of righteousness when he passes over from the present life into the hereafter."[96]

Dhammapada, vv. 219,220

He who departs from the body thinking of Me alone, even at the time of death, attains My state; there is no doubt about it.

Bhagavad Gita, VIII.5

These two paths of the world, the bright and the dark, are considered to be eternal. Proceeding by one of them, one reaches the supreme state from which there is no return; and proceeding by the other, one returns to the mortal world, and becomes subject to birth and death once more.

Bhagavad Gita, VIII.26

By oneself, indeed, is evil done; by oneself is evil left undone; by oneself is one purified. Purity and impurity belong to oneself. No one purifies another.[97]

Dhammapada, v. 165

A person consists of desires, and as is his desire, so is his will; and as is his will, so is his deed; and whatever deed he does, that he will reap.

Brihadaranyaka Upanishad, IV.4

---

[95]*Dhammapada*, v. 127. However, the above passage cannot be stretched to justify re-incarnation into the physical plane since the proponents of re-incarnation cannot explain the complete absence of memory of the individual's past existence. Claims for re-incarnation run contrary to both the perfection of the law of Karma and an intelligent 'First Cause' and have only had currency due to our desire in the past to explain physical misfortunes, the causes for which had eluded us. The Law of Karma operates just as perfectly in the higher planes of consciousness to which we evolve according to our acts here and there is no need to try and explain its operation by fallacies. For a detailed explanation of the concept of Karma and the meaning of re-incarnation the reader is referred to pp. 44-54 of *The Fallacy of Ancestor Worship* by the author (Bombay, 1965, Library of Congress Cat. Card No. SA 66-7067).

[96]Also *Dhammapada*, vv. 167,168,169.

[97]Also *Dhammapada*, vv. 172,173.

Self-control is the most difficult problem and only Religion provides us with the 'how' as well as the 'why' to motivate us to achieve this control of our self by our self. The reality of our true self must be recognized by us first before we can transcend the limits of personal attachments and view humanity as one indivisible whole deserving of our unconditional love. It is through that pure love for all life that we can eliminate the selfishness of self and, detached from its bonds, achieve unshakeable tranquility.

Destroy illusions and the contact with things will cease to beget misconception. Destroy misconception and you do away with thirst. Destroy thirst and you will be free of all morbid cleaving. Remove the cleaving and you destroy the selfishness[98] of selfhood. If the selfishness of selfhood is destroyed you will be above birth, old age, disease, and death, and you will escape all suffering. The Enlightened One saw the four noble truths which point out the path that leads to Nirvana: The first truth is the existence of sorrow. The second noble truth is the cause of suffering. The third noble truth is the cessation of sorrow. The fourth noble truth is the eightfold path that leads to the cessation of sorrow. This is the Dharma. This is the truth. This is religion.[99]

With your mind thus established in the Yoga of Renunciation (offering of all actions to Me), you will be freed from the bonds of Karma in the shape of good and evil consequences; and freed from them, you shall attain Me.

Bhagavad Gita, IX.28

Desire, aversion, pleasure, pain, the body, consciousness, firmness; this in brief is the field of consciousness with its modifications. Absence of pride, freedom from hypocracy, non-violence, forgiveness, straightforwardness, service of the preceptor, purity of mind and body, steadfastness, self-control, Dispassion towards the objects of senses, and absence of egoism, constant revolving in mind of the pain and the evil inherent in birth, death, old age, and disease.

Bhagavad Gita, XIII.6,7,8

We become illumined when we sever the bonds of the heart and rise above our limitations. Our true self directly experiences its own intrinsic identity and, shorn of all doubt, we enter that realm of total certitude. We recognize that our self is not merely an aggregate of our experiences but a thing over and above the manifestations of its emotions, perceptions, thoughts and actions. Nor is our self the intellect, although we possess intellect. The real 'we' is distinct from all these outward manifestations. It is pure consciousness—a mystery, which, while conscious and certain of its own reality, is not open to empirical analysis.

It would, indeed, be futile for one to attempt to define by 'rule and line' the nature and attributes of that imperishable self, that immortal soul, the mind. The *Brihadaranyaka Upanishad*[100] states that "the self can only be described

---

[98] The Buddha here does not ask for destruction of self or selfhood, but of 'the selfishness of selfhood' and this is the only way in which His references can be properly understood, if they are not to conflict with His other references concerning self—"Be as those who have the self as their light . . ." (*Mahaparinibbana Sutta,* 33).

[99] *Mahavagga,* i.6 (19-28). Also see *Dhammapada:* "Religion, Dharma and Truth are identical."

[100] *Brihadaranyaka Upanishad,* III.9, 26; IV.2, 4; IV.4, 22.

as, not this, not this. It is incomprehensible; so it cannot be comprehended."
To quote the *Taittiriya Upanishad:* ". . . the words turn back from it with the mind." The Buddha, too, observes silence about the nature and attributes of the self. However, from the foregoing (p. 68), we see Him telling the officer of Siha that learning and conduct effect the self or, as He calls it, the 'mind', and in order to enable our true self to rise above the world of *becoming* (birth and death) and attain to final liberation (Nirvana) we must subdue desire, conquer ignorance, pass beyond the world of the gods and beyond 'hell' and 'heaven'.

HEAVEN AND HELL

In Buddhism, too, as in all the great religions, one's actions determine which of the two roads one travels, and while heaven and hell are described by different allegories in the Hindu as well as the Buddhist faith, yet, certain characteristics concerning these two states are common in both Hinduism and Buddhism, namely, (*a*) both heaven and hell belong to the world of time; (*b*) Rebirth, or, in a more exact sense, continuous education and self purification, is man's destiny until he obtains true knowledge; (*c*) the reward for goodness and purity of heart is a clearer vision of Reality, which ultimately lifts one above ascent and descent. And the road to heaven lies through strict adherence to the Dharma:

The evil-doer grieves in this world, he grieves in the next, he grieves in both. He grieves, he is afflicted, seeing the evil of his own actions.
Dhammapada, v.15

Arjuna, people having no faith in this Dharma, failing to reach Me, revolve in the paths of the world of death.
Bhagavad Gita, IX.3

The righteous man rejoices in this world, he rejoices in the next; he rejoices in both. He rejoices and becomes delighted seeing the purity of his actions.
Dhammapada, v.16

Arjuna, Yogis, who partake of the nectar in the form of the remains of sacrifice, attain the eternal Brahma. To the man who does not offer sacrifice even this world is not happy; how then can the other world be happy?
Bhagavad Gita, IV.31

The evil-doer suffers in this world, he suffers in the next; he suffers in both. He suffers (thinking) "evil has been done by me". He suffers even more when he has gone to the evil place. The righteous man rejoices in this world, he rejoices in the next; he rejoices in both. He rejoices (thinking) "good has been done by me". He rejoices still more when he has gone to the good place.
Dhammapada, vv.17,18

Passion, anger and greed, these constitute the triple gates to hell leading to the damnation of the soul. Therefore, one should shake off these three.
Bhagavad Gita, XVI.21

A man released from these three gates to hell, Arjuna, works his own salvation and thereby reaches the highest goal (i.e. Myself).
Bhagavad Gita, XVI.22

THE GOD OF BUDDHA

And for those who mistakenly think that, unlike the other great Faiths, Buddhism is merely a loosely knit system of ethics and philosophy, indifferent to the imperatives of organization and unswerving allegiance to its Founder and His doctrine—the essential elements embedded in every great Faith, to enable it to outlast the merely human systems and artifacts, and span not only continents, but also aeons of time, the hall-mark of Religion and only Religion—let them ponder over the Buddha's following admonitions to His own cousin, Devadatta, who tried to supersede Him and eventually created the first schism, as well as note the Buddha's assurance of happiness to those who maintain unity or heal the divisions within Religion.

He who violates the one law (the Buddha's doctrine), who speaks falsely, scoffs at another world, there is no evil he will not do.
Dhammapada, v. 176
The foolish man who scorns the teachings of the saintly, the noble, and the virtuous and follows false doctrine, bears fruit to his own destruction even like the Khattaka reed.
Dhammapada, v. 164

They say: 'The world is without any foundation and altogether false, godless and brought about by desire; what else?' Embracing this view, these lost souls with little understanding, ill-disposed and devoted to cruel actions, are born for the destruction of the world.
Bhagavad Gita, XVI.8,9.

Do not let there be a schism in the Order, for a schism in the Order is a serious matter, Devadatta. He who splits an Order that is united sets up demerit that endures for an aeon and he is boiled in hell for an aeon. But he who unites an Order that is split sets up sublime merit (Brahmapunna) and rejoices in heaven for an aeon.
Vinaya-pitaka, II.184-198 (condensed)

What lies beyond life shines not to those who are childish, or careless, or deluded by wealth. 'This is the only world, there is no other,' they say; and thus they go from death to death.
Katha Upanishad, 2.6

May there be concord so that I may speak these blissful words to the masses of men.
Yajur Veda, 26

Even an evil-doer sees happiness so long as his evil deed does not ripen; but when the evil deed has ripened, then does the evil-doer see evil.
Dhammapada, v. 119

The joy which is derived from the contact of the senses with their objects, though appearing like nectar in the beginning (at the time of enjoyment), proves to be mischieveous like poison in the end. . . .
Bhagavad Gita, XVIII.38

And he who lives a hundred years, not perceiving beginning and end, a life of one day is better if a man perceived the beginning and the end (birth and death). And he who lives a hundred years not perceiving the deathless state, a life of one day is better if a man perceives the deathless state.
Dhammapada, vv. 113,114

The pleasures which are born of sense-contacts are verily sources of pain. They have a beginning and an end. Arjuna, it is for this reason that a wise man does not indulge in them.
Bhagavad Gita, V.22
Arjuna, I am the Self seated in the heart of all beings, so I am the beginning and middle and also the end of all beings.
Bhagavad Gita, X.20
Arjuna, I am the beginning and middle and end of all creations. . . .
Bhagavad Gita, X.32

78

And he who lives a hundred years not perceiving the highest law,[101] *a life of one day is better if a man perceives the highest law.*

Dhammapada, v. 115

He, who, having cast aside the injunctions of the scriptures, acts according to his own sweet will, attains not perfection, nor the highest goal, not even happiness.

Bhagavad Gita, XVI.23

This world is blinded, a few only can see here. Like birds escaped from the net a few go to heaven.

Dhammapada, v. 174

Abiding in the midst of ignorance, thinking themselves wise and learned, fools go aimlessly hither and thither, like blind led by the blind.

Katha Upanishad, 2.5

The Buddha is most emphatic on the condition for avoiding the suffering of hell through abstention from evil and this, according to Him, must require the belief in the next life, *another world* and His *dharma.* In essence, this condition, as stated in the *Dhammapada* (verse 176), shows that from our acceptance of the Buddha's Doctrine (*one law*), we are led to the belief in the existence of that *another world,* which the Buddha repeatedly acknowledges, and for the attainment of which the true disciple must lead a pure and truthful life. Thus, we have seen that both Krishna and Buddha declare that they who deny the reality of this *another world* are capable of committing every evil act. Religion (Dharma) is the greatest safeguard for the individual as well as society and also the greatest source of happiness, both here and in the hereafter,[102] happiness which, as the Buddha states, *is the food of the shining gods.*

THE WORLD OF DEVAS (GODS) AND SPIRIT BEINGS

The Buddha, in deference to the universal belief in His time in the various deities, e.g. Brahma, Shiva, Vishnu, Rudra, etc., acknowledged these as well as the other gods, angels and spirit beings but rejected any homage to be paid to them as a means of attaining salvation, which, He stated, could only be obtained through the Dharma. However, the following should show more clearly the Buddha's own views on such 'beings'.

Verily, the miserly do not go to the world of the gods. Fools, indeed, do not praise giving. But the wise man rejoicing in charity, becomes on that (account) happy in the other world.

Dhammapada, v. 177

O self-effulgent Lord, like a well-sewn armour Thou dost protect that man from all sides who is liberal, the man possessed of all means of subsistence, who remains ever engaged in gratifying others, who performs sacrifices for all living beings, who is really the type of gods.

Rig Veda, 1

---

[101] Dharma (Religion) is the highest law.

[102] *Dhammapada,* vv. 16,18.

THE GOD OF BUDDHA

By vigilance did Indra rise to the lordship of the gods. People praise vigilance; thoughtlessness is always deprecated.
Dhammapada, v. 30

Rudra gave to the gods their birth and their glory, He created the golden seed.
Svetasvatara Upanishad, III.4

Him I call a Brahmin whose path the gods do not know, nor spirits nor men, whose taints are extinct, and who has attained sainthood.
Dhammapada, v. 420

The wise Brahmin, who knows Thee thus, shall have the devas (gods) in his control.
Yajur Veda, 31

The disciple will conquer this world and that world of Yama with its gods. The disciple will find out the well-taught path of virtue even as a skilled person finds out the (right) flower.
Dhammapada, v. 45

Those who take to the worship of devas (gods) go to the devas; those who worship the manas reach the manas; those who adore the spirits reach the spirits and those who worship Me attain Me.
Bhagavad Gita, IX.25

The reader can see that what is talked about here is simply an order of beings, intrinsically neither higher nor lower, but in the spirit plane which, while able to manifest themselves in the physical, are also able to function outside the physical, and can, depending on circumstances, either act malevolently or beneficially. Their world or their own state of existence is not inherently superior or inaccessible to the devout followers of the Buddhas or the Avatars since these gods (devas) and other spirit beings are completely subject to the Law of Karma and must themselves adhere to the Dharma for their continued well-being and progress. Hence, the true followers of the Buddhas and the other Avatars can attain and even surpass the station of these gods, and from the afore as well as the following excerpts we see that any dedicated disciple, upon passing from the physical existence and having accumulated the necessary merits and qualities of purity of mind and deeds, can become a 'god' and function as such and continue to *dwell feeding on happiness.*

Even the gods emulate those wise men who are given to meditation, who delight in the peace of emancipation (from desire) the enlightened, the thoughtful.
Dhammapada, v. 181
Even the gods praise that mendicant who though he receives little does not overvalue what he receives, whose life is pure and strenuous.
Dhammapada, v. 366

This form of Mine which you have seen is exceedingly difficult to perceive. Even the gods are always eager to behold this Form. Neither by study of Vedas, nor by penance, nor by charity, nor by ritual can I be seen in this Form as you have seen Me.
Bhagavad Gita, XI.52,53

Let us live happily then, free from care in the midst of those who are careworn; let us dwell free from care among men who are careworn. Let us live happily then, we who possess nothing. Let us dwell feeding on happiness like the shining gods.
Dhammapada, vv. 199,200

Those whose wisdom has been carried away by various desires, being bound by their own nature worship other gods undertaking vows relating to each. Endowed with such faith he worships that deity and obtains through him without doubt his desired enjoyment as ordained by me. The fruit gained by these people of meagre intelligence, however, is perishable. The worshippers of gods attain the gods; whereas My devotees, in the end attain Me alone.

Bhagavad Gita, VII.20,22,23

Nothing stated above shows that these spirit beings, gods, angels, etc. are outside the frame of space and time. Their world, either separate or inter-mingling with heaven and hell, is viewed as within the empirical order of the universe, while the plane of the 'Ineffable', is yet beyond—and though not necessarily the birthright of gods or men, is attainable by both, as the final stage of freedom and liberation from the ephemeral, through a complete merging of one's individuality in the Dharma, in the eternal scheme-of-things. And so we must pass from hell and heaven and the world of the gods to the supreme state, Nirvana. However, the Buddha, too, like the other Avatars, leaves no doubt that this deathless state, the ineffable bliss, that supreme Nirvana, is not easily attained. Many fall by the wayside. Only a few arrive!

Him I call a Brahmin who has gone beyond this miry road of rebirth and delusion, who has crossed over, who has reached the other shore, who is meditative, unagitated, not doubting, not grasping, and calm.

Dhammapada, v. 414

I shall speak to you in brief of that supreme goal which knowers of the Vedas term as the Indestructible, which striving recluses free from attachment enter, and desiring which the celibates practice celibacy.

Bhagavad Gita, VIII.11

Few amongst men are those who reach the farther shore: the other people here run along (this) shore.

Dhammapada, v. 85

Not many hear of Him; and of those not many reach Him. Wonderful is he who can teach about Him; and wise is he who can be taught. Wonderful is he who knows Him when taught.

Katha Upanishad, 2.6

But those who, when the law has been well preached to them, follow the law, will pass to the other shore, (beyond) the dominion of death which is difficult to overcome.

Dhammapada, v. 86

May we light the sacred fire of Nachiketas, the bridge to cross to the other shore where there is no fear, the supreme everlasting Spirit!

Katha Upanishad, 3.2

But, while showing the path to Nirvana, the Buddha maintains a thunderous silence concerning its nature. No words can relate its glory.

3

NIRVANA

Long before the time of the Buddha, the thought of Indian religion, as expressed by the Vedas and the Upanishads, had seen through the pain and futility of physical existence and had sought and probed the mystery of eternity. Hence, it is obligatory for us to acquaint ourselves with the basic concepts of this mystic philosophy, originally expressed in the Upanishads, if we are to gain a correct understanding of the Buddha's ideas and teachings concerning these eternal mysteries, within whose depths even the most incisive mind can do no more than turn back on itself. This is a realm beyond rationality, where, while mind may enter, it must do so shorn of every parameter of reason or logic. For, such are the dimensions of the realm where these eternal mysteries hold sway that man's puny rationality is worse than useless, it is an impediment. And for rationality here to demand empirical proof of the ineffable state is for the cup to insist on containing the boundless ocean. It is simply not within its domain, and even a single fish could crack the cup, how much more those other objects that are contained within the ocean. Nor does this impossible insistence on the part of the cup preclude the existence of the ocean. It is in the light of this fact that we must appreciate the Buddha's well-nigh total silence on these matters which the human mind has no way of discovering except through faith; nor of ever being able to describe it, while yet being capable of experiencing it. Hence, we must not erroneously interpret the Buddha's extreme abstinence from words concerning these mysteries as a cloak for nihilism, agnosticism or ignorance.

The following discourse on the *Simsapa leaves* should succinctly clear up any confusion on this point and show that like the perfect parent, the *fully enlightened teacher*, the Buddha, too, as all other divine Manifestations, moderated His message of salvation in accordance with His pupils' capacity to digest the truths, instead of confounding them by a deluge of metaphysical nebulae.

At one time, the Exalted One was staying at Kosambi in the Simsapa grove. And the Exalted One took a few Simsapa leaves in his hand and said to his disciples: "What think ye, my disciples, which are the more, these few Simsapa leaves which I have gathered in my hand or the other leaves yonder in the Simsapa grove?" "The few leaves, sire, which the Exalted One holds in his hand are not many, but many more are those leaves yonder in the Simsapa grove." "So also, my disciples, is that much more which I have learned and have not told you, than that which I have told you. And, wherefore, my disciples, have I not told you that? Because, my disciples, it brings you no profit, it does not conduce to progress in holiness; because it does not lead to the turning from the earthly to the subjection of all desire, to the cessation of the transitory, to peace, to knowledge, to illumination, to nirvana: therefore have I not declared it unto you."[103]

When a man has heard and has understood and, finding the essence, reaches the Inmost, then he finds joy in the Source of Joy. Nachiketas is a house open for thy Atman, thy God.

Katha Upanishad, 2.12

In order to shower My grace on them I, dwelling in their heart, dispel the darkness born of ignorance by the shining light of wisdom. There is no end to My divine manifestations, O Conqueror of the foe (Arjuna). What has been declared by Me is only illustrative of My infinite glory. Whatsoever being there is, endowed with glory and grace and vigour, know that to have sprung from a fragment of My splendour. But what need is there, O Arjuna, for such detailed knowledge by you? I support this entire universe pervading it with a single fraction of Myself.

Bhagavad Gita, X.11, 40, 41, 42

We read that one of His listeners, Malunkyaputta, lists the metaphysical questions at issue here, and, stating his dissatisfaction at the Buddha's apparent evasion of these matters, says to the Buddha:

"If the lord answers them, I will lead a religious life under him: if he does not answer them, I will give up religion and return to the world. If the Lord does not know, then the straight-forward thing is to say, 'I do not know.'" The Buddha with courtesy relates a parable: "A man is hit by a poisoned arrow. His friends hasten to the doctor. The latter is about to draw the arrow out of the wound. The wounded man, however, cries: 'Stop, I will not have the arrow drawn out until I know who shot it, whether a woman, or a Brahmin, a Vaisya, or a Sudra, to which family he

Sri Bhagavan said: "Dear Arjuna, there is no fall for him either here or hereafter. For, none who works for self-redemption meets with an evil destiny."

Bhagavad Gita, VI.40

Sri Bhagavan said: "Arjuna, now listen how with mind attached to Me (through exclusive love) and practising Yoga with complete dependence on Me, you will know Me in full and freed from all doubts. I shall unfold to you in its entirety this wisdom along with the real

---

[103]*Samyutta*, v. 437.

belonged, whether he was tall or short, of what species and description the arrow was'.[104]

knowledge of manifest Divinity, having known which nothing else remains still to be known in this world."

Bhagavad Gita, VII.1, 2

Such a man would of course die and, in like manner, would perish the disciple who sought the painless state from the arrows of desire, ignorance and egotism, if he first insisted on having a complete description of that ineffably blissful state, which is devoid of all pain and suffering, without learning the cause of suffering and the way to eliminate it. However, notwithstanding this parable of the arrow, as expected, neither the Buddha nor Krishna (see parallel), or any other divine Teacher, can, by any way or to any least degree, describe that 'supreme state' or Nirvana or Brahmabhuta. They can only show the way to Its attainment and teach the willing disciple how to prepare himself for the journey on that path towards the salvation of his soul.

The distinctive genius of Buddhism lies in the achievement of its founder the Buddha in turning the attention of humanity in His day away from meaningless rituals and penances to unimaginable gods with indefinable attributes, and focussing it on freeing one's self from the mundane existence of endless rounds of birth and death; by a re-dedication of purpose for treading the path of righteousness—for attaining Nirvana.

This act of change consisted much more of a reinterpretation of the 'attributes' of those concepts, such as Brahma, Brahmabhuta, Brahmavihara, Brahmaloka, as well as Nirvana, rather than any new discovery about these ideas, since the essential nature of any and all these terms is, in every case, beyond definition. The Hindu concept of the highest goal, Brahmabhuta, or dwelling in Brahma, the Buddha acknowledged, but defined it as the state where the mind is free from hatred and malice and loves everything, while higher than the state of Brahmabhuta, according to the Buddha, was Nirvana which, He stated, could only be attained through the eight-fold path (Dharma) preached by Him. Nirvana was also well known to the Hindus of His day since this term occurs in the Upanishads and the *Bhagavad Gita* and denotes 'eternal bliss attainable after blowing out of all passions.' It also denotes the ineffable experience of reunion with the Supreme (Brahmanirvana).

One can go on endlessly in semantic futility, trying to interpret the Buddha's thoughts on the nature of these two concepts—Brahmabhuta and Nirvana—but, in the end, we can only return to a comparative analysis of the meaning of these words commonly accepted in His day to define these states. The following dialogue[105] will be helpful for our understanding:

---

[104] *Majjhima-nikaya,* 1.63.

[105] *Lankavatara Sutra,* 2.*XVIII*.

THE GOD OF BUDDHA

At that time, Mahamati, the Bodhisattva-Mahasattva, said this to the Blessed One: "Nirvana, Nirvana, is talked of by the Blessed One; what does this term designate? What is the Nirvana that is discriminated by all the philosophers?" Said the Blessed One: "Mahamati, listen well and reflect well within yourself; I will tell you." "Certainly, Blessed One," said Mahamati the Bodhisattva-Mahasattva, and gave ear to the Blessed One. The Blessed One said this to him: "As to such Nirvana as are discriminated by the philosophers, there are really none in existence. Some philosophers conceive Nirvana to be found where a system of analytic reasoning no more operates, owing to the cessation of the Skandhas (individuals), Dhatus (elements), and Ayatanas (sense organs), or to indifference to the object world, or to the recognition that all things are impermanent; or where there is no recollection of the past and present, just as when a lamp is extinguished, or when a seed is burnt, or when a fire goes out, because then there is the cessation of all the substrate—which is explained by the philosophers as the non-rising of discrimination. But, Mahamati, Nirvana does not consist in mere annihilation."

Arjuna, such is the state of the God-realized soul; having reached this state, he overcomes delusion. And established in this state, even at the last moment, he attains Brahmic Bliss.

Bhagavad Gita, II.72

Nowhere in the *Dhammapada*, if we investigate every paragraph where Nirvana is mentioned, will we find a single reference denoting Nirvana to mean annihilation. It is obvious from the above, as well as the *Sutta-nipata*, vv. 1093-94 *(see* page 89 below), that the Buddha is quite emphatic that Nirvana is *not annihilation* but *the extinction of aging and dying,* and one may also refer to the 'heavenly messenger's own words, *I search for that most blessed state in which extinction is unknown,* which galvanized and set the young Siddharta on His quest for this Supreme State (Nirvana), on towards His destiny (Buddhahood).

Essentially, it means the condition of bliss where all fires of passion are annihilated. It is where the causal order no longer operates and the liberated soul passes to a realm of bliss freed from the phenomenon of birth and death. Such a soul, while continuing to live in the world, and helping in the development of others, is no longer of the world. In the consciousness of such a soul, the phenomenal and the real, Samsara and Nirvana, have become merged in an identity with the Divine. The Tibetian meaning of the word 'Nirvana' also implies the state of the person who has been freed from sorrow. While in the *Lalita Vistara* the word occurs in a few passages and in none of those is the sense of annihilation necessary to understand its meaning.

Further, Mahamati, those who, afraid of suffering arising from the discrimination of birth and death, seek for Nirvana, do not know that birth-and-death and Nirvana are not to be separated the one from the other; and seeing that all things subject to discrimination have no reality, imagine that Nirvana consists in the future annihilation of the senses and their fields.
Lankavatara Sutra, 2.XVIII

Arjuna, whatever being, animate or inanimate, is born, know that as emanated from the union of sense-fields (Ksetra) and Spirit (Ksetrajna). Arjuna, as the one sun illumines this whole world, so the one Spirit (Atman) illumines the whole field. Those who by the eye of wisdom perceive the difference between the field and the Knower of the Field, and the negation of nature (Prakriti) with her evolutes, reach the Supreme.
Bhagavad Gita, XII, I.26, 33, 34

Those who achieve sainthood are in their own beings the manifestations of Nirvanic bliss regardless of where they dwell. However, the saints do not exist in merely contemplative isolation but lead an active life completely dedicated to the betterment of the human condition of the world around them. Theirs is a life of selfless endeavour and stainless example predicated on self-abnegation, utter simplicity and humanity born of the truth about their own being and purpose.

That place is delightful where saints dwell, whether in the village or in the forest, in deep water or on dry land.
Dhammapada, v. 98

To those wise men, who are free from lust and anger, who have subdued their mind and have realized God, Brahma, the abode of eternal peace, is present all around.
Bhagavad Gita, V.26

The saint is one who has passed beyond the cycle of *comings and goings* (births and deaths) and his consciousness has become merged in *the Eternal.* The Hindus call this condition paramam brahma or brahma-nirvana, and it is known to the Buddhists as nirvana-dhatu. The Buddha tells us that *all elements of being are non-self when one by wisdom realizes this, he heeds not sorrow.* We can never be truly content with wordly wealth or temporal power. Such things can never bring us lasting satisfaction since these are the things of time and have no intrinsic permanency. As the *Upanishad* states: "There is no joy in the finite. Only in the infinite there is joy." Nirvana means not extinction, but the absence of the three fires of passion. *Verily I say unto thee: The Blessed One has not come to teach death, but to teach life, and thou discernest not the nature of living and dying.*[106] Moreover, when the disciple Yamaka asserts that a mendicant, in whom evil has ceased to be, himself also becomes totally extinct upon death, he is promptly refuted by Sariputta who replies that such a belief is heresy since, even in life, the saint's intrinsic nature is beyond understanding.

---

[106]*Questions of King Milinda* (Discourse with the Brahmin Kutadanta of Danamati village).

THE GOD OF BUDDHA

No measure measures him who enters rest.
There is no word with which to speak of him.
All thought is here at an end and so are all
paths that words can take here closed.

Sutta-nipata, (Parayama Vagga.)

He who knows, O my beloved, that Eternal
Spirit wherein consciousness and the senses,
the powers of life and the elements find peace,
knows the All and has gone into the All.

Prasna Upanishad, IV.11

Ananda, this is the real, this the excelllent,
namely the calm of all the impulses, the
casting out of all 'basis', the extinction of
craving, dispassion, stopping, Nirvana.

Anguttara-nikaya, v. 322

Great souls, who have attained highest perfection, having come to Me are no more sub-
jected to rebirth, which is the abode of sorrow,
and transitory by nature.

Bhagavad Gita, VIII.15

Vigilance is the abode of eternal life,
thoughtlessness is the abode of death. Those
who are vigilant do not die. The thoughtless
are as if dead already. These wise ones,
meditative, persevering, always putting forth
strenuous effort attain to nirvana, the highest
freedom[107] and happiness.

Dhammapada, vv. 21, 23

Two paths lie in front of man. Pondering on
them, the wise man chooses the path of joy;
the fool takes the path of pleasure. There is the
path of wisdom and the path of ignorance.
They are far apart and lead to different ends.

Katha Upanishad, II.2

Not only was the description of Nirvana, as we have already noted, identical
to that known by the Hindus a thousand years earlier, but, as we see from the
following, even the Buddha's manner of expressing this *freeing of the heart,*
or *destruction of desires,* as told to the Brahmin Kutadanta, is identical: *All
good works whatever are not worth one-sixteenth part of Love which sets free
the heart. Love which sets free the heart comprises them.* The Buddha not
only proclaims the same meaning of Nirvana as that expressed by the Hindu
scriptures, He even uses the identical numerical fraction to denote the quan-
titative excellence of Nirvana!

Better than absolute sovereignty on earth,
better than going to heaven, better than
lordship over all the worlds is the reward of
reaching the stream. Even in celestial
pleasures he finds no delight. The disciple who
is fully awakened delights only in the destruc-
tion of all desires.

Dhammapada, vv. 178, 187

Whatever delight of satisfaction there is on
earth, whatever is the great delight in heaven,
they are not worth the sixteenth part of the joy
which springs from the destruction of the
desires.

Mahabharata (Santiparva, 6503)

It is of particular interest to note in the following an interchange of the terms
Brahma and Nirvana by the Buddha, who gives the term Brahma a meaning
akin to a state of existence similar to Nirvana. The earlier Hindu concept, as
voiced by the *Bhagavad Gita,* also separates the term "God" from the "abode
of eternal peace—Brahma", and it can be stated that Brahma like Nirvana is

---

[107]The reader should note the positive aspects of Nirvana stated in this verse.

a condition, 'It' rather than a sentient Creator. Brahma is also regarded as Nature (Prakriti) which emanates from the Supreme—God.

Ah, happy indeed the Arahants! In them no craving's found. The 'I am' conceit is rooted out; confusion's net is burst. Lust-free they have attained; translucent is the mind of them. Unspotted in the world are they, Brahma-become, with out-flows none. Comprehending the five groups, pasturing in their seven own mental states, worthy of praise, the true men, own sons of the Buddha. Endowed with the sevenfold gem, trained in the three trainings. These great heroes follow on, fear and dread overcome. Endowed with the ten factors, great beings concentrated, Indeed they are best in the world; no craving's found in them. Possessed of the adept's knowledge, this compound is their last. In that pith of the Brahma-faring they depend not on others. Unshaken by the triple modes, well freed from again-becoming. Attained to the stage of 'tamed', they are victorious in the world. Above, across, below, no lure in them is found. They roar• the lion's roar: 'Incomparable are Buddhas in the world.'
                              Samyutta-nikaya, III.83-84

Those whose mind and intellect are wholly merged in Him, who are constantly established in identity with Him, and are exclusively devoted to Him, their sins being wiped out by wisdom, go to whence there is no return. He, who, with reason firm and free from doubt, rejoices not on obtaining what is agreeable, and does not feel perturbed on meeting with the unpleasant, that knower of Brahma lives eternally in identity with It. He, whose mind remains unattached to external enjoyments, derives through meditation the unmixed joy which is inherent in the soul; then that Yogi, having completely identified himself through meditation with Brahma, enjoys eternal Bliss.
                              Bhagavad Gita, V.17, 20, 21

The Brahma-faring is lived for the plunge into Nirvana, for going beyond to Nirvana, for culmination in Nirvana.
                              Samyutta-nikaya, III.189

That monk of wisdom here, devoid of desire and passion, attains to deathlessness, peace, the unchanging state of Nirvana.
                              Sutta-nipata, v. 204

The sacrifice in which the ladle is Brahma, the oblation itself is Brahma, even so the act of pouring the same into the fire which is again Brahma, by the sacrificer, who is himself Brahma—surely the goal to be reached by him, who is absorbed in such sacrifice as Brahma, is also Brahma. Other Yogis offer sacrifice in the shape of worship to the gods. Others pour into the fire of Brahma, the very sacrifice in the shape of the self, through the sacrifice known as the perception of identity.
                              Bhagavad Gita, IV.24, 25

For those who in mid-stream stay, in great peril in the flood—for those adventuring on ageing and dying—do I proclaim the Isle: Where is no-thing, where naught is grasped, this is the Isle of No-beyond. Nirvana do I call it—the utter extinction of ageing and dying.
                              Sutta-nipata, vv. 1093-94

The Yogi, knowing this secret, doubtless transcends all the rewards, promised in the scriptures, of the study of the Vedas, and of the performance of Sacrifices, austerities and charities, and attains the supreme eternal state.
                              Bhagavad Gita, VIII.28

From the foregoing, we can see that *Brahma-faring* is described as both synonymous with *Nirvana* and *attaining to Nirvana,* and, while the Buddha uses this metaphor, a little reflection should tell us that, since both Nirvana and Brahma-faring are by their very nature outside the realm of description, to the Hindus of His day this was the best way to show that Nirvana was in essence the same state of ineffable bliss which they hoped to experience through Brahma-faring. However, the method or path of achieving Nirvana and hence also Brahmabhuta or Brahma was now, according to Him, only possible through assiduous adherence to His Teachings (Dharma). As He declares *there is no path in the sky, there is no recluse outside, mankind delights in worldliness; the Buddhas are free from worldliness.*[108] Alternately, the Buddha uses the words *Brahmaprapti* and *Brahmabhuta* for *Nirvana* and states that it is possible to attain it in this very existence, even before physical death:

In this very life he is allayed, becomes cool, he abides in the experience of bliss with a self that has become Brahma.[109] Majjhima-nikaya, i.344	He, who is able to withstand, here on earth, before casting off this body, the urges of lust and anger, he is a Yogi—a harmonized soul; he is a happy man. Bhagavad Gita, V.23

We have seen that the Buddha did not deny the existence of Brahma but described him as only the chief of the gods instead of the 'Supreme Cause' behind the entire cosmos; *Who is worthy to blame him who is like a gold coin from the Jambu river? Even the gods praise him; he is praised even by Brahma.*[110] However, we have also noted from references in *Sutta-nipata, Samyutta-nikaya,* etc. that this concept of Brahma was further modified by the Buddha, who, while continuing to reject Brahma as a transcendent source of all reality, transformed Brahma into a state of bliss akin to Nirvana. At times, even the *Bhagavad Gita* describes Brahma as 'It',[111] and gives it a meaning synonymous with the 'state of ineffable bliss'.

It is, therefore, essential for us to recognize the transformation of these terms in Buddhism or, in a real sense the Buddha's re-interpretation of the Upanishad concepts of Nirvana, Brahmabhuta or even Brahma, from that denoting the supreme bliss, to that signifying release from all desire, similar to the Upanishad concept of Moksa. It is a fundamental rule of logic that terms which are intrinsically unexplainable can only be 'explained' by other terms which are also unexplainable intrinsically! Therefore, Nirvana, too, can only be talked about as 'not this, not this,' or 'like that, like that,' since 'it is incomprehensible; so it cannot be comprehended.'[112] The Buddha

---

[108]*Dhammapada*, vv. 254, 255.

[109]Also see *Majjhima-nikaya*, ii.159; *Anguttara*, ii.211.

[110]*Dhammapada*, v. 230.

[111]*Bhagavad Gita*, V. 20.

[112]*Brihadaranyaka Upanishad*, III.9, 26.

sometimes equates it with Dharma, as He also equates it with Brahma (*Samyutta-nikaya* III.189) and then Brahma with Dharma (*Digha-nikaya* III.84).

The religious life (dharma) is embedded in nirvana, its goal is nirvana, its perfection is nirvana. We can make an end of pain in this life.[113]

Majjhima-nikaya, i.304

The gift of the law surpasses all gifts; the flavour of the law surpasses all flavours, the delight in the law surpasses all delights. The destruction of craving conquers all sorrows.

Dhammapada, v. 354

Now the self is the bridge, the separating boundary for keeping these worlds apart. Over that bridge day and night do not cross, nor old age nor death, nor sorrow, nor well-doing nor ill-doing. All evils turn back from it for the Brahma-World is freed from evil.

Chandogya Upanishad, VIII.4,1

On other occasions, the Buddha, describing how He Himself attained the incomparable supreme Nirvana where there is no *coming or going*, sickness or sorrow, declares Nirvana to be the 'highest',[114] higher also than heaven. As we see from references in the *Mahabharatta*, this too was acknowledged by the Hindus well before the time of the Buddha, and in *Visnu Purana*, the word Nirvana is used to denote the state of bliss that can be attained only through completely detached devotion to God.

Health is the greatest of gifts, contentment is the greatest wealth; trust is the best of relationships. Nirvana is the highest happiness.

Dhammapada, v. 204

Brahma is joy: for from joy all beings have come, by joy they all live, and unto joy they all return.

Taittiriya Upanishad, 3.1-6

'All created things are impermanent.' When one by wisdom realizes this, he heeds not sorrow; this is the path to purity. 'All created things are sorrowful.' When one by wisdom realizes (this) he heeds not sorrow; this is the path to purity. 'All the elements of being are non-self.' When one by wisdom realizes (this), he heeds not sorrow; this is the path to purity.

Dhammapada, vv. 277, 278, 279

Where there is creation there is progress. Where there is no creation there is no progress: Know the nature of creation. Where there is joy there is creation. Where there is no joy there is no creation: Know the nature of joy. Where there is the Infinite there is joy. There is no joy in the finite. Only in the Infinite there is joy: Know the nature of the Infinite.

Chandogya Upanishad, VII. (21-23)

Who sees all beings in his own Self and his own Self in all beings, loses all fear. When a sage sees this great Unity and his Self has

---

[113]Buddha's concurrence of the preaching of the nun Dhammadinno.

[114]*Dhammapada*, vv. 184, 203.

become all being, what delusion and what sorrow can ever be near him?

Isa Upanishad, 6.7

As far as the suns and moons extend their courses and the regions of the sky shine in splendour, there is a thousand fold world system. In each single one of these there are a thousand suns, moons, Meru mountains, four times a thousand continents and oceans, a thousand heavens of all stages of the realm of sense pleasure, a thousand Brahma worlds. As far as a thousand fold world system reaches, the Great Brahma is the highest being. But even the Great Brahma is subject to coming-to-be and ceasing-to-be.

Anguttara-nikaya, V.10, 29, 2

Arjuna, all the worlds from Brahmaloka (the Abode of Brahma) downwards are subject to appearance and disappearance. But, O son of Kunti, on attaining Me there is no rebirth. (For I am beyond Time, and regions like Brahmaloka, being subject to time, are impermanent.) All embodied beings emanate from the Unmanifest at the commencement of Brahma's day; at the commencement of his night, they merge in the same subtle body of Brahma, known as the Unmanifest.

Bhagavad Gita, VIII.16, 18

Here, we see from the above, both Buddha and Krishna implying that Brahmaloka and *Great Brahma* are not intrinsically eternal. Brahmaloka is the ultimate that can be conceived within the frame of unversal experience. There is nothing beyond it in the realm of manifestation, and Brahma is the spirit embodied in the cosmos and existing during the whole cycle of its life. These terms do not denote the Supreme Absolute beyond the Cosmos, but only the farthest limit before we are faced with the 'Unthinkable'. *The Absolute,* as the *Gita* continues, is outside the frame of any reference of Time and Space, while yet manifesting Itself to the experience of the purified mind through Its emanations of ineffable bliss, such as Brahmaloka or Nirvana. In a sense, the reader may visualize the whole creation as the aura emanating from the Supreme, just as light pulsations emanate from the sun, periodically advancing and receding. As Krishna tell us, "All embodied beings emanate from the Unmanifest at the commencement of Brahma's day; at the commencement of Brahma's night, they merge in the same subtle body of Brahma known as the Unmanifest." If one understands the Buddha correctly, what is meant by Nirvana is liberation from every bond holding us to the ephemeral and the mundane, in order to attain the ineffable realm of the soul, in the heart of *the Eternal.* Where, like birds, whose tracks in the atmosphere are completely obliterated, our paths too become trackless in that realm of *no becoming.*

There is no suffering for him who has completed his journey, who is freed from sorrow, who has freed himself on all sides, who has shaken off all fetters.

Dhammapada, v. 90

He, who is happy within himself, enjoys within himself the delight of the soul, and even so is illumined by the inner light, such a Yogi identified with Brahma attains Brahma, who is all peace.

Bhagavad Gita, V.24

Some enter the womb; evil doers go to hell; the good go to heaven; those free from worldly desires attain nirvana.

Dhammapada, v. 126

The seers whose sins have been washed away, whose doubts have been dispelled by Knowledge, whose mind is firmly established in God and who are actively engaged in promoting the welfare of all beings attain Brahma, who is all peace.

Bhagavad Gita, V.25

Spiritual insight does not involve physical escape from the world but is the release of the soul (the integral self) from the fetters of the selfish ego. The world continues around us as before except that we now view it from a higher plane of awareness. We are no longer attached to, or effected by, its tragedies and terrors for our non-objective consciousness has merged into a realm of serene certitude and quiescent bliss above the doubts and fears of existence. It is not the limitations of our physical body and natural laws (Prakriti) that hold us in bondage to the ephemeral and the mundane but our mental attitude.

Those whose minds are well grounded in the elements of enlightenment, who without clinging to anything rejoice in freedom from attachment, whose appetites have been conquered, who are full of light, attain Nirvana in this world.

Dhammapada, v. 89

Samsara, the transmigration of life, takes place in one's own mind. Let one therefore keep the mind pure, for what a man thinks that he becomes: this is a mystery of Eternity.

Maitri Upanishad, 6.24

Those who have no accumulation, who eat according to knowledge, who have perceived release and unconditioned freedom, their path is difficult to understand like that of birds through the sky. He whose passions are destroyed, who is indifferent to food, who has perceived release and unconditioned freedom, his path is difficult to understand like that of birds through the sky. Even the gods envy him whose senses are subdued like horses well tamed by the charioteer, who is free from pride and free from taints.

Dhammapada, vv. 92, 93, 94

Arjuna, even those devotees who, endowed with faith, worship other gods, they too worship Me alone, though not in accordance with rules (i.e. without proper knowledge). For I am the enjoyer and also the Lord of all sacrifices; but they do not know Me in reality, hence they fall and are subject to birth and death. I am equally present in all beings; there is none hateful or dear to Me. They, however, who devoutly worship Me abide in Me, and I also stand revealed in them.

Bhagavad Gita, IX.23, 24, 29

Here, the reader should note that the Buddha does not state that the birds are obliterated, but that their tracks are obliterated.

Thus, we can clearly see from the various excerpts in the Buddhist scriptures, which are further confirmed by the comparative quotes from Hinduism, that Nirvana is really a state of mind and not a spot in space. And, since Nirvana is acknowledged as eternal—an eternal experience for those who attain it—its corollary must be the confirmation of Buddha's assertion that 'mind', meaning also 'soul', as previously stated (see p. 67), exists, and that it, too, is an eternal entity and its immortality is not dependent on its state of being (hellish torment or nirvanic bliss) but is an intrinsic and inseparable attribute of its own essence. Otherwise, what is it that is in niraya hell or in nirvanic bliss, if not the mind? Moreover, the Buddha tells us that the attainment of Nirvana is also possible for the mind right here in the physical plane, during *this very life* those rare souls *who are full of light attain Nirvana in this world.*[115] Nirvana, as He explains, is *the realm of self-realization* and it exists where one views that *there is nothing but what is seen of the mind itself.*[116] As He states, it is *the stopping of becoming that is Nirvana*[117] and *the getting rid of craving,*[118] where *the steadfast go out like a lamp,*[119] which has *the wick pulled right out,* and that the *going out of the flame itself was deliverance of the mind.*[120] All of which as we see (from *Samyutta-nikaya,* III.83-84) is identical to having 'Brahma-become' *(Unspotted in the world, Brahma-become with outflows none).* Nor is Nirvana something which is empirically verifiable, about which, and in which, dispute and argument can occur, *understanding Khema*[121] *to be the place where there is no dispute.*[122]

So, however high a state Nirvana is conceived to be, whether attainable here or in the hereafter, it still remains a state—a condition—and, when equated with Dharma (Religion), it is the law—the divine law, acting in perfect accord with the principle of Causality (Karma). But, just as no law exists without a law-giver, no condition can exist without a cause, and it is precisely because Nirvana is a state of mind, a condition of bliss, that it is never referred to as an underlying Reality anywhere in the Pali canon.

We should also note that Krishna, too, differentiates between that state of supreme eternal bliss, which is Brahma, and Himself, the Supreme Being.

For, I am the abode of the imperishable Brahma, of immortality, of everlasting virtue and of unending bliss—*Bhagavad Gita,* XIV.27.

And that He, Krishna, is to be worshipped exclusively if the worshipper is to attain Brahma.

And he who constantly worships Me through the Yoga of exclusive

---

[115]*Dhammapada,* v.89.
[116]*Digha-nikaya,* II.157.
[117]*Samyutta-nikaya,* II.117.
[118]*Ibid.,* I.39.
[119]*Sutta-nipata,* v. 235.
[120]*Therigatha,* v. 116.
[121]*Nirvana.*
[122]*Sutta-nipata,* vv. 895-96.

devotion, transcending these three Gunas, he becomes eligible for attaining Brahma—*Bhagavad Gita*, XIV.26.

Thus, it can be said that Brahma, too, is not the underlying Reality or the 'transcendent Being' but a state, rather identical to what Nirvana itself is in Buddhist belief. Also Krishna speaking as the Supreme, states that He is "the abode of the imperishable Brahma." Hence, Brahma, which is a state, albeit the highest (just as Nirvana), is nevertheless contained within, and is a product of, the Supreme Being, and this Supreme State of ineffable bliss (Brahma), according to Krishna, is attainable only by him "who constantly worships Me through the Yoga of exclusive devotion . . ." This is the same method *(treading the path of Dharma)* inculcated by the Buddha for attaining Nirvana.

Now, if Nirvana is not the underlying Reality, we are left with only two choices: That something else exists, and 'It' is the underlying Reality, the 'ground' on which all else rests, the *Causeless Cause* of all causes and effects, including Nirvana, and that 'It', and not Nirvana, is the *Unoriginated* originator of the eternal Dharma. Or Nirvana, Dharma, 'Existence', and everything else are just meaningless and empty words and all end in extinction, total and complete, and that there are no ends worth striving for, and life is purposeless—a mirage. This latter concept is unequivocally rejected by the Buddha: *Nirvana does not consist in mere annihilation.*[123] *Nirvana is the unchanging state of deathless peace . . . the utter extinction of aging and dying.*[124]

Moreover it could not be said: 'There is not Nirvana.' Why is this? Because the practice of Dharma is not barren. For if Nirvana were not, there would be barrenness in regard to (spiritual) attainment in the three categories of Moral Habit and so on that begin with Right View. But due to the attainment of Nirvana, there is not this barrenness. Dispassion is called the Way (Dharma). It is said: 'Through dispassion is one freed.' Yet, in meaning, all these (renunciation, surrender, release, lack of clinging) are synonyms for Nirvana. For, according to ultimate meaning, Nirvana is the Ariyan Truth of the stopping of suffering. But because when that (Nirvana) is reached, craving detaches itself, besides being stopped, it is called Dispassion and it is called Stopping.

Visuddhimagga, vv. 507-09

Arjuna, he who always thinks of Me with undivided mind, to that Yogi always absorbed in Me, I am easily attainable.

Bhagavad Gita, VIII.14

Arjuna, that Supreme Purusa (God), in whom all beings reside, and by whom all this is pervaded, is attainable only by exclusive devotion.

Bhagavad Gita, VIII.22

When he does not know, yet is he knowing, though he does not know. It becomes like water, one, the witness, without a second. This is the world of Brahma.

Brihadaranyaka Upanishad, IV.3, 30, 32

[123]*Lankavatara Sutra*, 2.XVIII.
[124]*Sutta-nipata*, 204. 1093, 1094.

95

> For wise men endowed with equanimity,
> renouncing the fruit of actions and freed from
> the shackles of birth, attain the blissful
> supreme state.
>
> *Bhagavad Gita*, II.51

From all the foregoing excerpts, we have seen that the Buddha, just like the teacher of the Upanishads, also confines Himself to stating what Nirvana is not, rather than attempting the impossible by giving any descriptions or similes concerning its nature. Its reality is outside the realm of thought, for it is not 'existence' or 'being' in the sense of existence within the frame of space and time. Hence, words can give no meaning since thought cannot conceive it. And, by the process of eliminating those objects and aspects of existence which are subject to composition and decomposition and to 'time' itself, the Buddha, in the following famous discourse, leaves no doubts as to the reality of Nirvana:

There is, O monks, a state where there is neither earth, nor water, nor heat, nor air; neither infinity of space nor infinity of consciousness, nor nothingness, nor perception nor non-perception; neither this world nor that world, neither sun nor moon. That, O monks, I term neither coming nor going nor standing; neither death nor birth. It is without stability, without change; it is without support, without beginning, without foundation; just that is the end of sorrow.[125]

Now I shall speak to you at length about that which ought to be known and knowing which one attains immortality; that beginningless supreme Brahma is said to be neither Being (Sat) nor non-Being (Asat).

Bhagavad Gita, XIII.12

Beyond this Unmanifest, there is yet another eternal Unmanifest, that supremely Divine Substance, which does not perish even though all beings perish. The Unmanifest, spoken of as the undestructible, is called the supreme Goal; that is My supreme Abode, attaining which man does not return.

Bhagavad Gita, VIII.20, 21

But, as we see, it is a 'state', a 'plane', a 'condition'—a stage which can be reached and experienced even here on earth *(in this very life attain Nirvana).*[126] However, one must understand here that it (Nirvana) is not a condition or a product of our mind, or dependent for its creation on our correct actions and thoughts towards eradicating the last vestiges of craving and ignorance from our selves, but that it is a 'co-existent attribute' of the Primal Mind, the Supreme Soul, the *Causeless Cause* and radiating from It like light and warmth and life radiate from the sun. Hence, while light and

---

[125]*Udana*, 8.1-4 (80-81). In the second half of this famous discourse, the Buddha describes a condition very different from the above-quoted, which refers to a 'state', a 'plane', or a 'sphere', while the latter half strongly implies an 'Entity', with different 'negatives', denoting sentiency. That part of this same discourse is quoted and explained in the final chapter (p. 133).

[126]*Dhammapada*, v.89. *Majjhima-nikaya*, i.344.

warmth are co-existent with the sun and also a proof of the sun's existence, yet, these fields of emanations depend for their reality and existence on the sun, and only the sun and not on any viewer or other objects. Thus, the sun, and not its emanating aura (the field), is the underlying reality. Likewise, when by understanding the Dharma (Religion) and acting in strict adherence to the Buddha's Message, we remove the blindfold of ignorance and ephemeral desires, we can open our eyes to the glory of that ineffable light and, experience its bliss (Nirvana) without being able to explain it in words to others, who, in order to understand, must also experience it, since no amount of explanation can convey to the blind the experience of light. Moreover, the Buddha, in *Majjhima-nikaya*,[127] tells us that Nirvana is both different and higher than the doctrines of 'the sphere of Nothingness' taught to Him by Alara Kalama and 'the sphere of Neither-perception-nor-non-perception' taught to Him by Uddaka Ramaputta.[128]

"Thus, monks, though Alara Kalama was my teacher and although I was his pupil, he put me on the same level as himself and did me a great honour. However, monks, it occurred to me: 'This doctrine does not lead to aversion, detachment, cessation, tranquility, higher knowledge, enlightenment and Nibbana; it is only for the attainment up to the sphere of Nothingness.' Monks, I did not appreciate that doctrine and being repelled I left it."

"I, monks, while seeking for what was good and searching for the incomparable noble state of peace, went to Uddaka Ramaputa. Thus, monks, Uddaka Ramaputta, although he was my fellow recluse, placed me in the position of a teacher and did me a great honour. Then, monks, it occurred to me: 'This doctrine does not lead to aversion, detachment, cessation, tranquility, higher knowledge, enlightenment and Nibbana; it is only for the attainment up to the sphere of Neither-perception-nor-non-perception. I did not appreciate that doctrine and being repelled I left it.' "

Having left Alara and Uddaka, He then describes how He reached Uruvela where He eventually achieved Nirvana.

"That I, monks, while seeking for what was good and searching for the incomparable noble state of peace, and while travelling in Magadha by stages, came to the village of Senani at Uruvela. There I saw a pleasant, a delightful forest grove with a flowing river of clear water, a pleasant and delightful ford and a village near by for procuring food. Monks, then it

---

[127]*Ariyapariyesana Sutta (Majjhima-nikaya).*
[128]Sanskrit: 'Udraka Ramaputra'.

occurred to me: 'Pleasant indeed and delightful is the forest grove with a flowing river of clear water, a pleasant and delightful ford and a village nearby for procuring food. Indeed it is a most suitable place for a noble youth intent on spiritual exertion.' Monks, I sat down at that very spot thinking: 'This is a most suitable place for spiritual exertion' . . . Being myself subject to old age . . . illness . . . death . . . grief . . . mental impurities, while seeking for Nibbana which is not characterized by old age, illness, death, grief and mental impurities, which is incomparable and safety from bondage, I attained Nibbana which is not characterized by old age, illness, death, grief, and mental impurities, which is incomparable and is safety from bondage. Then this knowledge and insight arose in me: 'My emancipation is assured, this is the final birth for me and there is no other existence for me.' "

But, from the above description, Nirvana, too, seems to be the same as the concepts imparted to the Buddha by His mentors Alara and Uddaka. Furthermore, by reference to the well-known discourse from *Udana* (see p. 96) one can see that the 'state' or 'order' described by the Buddha in the first part of this discourse is identical to the concepts of the spheres of 'Nothingness' and 'Neither-perception-nor-non-perception' taught to Him by His two mentors. *There is, O monks, a state where there is neither earth, nor water, nor heat, nor air; neither infinity of space nor infinity of consciousness, nor nothingness, nor perception nor non-perception . . . just that is the end of sorrow.* (A part of this passage has been underlined to draw the reader's attention to the description of this state which is supposed to portray Nirvana.) Hence, while it is impossible to describe here what precise difference the Buddha saw between the states of 'Nothingness', 'Neither-perception-nor-non-perception' and 'Nirvana', one can nevertheless understand His reason for asserting that there is a difference between the first two 'dharmas' taught to him by human teachers and His own attainment to the understanding of Nirvana, which is an emanation from the Supreme. It was to show that Buddhahood is a thing apart, a divine bestowal, *an exaltation from the Absolute.*

Since we have now reached the penultimate step in our quest for that 'underlying Reality' behind Nirvana, behind the Dharma, and behind Buddha, the writer, at this point, would like to present the two perspectives of viewing Nirvana which are generally regarded by all schools of Buddhist thought as correct.

The first is from the discourse of Gautama the Buddha-to-be with the 'Holy Spirit', who appeared as a mendicant with the announcement of His coming Buddhahood. This episode from the *Jataka Tales* equates Nirvana with Dharma and gives the following allegories:

If the lake which is nearby is not sought to clean the filth into which one has fallen, it is not the fault of the lake. Even so when there is a blessed road leading the man held fast by wrong to the salvation of Nirvana, if the road is not walked upon it is not the fault of the road, but of the person. And when a man who is oppressed with sickness, there being the medicine to heal him, does not avail of the cure, that is not the fault of the medicine. Even so a man oppressed by the malady of wrong-doing does not seek the spiritual guide of enlightenment, that is no fault of the evil destroying guide.

It is true that the body is mortal, that it is under the power of death; but it is also the dwelling of Atman, the spirit of immortal life. The body, the house of the spirit, is under the power of pleasure and pain; and if a man is ruled by his body then this man can never be free. But when a man is in the joy of the spirit, in the spirit which is ever free, then this man is free from all bondage, the bondage of pleasure and pain. When the soul is in silent quietness it arises and leaves the body, and reaching the Spirit Supreme finds there its body of light. It is the land of infinite liberty where, beyond its mortal body, the spirit of man is free.

Chandogya Upanishad, 8.7-12

In every instance of the above discourse, except the dubious last—*the spiritual guide of enlightenment*—the description is one concerning a 'state', or 'condition', and not of an 'underlying cause', which, in the case of the lake, must be the cause for the creation of water; in the case of the road, the road builder; in the case of medicine, the maker of the medicine; and, if by the spiritual guide of enlightenment is meant a guide-book or righteous living, then the cause is the writer of that book, but if it refers to a person, e.g. a Prophet, or a Buddha, then the cause is the 'Creator' of that person. This discourse talks of the way as a path to be trod, to be known, and asserts that the result, in all instances, will be an approach to happiness of body and spirit. It does not claim for Nirvana any absolute conditions and is therefore closer in its concept to the Buddha's own views, since, if tradition is correct, they were patterned after this first discourse with His vision of the Holy Ascetic.

Moreover, interestingly enough, every simile given here in this earliest extant, and undoubtedly the first, discourse on Nirvana contained in the Buddhist Teachings is positive! It contains no negative descriptions, and if the account of this discourse, which occurred during the Buddha's youth, has been faithfully reproduced, then one can see that there is a subtle, but clearly discernable, deterioration in the simplicity of form and concept, of the 'effects' of Nirvana, as listed in this earliest discourse on the subject, to the more 'wordy', but also more confusing, discourse[129] 500 years later between Nagasena and King Milinda, assuming that it, too, was faithfully recorded. And the reader can see that many of the 'effects' ascribed to the qualities of Nirvana, by Nagasena, can also be accomplished by 'annihilation'—contrary to the Buddha's expressed views against nihility:

---

[129]*Sukhavativyah,* 15-19, 21-22, 24, 27, *Questions of King Milinda.*

"Its form, O king, cannot be elucidated by similis, but its qualities can."—"How good to hear that, Nagasena! Speak then, quickly, so that I may have an explanation of even one of the aspects of Nirvana! Appease the fever of my heart! Allay it with the cool sweet breezes of your words!" "Nirvana shares one quality with the lotus, two with water, three with medicine, ten with space, three with the wishing jewel, and five with a mountain peak. As the lotus is unstained by water, so is Nirvana unstained by all the defilements.—As cool water allays feverish heat, so also Nirvana is cool and allays the fever of all the passions. Moreover, as water removes the thirst of men and beasts who are exhausted, parched, thirsty, and overpowered by heat, so also Nirvana removes the craving for sensuous enjoyments, the craving for further becoming, the craving for the cessation of becoming.—As medicine protects from the torments of poison, so Nirvana from the torménts of the poisonous passions. Moreover, as medicine puts an end to sickness, so Nirvana to all sufferings. Finally, Nirvana and medicine both give security.—And these are the ten qualities Nirvana shares with space. Neither is born, grows old, dies, passes away, or is reborn; both are unconquerable, cannot be stolen, are unsupported, are roads respectively for birds and Arahats to journey on, are un-obstructed and infinite.—Like the wishing jewel, Nirvana grants all one can desire, brings joy, and sheds light.—As a mountain peak is lofty and exalted, so is Nirvana. As a mountain is unshakeable, so is Nirvana. As a mountain peak is inaccessible, so is Nirvana inaccessible to all the passions. As no seeds can grow on a mountain peak, so the seeds of all the passions cannot grow in Nirvana. And finally, as a mountain peak is free from all desire to please or displease, so is Nirvana."—"Well said, Nagasena! So it is, and as such I accept it."

King Milinda said: "In the world one can see things produced of karma; things produced from a cause, things produced by nature. Tell me, what in the world is not born of karma, or a cause, or of nature?"—"There are two such things, space and Nirvana."—"Do not, Nagasena, corrupt the Jina's words, do not answer the question ignorantly!"—"What did I say, your majesty, that you speak thus to me?"—"What you said about space not being born of karma, or from a cause, or from nature, that was correct. But with many hundreds of arguments has the Lord proclaimed to his disciples the way to the realization of Nirvana—and then you say that Nirvana is not born of a cause!"—"It is true that the Lord has with many hundreds of arguments proclaimed to his disciples the way to the realization (attainment) of Nirvana; but that does not mean that he has spoken of a cause for the production of Nirvana."

"Here, Nagasena, we do indeed enter from darkness into greater darkness, from a jungle into a deeper jungle, from a thicket into a denser thicket, inasmuch as we are given a cause for the realization of Nirvana, but no cause for the production of that same dharma (i.e. Nirvana). If there is a cause for the realization of Nirvana, we would also expect one for its production. If there is a son's father, one would for that reason also expect the father to have had a father; if there is a pupil's, teacher, one would for that reason also expect the teacher to have had a teacher; if there is a seed for a sprout, one would for that reason also expect the seed to have had a seed. Just so, if there is a cause for the realization of Nirvana, one would for that reason also expect a cause for its production."—"If a tree or creeper has a top, then for that reason it must also have a middle and a root. "Nirvana, O King, is not something that should be produced. That is why no cause for its production has been proclaimed."—"Please, Nagasena, give me a reason, convince me by an argument, so that I can understand this point!"

"Well then, O king, attend carefully, listen closely, and I will tell you the reason for this. Could a man with his natural strength go up from here to the Himalaya mountains?"—"Yes, he could."—"But could that man with his natural strength bring the Himalaya mountains here?"—"No, he could not."—"Just so it is possible to point out the way to the realization of Nirvana, but impossible to show a cause for its production. Could a man, who with his natural strength has crossed in a boat over the great ocean, get to the farther shore?"—"Yes, he could."—"But could that man with his natural strength bring the farther shore of the great ocean here?"—"No, he could not."—"Just so one can point out the way to the realization of Nirvana, but one cannot show a cause for its production. And what is the reason for that? Because that dharma, Nirvana, is unconditioned."—"Is then, Nagasena, Nirvana unconditioned?"—"So it is, O king, unconditioned is Nirvana, not made by anything. Of Nirvana one cannot say that it is produced, or unproduced, or that it should be produced; that it is past, or future, or present; or that one can become aware of it by the eye, or the ear, or the nose, or the tongue, or the body."—"In that case, Nagasena, you indicate Nirvana as a dharma which is not, and Nirvana does not exist."—"Nirvana is something which is. It is cognizable by the mind. A holy disciple, who has followed the right road, sees Nirvana with a mind which is pure, sublime, straight, unimpeded and disinterested."—"But what then is that Nirvana like? Give me a simile, and convince me by arguments. For a dharma which exists can surely be illustrated by a simile!"

"Is there, great king, something called 'wind'?"—"Yes, there is such a thing."—"Please, will your majesty show me the wind, its color and shape, and whether it is thin or thick, long or short."—"One cannot point to the wind like that. For the wind does not lend itself to being grasped with the hands, or to being touched. Nevertheless, there is such a thing as wind."—"If one cannot point to the wind, one might conclude that there is no wind at all."—"But I know, Nagasena, that there is wind, I am quite convinced of it, in spite of the fact that I cannot point it out."—"Just so, your majesty, there is Nirvana, but one cannot point to Nirvana, either by its color or its shape."—"Very good, Nagasena. Clear is the simile, convincing is the argument. So it is, and so I accept it: there is a Nirvana."

Now, despite the 'wordiness' of Nagasena, and his more easily refutable examples concerning the qualities of Nirvana, we would have still accepted his arguments as merely a more devious manner of stating what was more simply put 500 years earlier, but, then, Nagasena is asked about how Nirvana is produced, and he is obliged to reply that Nirvana is unproduced and unconditioned and, yet, the childish examples he gives to show this, indicates that he either did not know that such things as the Himalaya mountains, the wind, the farther shore, the ocean have a cause for their being (since these are poor examples indeed and it is not correct to describe the ineffable or its qualities by the qualities of the finite objects of the physical word), or, and this is more likely, that Nagasena had become a captive of his own prejudice concerning the non-existence of the underlying Reality, the Supreme, and could not move in that, the only correct, direction open to him, namely, to explain the reality of the world of light by the presence of the sun which is the real cause of light. Nagasena would then, of course, have had to admit the underlying Reality behind Nirvana, since Nirvana was not the 'ground' of all things, but was itself an emanation. By doing so he could have done away with all those contradictable examples which lack analytical insight, and shown that Nirvana, being the emanation from that Source of Reality, like the sun's rays from the sun, is co-existent and, therefore, 'ever-existent' and not subject to production by the mind of man or anything else within the whole fabric of space and time. The reader can see that, by inserting the 'Sun', the whole picture is complete, the aura (Nirvana) emanating from the underlying Reality can, when we by our efforts through righteous behaviour (Dharma) open our spiritual sight, light before us the straight path and free us from the craving for earthly things, the pitfall of ignorance, the sickness of the soul, and make us as purified forms, journeying on rays of light (Nirvana) towards the Sun of Reality—the Supreme.

Now, if one cannot describe these superlatives of unending bliss, everlasting virtue, immortality, embedded in the concepts of Nirvana or Brahmabhuta, how much less can one imagine the underlying Reality, the very 'ground' on which such states are predicated and without which they could have no existence.

Fully cognizant of the impossibility of defining any of the attributes of that Absolute Reality, and not wishing to merely add words to describe other words, the Buddha created instead, a dynamic and vibrant life of righteousness as the surest *escape* from the fleeting unreality of mundane existence with its accompanying sorrows and uncertainties.

I shall raise no temples, pagodes, palaces, or parks,
To proclaim Thy praise and tell Thy story.
But generate instead an endless stream of enlightened minds, shining
souls, purified hearts, Who acknowledge Thee and sing Thy glory.

Thus, making His whole life and entire Message into one continuous proof
and an immortal tribute of His belief in the existence of that *Unoriginated,
Unborn, Uncreated, Unformed* underlying Reality.

4

THE GOD OF BUDDHA

POINT AND COUNTER-POINT

Through the slow aeons of progress, Man is gradually beginning to recognize that he is still very far from contact with Ultimate Reality and that all his knowledge of the phenomenal world is only knowledge about its form and not of the intrinsic content, whose subtle essence continues to evade him as completely as it did his beetle-browed ancestor of a billion years ago. But, unlike our past foolish attitude, which demanded empirical verification for accepting any phenomenon, we are now progressively becoming 'wise' to the reality of the absolute limits of our faculties and gadgets for acquiring any true concept of Ultimate Reality. And, thus, in contrast to the fool who believes in nothing till it is proved, modern man cognizant of the limitless possibilities of phenomenal existence, totally outside his references of proof, is wisely beginning to accept the possibility of everything until it is disproved.

We shall now take up some of the standard Buddhistic arguments concerning their non-belief in the existence of the Supreme, *the Absolute,* Allah, or God. Such Buddhistic arguments are not predicated on the Buddha's own original concepts or teachings; yet they are an outgrowth from misunderstanding those same concepts and teachings, and, hence, it is our bounden duty to re-examine these and, where no ground exists for their acceptance, to discard them.

'GODS' IN OUR IMAGE AND
THE UNMANIFEST BRAHMA

We will not concern ourselves here with Buddhistic disputations against the impotency of Agni, the fire-god, or about water having no sentient quality, for such beliefs are simply manifestations of the superstitious mind to 'cover all bets' and to provide the maximum insurance against the ominous future, just as the worship of images in the Buddhist Faith (expressly forbidden by the Buddha), which is also found in the Hindu and other faiths, or the practice of necromancy, of fortune telling, wearing of charms and amulets, supplication to statues, etc. all of which, according to the Buddha as well as Krishna and all other Manifestations, have no real or intrinsic potency, since they are merely the creations of our own minds and can thus only effect us in and through our imagination—as the mind plays on the mind and its senses. The following words of the Buddha should be sufficient on this aspect: *Well, Kevatta! It is because I perceive danger in the practice of mystic wonders, that I loathe, and abhor, and am ashamed thereof.*[130]

Nor can we accept such naive methods of attributing qualitative inferiority of status to the Vedic gods, such as Indra, Varuna, Brahma, etc. just by asserting that they paid homage[131] to the Buddha, and hence He must be greater than them. Even a cursory reading of the Upanishads[132] will show us many such similar references—of Indra paying homage to the god Prajapati, and being tutored by him for 101 years! or Brahma and Indra acknowledging the superiority of Krishna, and Krishna admitting that He is the father and grandfather of Brahma and all the other gods. Would that not make Krishna and Prajapati at least equal to the Buddha, if not superior? Or, all this could mean that Indra is simply a rather dull fellow and of no great consequence unless one wants to emulate his humble frankness. For, he is at least not lacking in humility! And, as we learn from the *Jataka Tales,* he is also not without a streak of generosity, since he pleaded with the gods to return to Gautama, his wife and child, when in a former birth, Gautama was an aspiring Boddhisattva (See p. 175, under *'Vessantara Jataka').* As another

---

[130] *Digha-nikaya,* Part I, Kevatta Sutta.

[131] *Samyutta-nikaya,* 48, 57. V. p. 233.

[132] *Chandogya Upanishad,* 8.7-12. Moreover, despite any claims to the contrary, the Hindus of those times also knew full well that these different names and attributes were merely various aspects of the one indivisible and unknowable Supreme. Brahma, Vishnu, Siva are simply references to the three functions of creation, maintenance and dissolution, depicting the Supreme. "You, O Agni, are Varuna when you are born. You become Mitra when you are kindled. In you. O son of strength, are all gods. You are Indra for the pious mortal." *Nayamanjari,* I.242 (Jayantabhatta).

sign of the Buddha's superiority over the Vedic gods, we are told that Brahma had to plead before the Buddha, upon Gautama's attainment of Enlightenment (Buddhahood), by urging the newly established Tathagata to go down amongst suffering humanity and *work the weal of the world,* and that the Buddha eventually decided to do so.

To me, monks, this thought occurred: "I have attained this Dhamma which is profound, difficult to understand and comprehend, peaceful, exalted, beyond the reach of logic, subtle, conceivable only by the wise. This doctrine, the conditioned origination, is also difficult to be understood by the wordlings. ... This doctrine, the cessation of the formative tendencies, relinquishment of all the bases of attachment, wearing out of craving, absence of passion, cessation of all suffering, and Nibbana, is also difficult to understand. And, moreover, were I to preach the Dhamma and if others would not understand it, it would be weariness and trouble for me. And so, monks, these verses, not heard of before, occurred to me:

'This that I've won through many arduous days,
What profit lies in now expounding it?
The lustful, haters, will not understand;
Will comprehend not that which goes against
The current of their craving, and the mass
Of murky ignorance in which they're sunk
This Teaching rare, deep, subtle, hard to see.'

Monks, as I was pondering thus, my mind tended towards absence of eagerness and not for preaching the Doctrine. Thereupon, monks, it occurred to Brahma who knew my reflection with his own mind: "Alas, this world is perishing, alas, this world is being destroyed, inasmuch as the mind of the Tathagata, the Arahat, the Perfectly-enlightened Buddha is tending towards absence of eagerness and not to preaching the Doctrine." Then, monks, just as a strong man might stretch out his bent arm or bend his outstretched arm, even so Brahma vanished from his Heaven and appeared in front of me. . . . and entreated: "May the Exalted One preach the Doctrine, may the Happy One preach the Doctrine. There is a class of beings with little dust in their eyes who, not hearing the Doctrine, are degenerating, but if they are learners of the Doctrine they will grow."
Then Brahma added further:

E'en so, O Wisdom-won, self-freed from grief,
Climb to the topmost of thy Doctrine pure,

Look around and see the wordlings sunk in grief,
Oppressed with birth and its result, decay.
O hero! O Conqueror in battle!
Rise up! O Leader of the Caravan,
Now free from debt, move freely in the world!
Preach, Noble One, to those who'll understand!"

Then I, having known the entreaty of this god and out of compassion for beings, surveyed the world with the eye of an Awakened One. . . . even so, surveying the world with the eye of an Awakened One, I saw living beings with little dust in their eyes . . . a few looking with fear on sinfulness and the world beyond. Then I, monks, addressed Brahma in verse:

"The doors to the deathless are open!
Let those who will hear leave wrong doctrine!
That 'twould be but weariness, useless;
So thinking I taught not, O Brahma,
This Doctrine sublime and transcendent."

'Ariyapariyesana Sutta' (Majjhima-nikaya)

Does this not imply a higher wisdom and foresight on the part of Brahma as well as a greater sense of care for the salvation of humanity? Otherwise, what had Brahma to gain from the Buddha's attainment of enlightenment, or whether He went amongst humanity or not.

In whatever manner we wish to view this episode, it does bring out some salient points concerning the power of Brahma in relation to the newly-become-Buddha. We note that, while on occasions the Buddha states that He is incomprehensible to beings, it obviously cannot include Brahma among them, for He knew well the Buddha's mind and understood that the Buddha, being apprenhensive of failure, was hesitating to preach His Dharma. It should be obvious from this that, being able to read the Buddha's mind, Brahma knew all that was to be known about the Buddha including His Dharma and His concept of Nirvana, and, since the Buddha was to claim omniscience later on, Brahma, too, was and had been omniscient. Being all-knowing, Brahma knew not only that those beings with *little dust in their eyes* would be liberated if they heard the Buddha preach His doctrine, but also that the Buddha would, upon being urged by Brahma, accede to Brahma's wish and commence His mission *to beat the drum of Brahma, to work the weal of the world.* Moreover, as the Buddha recounts, Brahma, upon knowing the Buddha's mind, left his Heavenly Abode and appeared before the Buddha. Now, if the Buddha, too, could have known Brahma's mind, there would be no need for the Brahma to appear before Buddha either in vision or form. We read later that the Buddha with newly-won divine vision recognized what Brahma had urged upon Him and acceded to it. The whole episode is very similar to that which occurred in Buddha's youth—the vision of the 'Holy Spirit' coming to assure Him of success if He persevered in His quest for Buddhahood.

If the popularly understood Buddhist version of the natures and the states of these Vedic gods is correct, namely, that a true mendicant in the path of the Buddha-dharma has a more exalted station than Brahma, Indra and the other gods, then, by the Buddha preaching His Dharma to humanity and the consequent rise of more mendicants, Arahats and even Boddhisattvas, all attaining to heights of spirituality above the gods—Brahma and Indra had nothing to gain but a great deal to lose. They would have been better off to have kept the Buddha with them in heaven and not advised Him to go down and *work the weal of the world;* especially since the Buddha, as the story goes, was hesitant to do so. Obviously, these two points—Brahma pleading with the Buddha to preach His doctrine for liberating humanity and the Buddhist concept of the nature and purpose of these Vedic gods—are self-contradictory. Some may question that if Brahma was as great as Buddha, why didn't Brahma go and preach the Dharma. The answer can be better understood if we realize that Brahma is not a personal entity but a principle, the eternal factor which confronts and confirms all the Buddhas gone before and those yet to come. And, that Buddhahood is essentially a Divine mission, something *no worldling can attain* and not attainable *by disciplined conduct, and vows, not only by much learning.* Once having attained to cognizance of His station the Prophet, through some recognizable mechanism of Divinity, either through Divine insight, or through a 'holy spirit' in some instances, and in the case of the Buddha, through Brahma, is 'commanded' or urged to commence His Mission of effecting the salvation of humanity. As the story goes, of this 'Divine urging', the Buddha arose and came down to earth *to work the weal of the world, to turn the wheel of Dharma, for Brahma-faring.*

We can see a striking similarity between the Buddha's declaration concerning His own encounter with Brahma upon achieving enlightenment and that of one of the Arahats named Anuruddha.

The venerable Anuruddha spent the rainy season in the Eastern Bamboo Forest of the kingdom of Ceti.

There, dwelling alone, solitary, earnest, strenuous, resolute, he attained, in no long time, by the knowledge gained in the practice of insight-development, the realization, in this world, of the cessation of suffering, for the sake of which householders rightly go forth from their homes to the homeless life. He realized: "Rebirth is no more; I have lived the holy life; I have done what was to be done; I have nothing more to do for the realization of Arahatship."

And the venerable Anuruddha[133] was numbered among the Arahats.

Now at the time of attaining Arahatship, the venerable Anuruddha uttered these verses:

"The Master knew what thoughts were in my mind.
With power supreme He then appeared before me.
Great were the thoughts I'd had anent the goal,
But what was still unthought He taught to me.
He who had first attained defilement's end,
Taught me the way to reach that selfsame goal.
Hearing, I followed close the Path He showed:
Won is the Threefold knowledge by His Way,
Done is the task the Buddha set for me!"

'Anuruddhamahavitakka Sutta' (Anguttara-nikaya)

The description and conditions of these two episodes clearly indicate a pattern. The pattern of the rise of Buddhahood, of Divine Manifestation, where enlightenment flows down from *the Absolute* upon the *exalted* conveying the *task* (mission) that has been *set* and which must be *done* (accomplished). The Buddha, too, in His last conversation with Ananda acknowledges in a rather cryptic manner that He, too, was set a *task:*

Why should I preserve this body of flesh, when the body of the excellent law will endure? I am resolved, having accomplished my purpose and attended to the task set me, I look for rest.—Mahaparinibbana Suttanta

If Arahat Anuruddha had his task set for him by the Buddha, then 'whom' or 'what' was the Buddha alluding to as the 'setter' of His own task? Obviously it had to be 'someone' or 'something' higher. The Unmanifest Brahma? *The Absolute? The Uncreate?* These words can convey no meaning and all attempts towards the crystallization of concepts regarding the forms and attributes of *the Absolute* are merely symptoms of decay in the pristine purity of Religion. Hence, these gods of the Vedic pantheon, as well as their symbolic representations, are merely the outward and evident efforts of the seeking mind to relate, by worship, rituals, sacrifices, etc. to the Unthinkable Essence behind it all. Just as latter Buddhism, too, envisaged a number of such qualitative super-personal Buddhas e.g. Amitabha, Vairocana,

---

[133]It is worth noting that though many achieve Arahatship, they are not transformed into Buddha. Buddhahood is a very rare occurrence indeed.

THE GOD OF BUDDHA

Akshobhya, Avaloketisvara, etc., all emanations from the Adi-Buddha Vajrasattva. Names upon names and qualities upon qualities, to create some sort of satisfying tangibility for the finite to relate to the Infinite, the intangible *Absolute*. Eventually, the finite mind endows these its own creations, with concepts and powers the mind only vaguely imagines but does not itself possess, thus completing the 'god-in-man's-image' absurdity to which the Buddha was completely opposed. The Buddha exposes the fallacies of those that concoct God after their own imagination, a kind of overlord of a pantheon of lesser gods and beings, by giving the example of recurring world systems (the destruction and renewal of planets and galaxies) and shows how such ideas of 'overlord' and a 'personal God' are born in the mind. But the Buddha casts no doubts on *the Eternal* and He also acknowledges here that above this 'heaven' (plane of the 'personal God') there is yet another plane, the plane of radiant spirits and this goes on *ad-infinitum*. Only relative phenomena (creations) are discussed in the following passage and the Buddha by this example cautions us not to equate the creations of our mind with the reality of *the Absolute*.

Monks, at one time or other, after the lapse of many ages, this world-system comes to an end. This kind of time exists. When the world-system is destroyed, beings have mostly been reborn in the plane of radiant spirits; and there they live, made of mind, feeding on rapture, radiating light from their bodies, dwelling in the air, occupying glorious positions. Thus they remain for many ages.

Monks, at one time or other, after the lapse of many ages, this world-system begins to spring up. This kind of time exists. When this happens a plane of God appears, but it is empty. At that time some being, either because his span of life comes to an end or his merit is exhausted, falls from that radiant spirit plane and is reborn in the God plane which is empty. And there he lives made of mind, feeding on rapture, radiating light from his body, dwelling in the air, enjoying a glorious position. Thus does he remain for many ages.

That God, who, after spreading out one net after another and in various ways draws it together in that field, the Lord, having again created the lords, the great self, exercises this lordship over all.

Svetasvatara Upanishad, V.3

Matter in time passes away, but God is for ever in Eternity, and He rules both matter and soul. By meditation on Him, by contemplation of Him, and by communion with Him, there comes in the end the destruction of earthly delusion.

Svetasvatara Upanishad, I.10

Those who followed after meditation and contemplation saw the self-power of the Divine hidden in its own qualities. He is the one who rules over all these causes from time to the soul.

Svetasvatara Upanishad, I.2,3

A similar phenomenon is described in the Upanishad (p. 80 of this text). The Buddha, moreover, does not explain the cause for the world system springing up again, since His purpose in the foregoing and following excerpts is merely to show the futility of creating theories about such 'ultimates'.

Now there arises in him, from his dwelling there a great length of time alone, unsatisfac-

Truly Rudra is one, there is no place for a second, who rules all these worlds with his

toriness and a longing: 'O! would that other beings might come here.' And then, because their span of life had expired or their merit become exhausted, other beings fall from the radiant spirit plane and arise in the God plane as companions to him. They live made of mind, feeding on rapture, radiating light from their bodies, dwelling on the air, occupying glorious positions and remain for many ages. Then, monks, the one who was first reborn thinks to himself: "I am the Supreme God, God Almighty, the Conqueror, the One who cannot be conquered by others, surely All-seeing, All-powerful, the Ruler, the Creator, the Excellent, the Almighty, the one who has already practical Calm, the Father of all that are and all that are to be. I have created these other beings, because awhile ago I thought: 'Would that they might come'. Thus on my mental aspiration, these beings arise in this Heaven."
'Brahmajala Sutta' (Digha-nikaya)

ruling powers. He stands opposite creatures. He, the protector, after creating all worlds, withdraws them at the end of time. He who is the source and origin of the gods, the ruler of all, Rudra. . . . may he endow us with clear understanding. Higher than this is Brahma, the Supreme, the great hidden in all creatures according to their bodies, the one who envelopes the universe, knowing Him, the Lord, men become immortal. That which is beyond this world is without form and without suffering. These who know that become immortal but others go only to sorrow.
Svetasvatara Upanishad, III.2,4,7,10

All His discourses on this subject of the man-conceived Supreme, or Brahma, are clearly directed towards smashing these idols of vain-imaginings, and to show His own inherent superiority to such all-too-human gods! Just as a man of the twentieth century, equipped with his modern weapons and artifacts, could walk into a primitive settlement, discredit and smash their impotent gods, or 'God', and either set himself up as the only 'God', or tell them that he, too, is a man like themselves and that there is neither 'God' nor 'Devil'. In neither case would he expect to meet any real challenge to his claim, since the 'challenger' is totally impervious to such fleeting aberrations within the grand order of the cosmos, operating on the perfect law of Causality (Karma) and inexorably balancing any passing imbalances, whether of mind or matter. It is these vain imaginings concerning Brahma that, in the *Digha-nikaya*,[134] we find the Buddha refuting:

Are all paths paths to salvation, and do they all lead to a union with Brahma? And the Blessed One proposed these questions to the two Brahmins: "Do you think that all paths are right?" Both answered and said: "Yes, Gotama, we think so." "But tell me," continued the Buddha, "has any one of the Brahmins, versed in the Vedas, seen Brahma face to face?" "No, sir!" was the reply. "But, then," said the Blessed One, "has any teacher of the Brahmins, versed in the Vedas, seen Brahma face to face?" The two Brahmins said: "No, sir." "But, then," said the Blessed

---

[134] *Digha-nikaya, i.235. Tevijja Sutta.*

One, "has any one of the authors of the Vedas seen Brahma face to face?" Again the two Brahmins answered in the negative and exclaimed: "How can any one see Brahma or understand him, for the mortal cannot understand the immortal." And the Blessed One proposed an illustration, saying: "It is as if a man should make a staircase in the place where four roads cross, to mount up into a mansion. And people should ask him, 'Where, good friend, is this mansion, to mount up into for which you are making this staircase? Knowest thou whether it is in the east or in the south, or in the west, or in the north? Whether it is high, or low, or of medium size?' And when so asked he should answer, 'I know it not.' And people should say to him, 'But, then, good friend, thou art making a staircase to mount up into something—taking it for a mansion—which all the while thou knowest not, neither hast thou seen it.' And when so asked he should answer, 'That is exactly what I do; yea I know that I cannot know it.' What would you think of him? Would you not say that the talk of that man was foolish talk?"

"In sooth, Gotama," said the two Brahmins, "it would be foolish talk!" The Blessed One continued: "Then the Brahmins should say, 'We show you the way unto a union of what we know not and what we have not seen.' This being the substance of Brahmin lore, does it not follow that their task is vain?" "It does follow," replied Bharadvaja.

Said the Blessed One: "Thus it is impossible that Brahmins versed in the three Vedas should be able to show the way to a state of union with that which they neither know nor have seen. Just as when a string of blind men are clinging one to the other. Neither can the foremost see, nor can those in the middle see, nor can the hind-most see. Even so, methinks, the talk of the Brahmins versed in the three Vedas is but blind talk; it is ridiculous, consists of mere words, and is a vain and empty thing." "Now suppose," added the Blessed One, "that a man should come hither to the bank of the river and, having some business on the other side, should want to cross. Do you suppose that if he were to invoke the other bank of the river to come over to him on this side, the bank would come on account of his praying?" "Certainly not, Gotama." "Yet this is the way of the Brahmins. They omit the practice of those qualities which really make a man a Brahmin, and say, 'Indra, we call upon thee; Soma, we call upon thee; Varuna, we call upon thee; Brahma, we call upon thee.' Verily, it is not possible that these Brahmins, on account of their invocations, prayers, and praises should after death be united with Brahma." "Now tell me," continued the Buddha, "what do the Brahmins say of Brahma? Is his mind full of lust?" And when the Brahmins denied this, the Buddha asked: "Is Brahma's mind full of malice, sloth or pride?" "No, sir!" was the reply. "He is the opposite of all this." And the Buddha went on: "But are the Brahmins free from these vices?" "No, sir!" said Vasettha. The Holy One said: "The Brahmins cling to the five things leading to worldliness and yield to the temptations of the senses; they are entangled in the five hindrances, lust, malice, sloth, pride and doubt. How can they be united to that which is most unlike their nature? Therefore the threefold wisdom of the Brahmins is a waterless desert, a pathless jungle, and a hopeless desolation."

It is evident from this discourse, quoted at length, that the Buddha is discrediting not the Unmanifest Brahma or *the Absolute* but only those forms and attributes of Brahma concocted by the Brahmins, in their vain imaginings, to assert their superiority over the masses through their claim to portray the Supreme. But, on the other hand, the Buddha Himself is not diffident about claiming to know the way to Brahma. The very thing He proclaimed was impossible for the Brahmins:

When the Buddha had thus spoken, one of the Brahmins said: "We are told, Gotama, that the Sakyamuni knows the path to a union with Brahma." And the Blessed One said: "What do you think, O Brahmins, of a man born and brought up in Manasakata? Would he be in doubt about the most direct way from this spot to Manasakata?" "Certainly not, Gotama." "Thus," replied the Buddha, "the Tathagata knows the straight path that leads to a union with Brahma. He knows it as one who has entered the world of Brahma and has been born in it. There can be no doubt in the Tathagata." And the two young Brahmins said: "If thou knowest the way, show it to us." And the Buddha said: "The Tathagata sees the universe face to face and understands its nature. He proclaims the truth both in its letter and in its spirit, and his doctrine is glorious in its origin, glorious in its progress, glorious in its consummation. The Tathagata reveals the higher life in its purity and perfection. He can show you the way to that which is contrary to the five great hindrances.

Hence, from the above discourse, three things become clear. First, there is not a single assertion here that the Unmanifest Brahma does not exist. But He is not imaginable by the Brahmins, since the Brahmins themselves, by their actions, have proved to be most unlike the Brahma, whom they claim to know. Secondly, that it is the Buddha, who by His acts and achievement can show the *straight path to a union with Brahma,* since the Tathagata is a denizen of that Divine World, the World of Brahma. Lastly, the Brahma, which the Buddha claims to know, is the Unmanifest Brahma, which, according to the Buddha's assertion, the Brahmins had never known. There would be no point to this discourse, or such assertions by the Buddha, if the Unmanifest Brahma did not exist or if the Buddha did not know the way to 'It'. For, then, both He and the Brahmins would be equally wrong, or equally right, since each could permit his own claim to gallop on, astride his own imagination, in endless futility. Hence, one should understand that when the Buddha ridiculed the Brahmin-concocted concepts concerning Brahma, He was not referring to the Unmanifest Brahma.

CREATION AND CREATOR

Some Buddhist philosophers have directed their attack[135] against the Creator being the sole cause of Creation by objecting, strangely, to the perfectly valid condition for the Supreme, the Primal Cause—that, if all creation is reduced to God as the sole Cause, all would have had to be created at the same moment *(yagapat servena jagata bhavitavyam)*.[136] This is precisely what must be if there is a Creator-God at all. And, at least two reasons become evident for the inability of these philosophers to understand this vital principle of instantaneous creation from the Supreme Mind. The first reason is their inability to recognize, even in the simple creations of the finite human mind, the real cause of the various devices and artifacts that the mind creates for itself. The real cause of these effects (artifacts), our creations, is totally outside every frame of empirical verification by these objects that we create. This real cause—an indefinable 'thing' even to our own selves—is our 'thought' born of our mind from a desire for that object that we wish to bring forth or create. The other reason why these philosophers cannot understand that this phenomenon of instantaneous creation is the first condition for any proof of the existence of the Supreme Mind, is that they are unable to visualize the time-compression phenomenon, even in its simple form, in the operation of 'bringing forth' (creating) the objects of our own desire from the realm of thought into the objective world, the physical realm. The real cause, our mind, creates the essential effect (the object) in an instant of time, within its world of thought. A mechanical aeroplane or a paper one takes the mind the same amount of time to create in its own world of thought. But, the actual 'transference' of such objects from the mind's world of thought into the physical realm, depending on the nature of the object (a paper aeroplane takes less time than the mechanical one) and its form and substance requires a considerable amount of finite time, since our finite minds have only slowly begun to learn the art of creation to a finite degree! As we progress, we will naturally shorten the time-gap between the instantaneous creation of objects in our thought world and their appearance in the physical realm.

---

[135]*Abhidharma Kosho*, 2, 64d. I. pp. 311-13, Also *Sphutartha*, p. 237.
[136]*Sphutartha*, pp. 237, 23.

We can appreciate now that no such restriction can bind *the Absolute,* for, if It is bound by any restriction, especially that of time, It would cease to be *the Absolute,* and be merely 'relatively superior' to the human mind. However, our purpose here is not to acknowledge the existence of minds superior to ours, although they must surely exist, but to pursue our quest for an inkling of the Supreme Mind which demonstrates through Its effects *(It is through Its attributes that It is taught and heard)[137]* in the whole of creation, "the presence of an Intelligence of such superiority that compared with It, all the systematic thinking and acting of human beings is an utterly insignificant reflection." Nor "is there any likeness of Him whose glory is infinite."[138] For, "veiled by My creative Power (Yogamaya) I am not revealed to all, this bewildered world knows Me not."[139] It should not be too difficult to understand, therefore, that there is only one perspective from which *the Absolute* can act, to fulfil this vital aspect of Its Reality—instantaneous creation—and that perspective must be absolutely outside the whole space-time continuum, where neither space nor time exist, except as products of that inconceivable Mind. For "He is pure consciousness, the creator of time"[140] and *there, is no coming to be, or ceasing to be![141]*

The Creation is the instantaneous product or emanation from *the Absolute.* While it is perfect, and therefore complete, in every detail 'within' its true Cause, *the Absolute*—which is the only Reality—yet, as 'manifesting effect', within its own frame, the space-time continuum, it is in constant operation according to the perfect law of causality (Karma), which acts infallibly (being itself the result of Absolute Infallibility) for the operation of Its perfect product, the Creation. To simplify, 'thought', or to think, is the very nature and essence of the mind. We do not say to ourselves, 'we shall now think'; we know that in reality every operation of the mind is 'thought'. Now, as stated before, since our minds are finite, and not all-powerful, the step from 'thought' to 'action' involves a time-lapse, since time is a real property of the frame in which we exist. But for That *(the Absolute)* which by its very condition is outside time, since time itself must be inside *the Absolute,* no such time-lapse between thought and creation can exist. Hence, Creation is both instantaneous and co-existent with *the Absolute,* just as the rays of the sun[142] are with the solar orb. Here, physical laws, the law of

---

[137]*Madhyamuka Vitti,* p. 264.

[138]*Yajur Veda,* 32.

[139]*Bhagavad Gita,* VII.25.

[140]*Svetasvatara Upanishad,* VI.1,2.

[141]*Udana,* 8.1-4.

[142]The total sun is not just the glowing orb visible to our sense of sight, but, far larger. It is its total electromagnetic spectrum and its gravitational aura which stretches on to the farthest limits of the solar system and contains all those planets and objects within it. For, without the sun none of those objects could exist.

dependent origination (causality), free-will, etc. all function according to perfect laws, with no interference from *the Absolute,* just as the perfect painting needs no alteration from its creator—the human mind. The electrons within the painting's canvas are in eternal motion and change, according to perfect laws, yet the perfection of the whole painting is not affected, either by the constant change of every particle of itself, nor by the perfection of the laws that govern that change. The whole creation (i.e. the painting) is in dynamic motion to every single particle within its frame of existence, and, yet, to the 'eye' of the artist's mind—its creator—it is in perfect rest. As the Buddha states, *it is without stability, without change.*[143] Now, even if the painting could have eyes to see the three-dimensional form of the artist, it could still not describe its creator, its true cause—the mind. And by describing the physical form of the artist and ascribing its own existence to the physical attributes it saw in him, such as his eyes, his fingers, his hands, etc. it would be in total error, since other creatures, e.g. monkeys, also possess these identical physical attributes, but do not create paintings! Only the 'mind', inconceivable by the painting, not possessed by monkeys and other animals here on this planet, and also indescribable by the artist himself, is the real cause of the painting. Long before the mind saw the painting on the canvas, it saw it in its own world of 'thought'. But, the painting can never 'see' the mind. *Has any one of the authors of the Vedas seen Brahma face-to-face?* The Buddha knew only too well that the Unmanifest Brahma was like nothing the Brahmins conceived him to be. And the Buddhist apologists and philosophers should also recognize that their extrapolations for deriving and then denying the existence and attributes of *the Absolute* are in the same category of thought as the endless futile assertions of Its form and attributes by the Brahmins themselves, namely, the impossible conditions of the finite mind demanding that the Infinite conform and submit to finite yardsticks. For, by this same token, one can easily negate the reality of existence of the Karma, the Dharma, the Buddha and Nirvana, since in none of these concepts is any empirical proof or deductive logic possible for the verification of reality, as all of these concepts are larger than any references at our disposal for ascertaining their nature. We have only the Buddha's words for them and as He, too, was essentially beyond our understanding, *since a Tathagata, even when actually present, is incomprehensible,*[144] we must admit that we are left with no choice but to accept the whole package on faith! Finally, if the electrons in the painting were themselves possessed of mind, then slowly, but surely, these minds would develop degrees of freedom outside their two dimensional universe and, passing through various other

---

[143] See p. 96.

[144] *Samyutta-nikaya,* III.118.

dimensions, ultimately attain that liberation of the mind in the recognition that *mind is everything*.

LAW AND LAW-MAKER

To imply that the Buddha was not concerned with ultimates is not merely to misread His Message, but to relegate Him to a status less than human. For, every thinking being, be he savant or savage, is deeply concerned about ultimates when he sits down to really 'think'. A very large portion of every person's conscious thoughts, as well as subconscious, concerns ultimates—death, immortality and its nature, the law that governs the scheme-of-things-entire, and, most assuredly above all, the Law-Maker. The fundamental test of qualification, as well as success, of every Religion, including certainly Buddhism, is its ability to satisfy the cravings of the soul (mind) on questions concerning ultimates. There are no exceptions concerning this most fundamental of all requirements for any religion, if it is to obtain, from the depths of the human heart, that inexplicable allegiance to its tenets—the phenomenon of faith. Faith that outlasts centuries smiles in the face of death and willingly shoulders every sacrifice because of the belief in the vision concerning ultimates—the ultimates of immortality, of purpose, of goodness, of law (Karma) and, first and foremost, God, the Law-Maker. Those who exclude Buddhism from this fundamental qualification of Religion simply do not understand the Buddha or His Message and, somehow, continue to believe in the absurdity that the existence of the Law-Maker is inimical to the existence of the Law, instead of the rationale that the purpose of the Law-Maker are laws that function, and the more perfect the laws, the greater the Law-Maker. Buttressing this absurdity of the Law-Maker being inimical to laws (or vice-versa) are the equally ridiculous anthropomorphic concepts and characteristics that are invariably attributed to the Supreme, especially by western writers, instead of the obvious, that nothing can describe or give form or quality to *the Absolute*.

Those who talk about a moral law immanent in nature, and say that it is also the first principle, self-originated and self-operative, and not a product of 'Mind', are just as far off the mark of credibility as those who would claim that traffic laws, lights and patterns, have created roads, pedestrians and vehicles or that judiciary laws have created judges, jurists, criminals, policemen, and prisons. We know, and no thinking being can deny, that the 'creator' of laws, whether for regulating society or vehicular traffic, is the human intellect—the rational soul, the mind, or whatever other names we wish to give ourselves, including, of course, Homo sapiens! Likewise, the laws governing the microcosm as well as the macrocosm worlds and the mind-boggling grandeur of the infinitely varying phenomenon of life, moving and growing and transmuting within those physical planes, as well as above them, into the dimension of the mind itself, are the products of the Higher Mind, *the Absolute,* the Supreme, the Creator, the Ultimate Reality, Cause of all Causes—God. And, however nebulous the concept that each and every one of us may have of the Ultimate Reality, it is still the real sustaining power for our beliefs, our acts, our hopes in the ultimate of 'immortality', which nothing else, however substantial and seemingly real, has ever truly succeeded in supplanting. The Buddha, too, neither could nor did deny that *Absolute,* nor did He conceive Karma, or Dharma, or Truth, or Nirvana as the Ultimate Reality—the *Causeless Cause.*

OBVIATING THE ABSURDITIES

Now to deal briefly with a few representative examples of some of the other patent absurdities of the finite mind in its naive efforts, born of a peculiarly primitive pride as well as a childish fear, to negate 'ostrich-like', the existence of anything higher than itself—absurdities which have gradually taken root in Buddhistic philosophy.

Absurdity: The idea of God is based on imagination and has no more reality than the idea of the son of a barren woman.

Response: The 'idea' of any 'intangible' (such as God, Nirvana, Dharma, etc.) must be based on imagination. He who has no idea and cannot imagine also cannot think. For, thought itself is imagination (forming of images in the mind concerning tangible objects and intangible concepts). The difference between animal and man is that the animal is incapable of imagining and it knows nothing about intangible concepts. It has no mind, since the mind itself is 'an intangible' which reaches out through its thought processes of imagination, concentration, etc. to probe and understand other intangibles, at least as real as itself, if not more so. To equate this reality of imagination with the fiction of the son of a barren woman is indicative of ignorance. For, in truth, once the simple biological cause for barrenness in any reproductive system is mastered, and hence eliminated, the system will produce both sons and daughters, not one but many! The inability in any specific case to do so is simply the product of our present state of knowledge (or ignorance). Perhaps, imbued with too much Karma, the conceiver of such similes had no thought of his own ignorance of this simple biological function. We do.

Absurdity: That it is a contradiction in terms to suppose that from something incomprehensible to us there can derive something we can conceive. And it is, therefore, better to stick to what we know—for example, the elements—when we consider a first cause.

Response: It is not at all a contradiction in terms to know as well as conceive something derived from the incomprehensible. We do it all the time, with perfect ease. We know and understand every object and artifact which is made by the power of our mind. We not only conceive such objects completely, but we also create them! Yet, we can neither conceive nor comprehend the nature or meaning of our mind, that intangible entity within our make-up, the 'real we'. Likewise, in the physical world of nature, we can easily conceive, understand, and even manipulate for our own use, phenomena and laws, but we cannot conceive of the 'nature' of that Mind behind the physical Creation, except to know from Its effects that It exists. Even though that 'philosopher' thought he knew the elements as something fundamental and, therefore, wanted to stick to what he knew, he was only sticking to his own ignorance and not to any essential truth. For we know now that the elements are far from solid and, when probed further, disappear into realms of energy. The elements are no 'first cause'.

All elements of being are non-self. When one by wisdom realizes this, he heeds not sorrow.
Dhammapada, v. 279

Those who by the eye of wisdom perceive the difference between the Field and the Knower of the Field, and the negation of Prakriti (nature) with her evolutes, reach the Supreme.
Bhagavad Gita, XIII.34

The permanent is that being which is un-caused.
Brahma Sutra, IV.I.1

The elements are only primitive effects of more remote causes, and even we, having learnt about them, can now create these elements. But that does not make us God.

Nor can there by any basis in the supposition that 'Creation' is a chance product, since chance itself is a non-entity, an expression from our mind concerning a set of occurrences, the 'cause' of which is unknown to us. Chance has no intrinsic reality and is simply a word without any other existence at all. It is 'nothing', and nothingness cannot generate any existence, since it would be totally negated by it. Thus, if something cannot co-exist with, or emanate from, absolute nothingness, then it should be obvious that the mind cannot emanate from mindlessness but only from a greater Mind. Just as the whole is greater than the part, the 'cause' must be always greater than its 'effect', since 'perfect efficiency of transmission' and 'something out of nothing' are impossible by definition. Therefore, explanations for organization, mind, law in the cosmos will not be found in states of existence below these realities but above, since the cause must always be greater than the effect, and whatever characteristic or attribute is possessed or is evident in the effect, a greater degree of the same phenomenon or attribute must be present in its cause.

The very act of questioning establishes the existence of reason, and reason presupposes something, since non-existence or 'nothing' is devoid of everything including reason. Creation and the cosmos are real even in the absolute sense for they are emanations of the underlying Reality and even if, as the Buddha states, *the mind is everything,* the reality of the cosmos remains unchanged since it is portrayed as an extension of that everything (Mind) into the realm of the physical. However, while the Mind may project itself to bring forth the cosmos, the Mind is not the creation, and the creation is not the Mind. One is a product of time and within the bounds of infinity, while the 'Cause', the 'Real', is outside any such parameters since even those parameters of time and space constitute creation and hence, by definition, are contained within the Absolute Mind. Thus, Creator and creation are separate both in eternity as well as within the spatio-temporal frame. As Krishna tells us in the following verses immanence must not be confused with identity.

All this is permeated by Me in My unmanifest aspect and all beings abide in the idea within Me. Therefore, really speaking, I am not in them. Nay, those beings abide not in Me; but look at the wonderful power of My divine Yoga, though the Sustainer and Creator of beings, My Self in reality dwells not in those beings.—*Bhagavad Gita,* IX.4,5

Absurdity: If God is absolutely pure and perfect, how is it that the world He created and rules is impure and imperfect?

Response: We find in a passage from the *Jataka Tales* this same mode of questioning, put in the form of a ditty by an early Buddhist poet:

He who has eyes can see the sickening sight;
Why does not Brahma set his creatures right?
If his wide power no limits can restrain,
Why is his hand so rarely spread to bless?
Why are his creatures all condemned to pain?
Why does he not to all give happiness?
Why do fraud, lies and ignorance prevail?
Why triumph, falsehood, truth and justice fail?

This rather unjust tirade of that early Buddhist poet against Brahma appears more as partisan propaganda for his new found Faith, rather than any real defect in the behavior of the Supreme in relation to His Creation. For the author of the above poem, had he truly understood *the Absolute,* would have realized that the Creator, or Brahma, or God, works through perfect laws and not as a charlatan, capriciously wiping the slate clean and creating rose-coloured visions through bribes or supplications, irrespective of the cause and effect of our actions. Having given humanity the power of free will and, thus, the options to create its own heaven or hell, it would indeed be a demonstration of His short-sightedness and imperfections were He constantly interfering to right the many wrongs that we are continuously perpetrating against each other. This is a very one-sided and ridiculous condemnation of Brahma indeed, seeing, as this Buddhist poet did, the seeming injustice within the physical world and the accompanying trials and tribulations of life itself and then comparing it with the Nirvana of his imagination, which he hoped to attain. His enthusiasm in his new found nascent Faith seems to have clouded his mind to the reality of the Buddha's words, that *all things decay* and even *dharma is lost and forgotten and has to be found again.* This Buddhist poet seems to be unaware of schism which, by then, had already raised its ugly head within the fabric of the Sangha. But objectivity is difficult for those flushed with the pride of some new discovery, especially the discovery of a new Faith!

We know that Buddhism, too, soon suffered that same deterioration in the pristine purity of its doctrine and in the simplicity of its practice as had Hinduism and the other religions. The picture is identical in each case. It is in the very nature of man not to be able to remain on the peak of achievement, but to slowly retrogress, to lose a portion of his achievement and the vitality of any movement as time goes on. It is the story of life itself. Progress in human affairs, both material and spiritual, is not a natural law of the species, and any advances made by one generation can be negated by a succeeding one, as we have all too often witnessed. However, the Buddhist poet should have known that truth and justice do not fail and, in the long run, falsehood comes off second best. For, on the side of truth and justice is the only metaphysical law enveloping the whole fabric of human society, and constituting the master emotion of the ever searching soul of man, the continuously recurring phenomenon of Religion, the inexorable rise of the spiritual Sun. Such a one for His time was the Buddha, and that early Buddhist poet would have been more correct in his comparisons if he had understood the Buddha's own claim of being one of a succession of Buddhas and then compared the 'dawns' of these two great religions instead of comparing the 'dusk' which had by then enveloped Hinduism with the 'dawn' of Buddhism.

THE GOD OF BUDDHA

Absurdity: If God is considered omnipresent, then He must also be present in unclean places, for example, in the hells. And how can it even be conceived that a good and kind being creates such terrible places of punishment and causes sinners to suffer the most frightful tortures?

Response: Just as darkness is merely the non-existence of light, and not a positive state of being, likewise ignorance is simply the absence of knowledge, and evil, which is born of the ignorance of the consequences of one's actions, mental or physical, is, similarly, a negation—the negation of good. It has no independent existence in reality, in *the Absolute,* and hence, while, in the objective world, we are constantly meeting with so-called evil persons and their evil acts, these are, as we see, contained within our premise, since the doers of those short-sighted acts are themselves only finite minds looking for *a pleasure of little worth* and unmindful of *the larger pleasure.*[145] We read that even Mara, the 'Tempter', falls into this same category and often-times relents when he is shown the right path. Hence, it is obvious that, since *the Absolute* is All Knowledge and All Power, where no ignorance can be, there cannot exist any primordial source of evil, the 'Devil', within *the Absolute,* just as no darkness can exist within a perfect source of light. Nor can a primordial source of evil exist outside *the Absolute* since *the Absolute,* by definition, must encompass all existence, and the presence of another 'underlying reality' would automatically negate *the Absolute.* Therefore, by definition, there can only be one *Absolute,* underlying Reality, and that underlying Reality can entertain no partners to Itself. We can either have God or Devil, not both. 'Which' shall we choose? Ask the Buddha, Krishna and the other Avatars and look around. So much for 'original evil' and that much maligned but unreal, and hence totally innocent, old rascal, the Devil. Therefore, such places as 'hell' can have no positive existence in Reality and must be only mental states and conditions experienced by those minds which, through a lack of knowledge, are still attached to the things that perish. And adjectives, such as 'unclean', 'torturous', 'dark', and 'fearful', denoting that state (hell) are simply similes to define the experiences of such minds in that state. Since a little reflection should tell us that all such descriptions of hell refer to the physical, and as only the mind exists (since the physical body is dissolved here), no physical objects could relate to it. And, as these are conditions which only the finite mind experiences, as a consequence of its erroneous choices in life, it should be clear that *the Absolute,* which is all knowing and hence free of any error or ignorance, does not have any 'hell' or 'unclean places' or 'fearful punishments' present in Its Mind.

While it is impossible to define the bliss within the Mind of *the Absolute,* we are told that it is the recognition of that ineffable, blissful emanation from

---

[145]*Dhammapada,* v. 290.

the Absolute Mind by our own finite minds (which through striving and detachment can tune to It) that constitutes for us that indescribable experience of heaven or Nirvana.

Absurdity: That the world process is founded on the action of matter (Prakriti), which, without being itself conscious, is nevertheless regulated by Karma, and it is the cause of everything, just as the flowing of milk is the cause of the calf's growth.

Response: Since mind exists in creation (otherwise this book would neither have been written nor read) and, according to the Buddha's own assertion (see p. 69), it is also immortal, it cannot have emanated from mindlessness, but only from greater Mind. Now the above absurdity admits, and rightly so, that Prakriti has no mind (since it is not conscious) and nowhere in Buddhist scriptures has Karma been endowed with mind. Then 'who' or 'what' is the source of Mind? The answer is simple if we understand: that the flowing of milk has nothing to do with the calf's growing because the milk may flow but the calf may not like to drink it. Or the calf may even chew grass or have other nourishment and still grow, although perhaps not as perfectly. It is impossible to demonstrate the operation of Causality in the total cosmos by the use of such restricted similes. The better example would be to explain the causes of the calf's birth, growth and decay within as large a frame of the mineral, vegetable, and animal cycle as we can conceive, taking into account as much as we have already learned of the fantastic, but real, cause-effect operation, unimaginably intricate but nevertheless perfect, regulating the entire birth-death cycle *(comings and goings)* of the calf and the whole order of things surrounding it and beyond. From such a study of the calf's existence within that wider frame of reality, we must agree that if there are regulatory processes at play within the frame of investigation, they would have to be predicated on order (organization), and order presupposes intelligence, and intelligence emanates from the 'mind'. Of course, there is room in all this for both Prakriti and Karma, just as there is place for the physical substance called the calf and the cause-effect relationship (law) that controls its birth, growth and death. But that room for Prakriti and Karma is not at the 'top'—in the domain of 'volitional motivation'. For there only Mind exists, manifesting Itself below by bringing forth Prakriti (Nature or Cosmos), organized and operating according to perfect Law (Karma) throughout the various domains of existence, from inanimate matter on to the highest realm of rational thought. Hence, while Rita or law (Karma) embraces all things in Prakriti, there is nothing in that concept to suggest that the law precludes the presence of the Law-Maker. On the contrary, causality and logic dictate otherwise and, long before the advent of the Buddha, the Hindus of the time of the Rig Veda viewed Nature as being controlled and operated by the Law which emanated from the Mind of the Supreme. Creation itself is simply 'congealed thought' from the Primal Mind.

The reader may himself work out an interesting corollary of this proposition, namely, the wider the frame of reference that we are able to give the investigation of any process or phenomenon, the larger looms the role of the Mind, with commensurate reduction in the importance of the role of Prakriti and its 'operative' (Karma). While the narrower our frame of reference, the reverse becomes emphasized. When the limit of investigation is narrowed down to the microcosm, even a piece of cheese, if probed to its ultimate composition of packets of energy (quanta), resembles the human brain, also scrutinized to the same limit. No difference is found to exist in their fundamental content. It is only when we step back and see the total entity that we can separate the 'rational being', from the mindless cheese. Now, as we widen the frame still further and see the artifacts and creations of the rational being, we are even more convinced of the existence of its rationality, of the intelligence within him manifested in his handiwork, of mind. And, more clearly than ever, we see the abysmal difference between the rational being and the cheese!

Absurdity: There is no God and no outside world. Everything one perceives, imagines, or thinks is but a reflection of one's own I.

Response: The above absurdity is diametrically opposed to the Buddha's own teachings concerning the impermanence of such an 'I' (atta):

Lord, he who has reached enlightenment has utterly destroyed the fetters of becoming. Who is by perfect wisdom emancipated, to him there does not occur the thought that anyone is better than I or equal to me or less than I. "Even so," replied the Buddha, "do men of the true stamp declare the wisdom they have attained. They tell what they have gained, but do not speak of 'I'."
Anguttara, iii.359

Whenever the soul has thoughts of 'I' and 'mine' it binds itself with its lower self, as a bird with the net of a snare.
Maitri Upanishad, 3.2

He who abandons all desires and acts free from longing, without any sense of mineness or egotism, he attains to peace.
Bhagavad Gita, II.71

We can also recognize this absurdity by a simple phenomenon, namely, that if that rather inflated ego 'I' was obliterated from this physical dimension, we who witnessed its (ego's) passing would see that nothing else has changed and, if this process is continued to its final but rather horrifying conclusion, namely the annihilation of all 'I's', there would still not be any really discernable change in the cosmos around us, simply because, and this may hurt our ego, the cosmos or the physical world is a creation not of our minds, but of the Absolute Mind, of which we, too, are creations. Hence, while creation may be in a constant state of flux, according to regulatory principles of its own organization, yet, its intrinsic reality, since it is a product of *the Eternal,* is not subject to annihilation. This concept, and not the above absurdity, contains the premise of the Pali Canon that the great laws of existence, as distinct from the act of creating to bring forth creation, are immanent in the nature of the world and independent of a Buddha. As we have pointed out (pp. 114-6), creation is the instantaneous product of the Creator and this creation is 'everything': the field of matter and its laws, the field of mind and its laws, the law of the periodic appearance of Manifestations to reveal to the rational soul the higher law of Causality, operating in the realm of free will and having for its corollary the law of hell and heaven and Nirvana.

Absurdity: Time directs the whole cosmos and creation is a product of Time!

Response: Real Time is a non-entity. No such thing as Absolute Time can exist. Time is a relationship; it is a function of space and related to it or, more correctly, 'joined' to space. It exists literally only in the plane of relativity—it is the extra dimension to three dimensional space and it is the measure by which we define incremental changes in the ever changing cosmos. From this we can understand that 'Absolute Time' is a self contradictory term. Time cannot exist as an 'Absolute', nor can *the Absolute* exist in Time. However, Time can exist 'in' *the Absolute* and there is no contradiction here. Likewise, 'creation' itself cannot be a product of Time. For without 'creation', Time would have no reality. As we have noted, one without the other could not be defined. Both exist as co-equals; aspects of the same four dimensional space-time continuum. They exist simultaneously or dissolve simultaneously; neither can nor does create the other, unless it can be said that one side of a cubical object creates the other side of the same object! They are not absolutes but are contained within *the Absolute.*

Some sages speak of the nature of things (Prakriti) as the cause of the world, and others in their delusion, speak of Time. But it is by the glory of God that the wheel of Brahma revolves in the universe. The whole universe is ever in His power. He is pure consciousness, the creator of time: all-powerful, all-knowing.—*Svetasvatara Upanishad,* VI.1,2

Absurdity: There exists no personal creator but a 'personal being', regulating the cosmic moral law which rules all things in the cosmos.

Response: If a 'personal being' is necessary to regulate the operation of the cosmic moral law, then the law is not perfect, even though it may be universal and the 'personal being' is higher, for 'it', not the law, is the controller of the other. If the law is infallible and operates perfectly, then, no 'personal being' is necessary. The paradox is created because once again we are creating 'personal' images of *the Absolute,* e.g. 'personal being', and pitting 'it' against an 'intangible'—one (personal-being), semi-conceivable, against the other (law), intangible, and come up with a mental image somewhat similar to a mechanic (personal-being) keeping a machine (law) operating with periodic supervision. But, if the machine is perfect, then there is no need for the 'personal being'. If we can only get away from such primitive anthropomorphic images of God as a 'personal being' and conceive of things mental, e.g. the Mind, then the machine (a creation of Law), operating perfectly, reflects the perfections of it's Creator, who neither interferes in His handiwork nor has any need to supervise or correct its operation since it is perfect.

Absurdity: There are no eternal substances or permanent entities of any sort and, since all that exists is conditioned on its cause *ad infinitum,* a first beginning is as impossible as a definite end. The whole universe with everything *in* it reveals itself as a strictly ordered sequence of dynamic process, as a play of the forces of Dharma.

Response: The most important word in this proposition is 'in' (italicized above). If this proposition confines itself to being 'in' the space-time continuum and admits that it cannot explain the presence of Mind or minds (as apart from personality), then, in the light of our previous explanation (p. 118), there is no contest with this simple, but far from correct, mechanical model of the universe. The universe is enveloped and permeated by order. And while to the primitive man its diversity of life forms may have suggested a variety of causes (gods or demons), to the mature mind, the underlying thread of order and organization running through every aspect of it, from the mineral on to the mental, clearly indicates a single Cause and Governor.

Absurdity: God could not have created the world because He is not selfish and lacks nothing, nor could He have created it out of kindness because all His creatures are most unhappy in this world.

Response: As the Buddha has clearly demonstrated, we neither know nor understand the whole range of the meaning of such words as 'selfishness' or 'selflessness' and their manifestations in the world of sense perceptions in the form of cruelty and kindness, even within the context of human thought and action. So, to impute such limited concepts of these dimly understood emotions within our own finite minds to the Infinite and Supreme Mind is once again to make God in our own image and state that such a God could not exist. There can be no comment on such 'puppet play' of thought, which, as one sees, is obviously predicated on the patently ridiculous.

Absurdity: If God or the Supreme exists, it is not necessary for Him or It to continuously proclaim (witness the Vedas, Upanishads, *Gita,* etc.) His own virtues.

Response: This is a rather emotional and envious remark, for this is precisely what we are taught even in Buddhism, namely, to proclaim the virtues of the Buddha-Dharma (witness the *Dhammapada, Nikaya,* etc.). The answer is simple: Man's mind, as the Buddha and the Upanishads tell us, *is fidgety* and wavering and it is difficult for the mind to concentrate 'single-mindedly' on any object, let alone such intangibles as the Supreme or Dharma. Hence, constant recitations of His glory, or the virtues of the peerless Dharma, are absolutely essential to keep these intangibles in focus before one's mind's eye at all times, so that the mind, wholly absorbed in the *eternal,* can become free from all things ephemeral and experience the *ineffable bliss of Nirvana.*

As with the individual, so with the collective mind of society, these 'Intangibles' (the Supreme, Dharma, etc.) must be continuously acknowledged as our highest aspirations, their glories constantly sung in order to establish 'Them' as the perfect and unwavering standard by which all behaviour, of the individual as well as of society, must be measured, and towards which all allegiance and cohesion of conscience and purpose must be directed. Human history confirms this and shows that this master emotion is the principle instrument for the flowering of cultures and the establishment of civilizations.

THE UNDERLYING REALITY—GOD

It is hoped that from a comparative analysis of the Buddha's sayings with the teachings of Hinduism as already presented in the preceding chapters, concerning the most important aspects of His Message, the reader will have been able to accept the historical Buddha (Siddharta Gautama) in His correct setting—a Hindu among Hindus; not an iconoclast, but a gentle teacher; not a militant rebel, but an erudite reformer; not an abolisher of past precepts, but a wise innovator; a reviver of the pristine purity of religion, Who endowed it with a hitherto unknown breadth of vision and provided it with the motive force to propel His message far beyond the confines of India, to take root in the hearts of a humanity many times larger than that of His native land.

We know of no power that has succeeded in influencing the course of human history, nay, even initiating man's progress and guiding it along a broad and clearly defined route, above the power of religion. The Buddha's message, by His own admission, was one such religion—*now is the time to seek religion.*[146] One can hardly accept that this unique motivation demonstrated by the power of religion has been achieved without cognizance of the nature of the very instrument needed to accomplish it, namely, the human psyche.

Not by mere periodic reiteration of the age-old Golden Rule—*practice the truth that thy brother is the same as you*[147]—could one hope to capture and transform the leaden mass of humanity into a living, dynamic and irresistible force, capable of raising up cultures and civilizations, that, more than any other achievements of human history, continue to withstand the ravages of the centuries. The Golden Rule was only the means, the motive had to concern itself with something much more intrinsic in the human make-up, that deepest of all cravings of the human psyche, its passion for immortality, at once the strongest desire and the most ardently sought-after goal. This, too, the Buddha clearly defined and promulgated.

Walk in the noble path of righteousness and thou wilt understand that while there is death in self there is immortality in truth.[148] *The doctrine of the conquest of self . . . is not taught to destroy the souls of men, but to preserve them.*[149]

Just as no condition can exist without a cause, so also immortality becomes meaningless without a firm belief in the existence of its source, however indefinable and incomprehensible such a source may be. For, immortality itself is merely the ultimate limit of time and, in order to be meaningful, it must continue to be a function of time. On the other hand, that underlying Reality from which time and space are generated must by Its very nature be outside the space-time continuum—beyond the outermost limits of infinity and indefinable by any parameters within the infinity of space or the eternity of time.

But nowhere in the old Buddhist scriptures are Nirvana[150] or Dharma

---

[146]*Jataka Tales; Mahavagga,* 1.6, 19-28. "This is the Dharma. This is the Truth. This is Religion." Also *Dhammapada.*

[147]*Questions of King Milinda.* Also *Dhammapada,* vv. 129, 130, 131, 132, 133.

[148]*Udana.*

[149]*Mahavagga,* VI.31. Also *Questions of King Milinda,* p. 256.

[150]In Pali literature, Nirvana is viewed both as a condition of the mind attainable by a person still in his physical body and also as asamskrita (unconditioned origination). It is, however, important to know that in many of the older schools of Buddhism other entities such as empty space, the Four Noble Truths, Dharma, and the fundamental law of all existence are, besides Nirvana, also regarded as asamskrita. It is possible to understand how these various entities could be viewed as 'unconditioned' while not being themselves the ground of being, only if we

mentioned as the underlying Reality, that ground of being, that many mistakenly believe them to be. And, yet, the Buddha could not have left any doubt of His acknowledgement of the existence of that Absolute Reality, if His Message was to have any meaning and attract the masses of His day, themselves completely saturated with the belief in the existence of this underlying Reality, the Supreme, God. Otherwise, one would have to conclude that the arduous life of effort and renunciation led nowhere, His doctrine was without a 'ground', lacking any foundation, and the goal was annihilation. This, of course, was not the case, since the Buddha, as we have already seen, unequivocally rejected such nihilistic conclusions about His doctrine. Hence, the question we have before us is not 'whether' the Buddha acknowledged the existence of the *Causeless Cause, the Absolute,* but 'what' words He used to describe It and convey Its meaning to His disciples. The founding of a major Faith would have been impossible from the outset had He preached any kind of atheism and thus negated any reason at all for humanity to strive on the path of righteousness and renunciation. In the history of civilization, not even a single society predicated on atheism has been able to sustain righteousness of conduct and unity of conscience and purpose even for a hundred years, unless the citizenry was terrorized by the overwhelming power of the government. The cardinal fact of human culture seems to be irrefutable: In the affairs of men, there simply does not exist the possibility of achieving any great good without God.

By comparing the essential teachings of these two great Faiths, Hinduism and the gospel of the Buddha, both rising from the same spiritual soil, although separated in time by milleniums, we have already witnessed the extraordinary similarity in their concepts and their harmonious identity with the timeless culture of India. While it would have been quite possible to correlate the teachings of the Buddha with the message of the Upanishads and the *Bhagavad Gita* even in minor aspects, it should suffice for the purpose of our quest to have noted this remarkable resemblance in terminology as well as conceptual identity on the fundamental and essential matters concerning all religions, i.e. the nature of the real man; his soul or mind; the meaning and purpose of life; the path of attaining that 'higher stage' beyond the recurrence of births and deaths; the nature of that 'ineffably blissful state'; and, above all, the reason for striving at all, nay, even more elemental, the why and wherefore of life itself and all its ramifications, physical and metaphysical, the scheme-of-things-entire, the *Unoriginated, Cause* of all causes—God.

However, before we proceed further, the essential point to note is that

---

recognize (as suggested on p. 102) that these are emanations or aspects of the Ultimate Reality and therefore co-existent with It. Hence, nowhere in the Pali Canon is Nirvana or any of the other asamskritas viewed as the ground of being.

modern man in the twentieth century is no closer to a description of Soul, Mind, Nirvana, Primal Cause, God, or an analysis of the concepts concerning these 'entities', than his learned counterpart of 5000 years ago, since words are our only means of communicating ideas concerning these subjects, and perhaps these subjects will, by their very nature, always remain outside the scope of direct human verification or grasp. Hence, we see people using different words to give these same ideas different or even identical attributes to describe the same thing, to wit, the Buddha's use of Mind instead of Soul; Nirvana instead of Brahmabhuta or Brahmaloka; the *Unoriginated, Unborn, Uncreated, Unformed,* instead of the Primal Person or God. For, in the final analysis, words are all we have to communicate the nebulous concepts concerning these subjects envisaged by the Buddha's mind. And, in this field, the only way open to us for determining the degree of agreement or disparity concerning these concepts is to compare the effects and attributes ascribed to them by the Buddha and the other Hindu Avatars, or for that matter, the Founders of all religions, and, taking into account the reasonable differences of language, mannerisms and the times of each of these Divine spokesmen, to determine if essential correlation exists concerning the description of their attributes, conditions and effects. That is the principle employed by this thesis. There was no other way to demonstrate the near identical relationships that exist between the actual concepts concerning Mind, Nirvana and the *Uncreated, Unoriginated, Causeless Cause* described by the Buddha and the Soul, Brahmaloka, the Primal Person or God referred to in the Upanishads, especially the *Bhagavad Gita.*

By relating the Buddha and His doctrine to His own time and environment, we can see that He acknowledged a self, or soul, or mind, over and above the empirical combinations and that this self passes on in full consciousness to the fruits of its action, namely, to hell, heaven, or Nirvana and that these are real states and not just negations. If this were not so, and there was no essential reality to the human self (or soul or mind), or to the three states (hell, heaven or Nirvana) that it experiences in accordance with its acts, the Buddha would not have made any distinction between these states and simply lumped them into one: *extinction.* Then, there would be no point in predicating their existence as well as the *escape of the self from the world of the originated, born, created, and formed* on the existence of that deeper Reality which, He described as being *Unoriginated, Unborn, Uncreated, Unformed.* Even though the Buddha's emphasis is on the pathway and the mode of conduct rather than on the goal, we see that He has often-times implied the existence of this universal essence, for unlike and apart from the changing universe, this *Element* or *Causeless Cause* constituted for Him the source from which all Buddhas and Dharmas originate.

The Element (Cause) is without beginning in time. It is the common foundation of all dhammas. Because it exists there also exist all places of rebirth and the full attainment of Nirvana.

> *Ratnagotravibhaga, pp. 72-73*
> *Abhidhamma Mahayanasutra*

There was something formless yet complete that existed before heaven and earth, Without sound, without substance, dependent on nothing, unchanging All-pervading, unfailing.

> *Isa Upanishad, I.14*

You are the supreme Indestructible worthy of being realized; You are the ultimate resort of this universe; You are the protector of eternal Dharma; I consider You to be the eternal, imperishable Being.

> *Bhagavad Gita, XI.18*

The Buddha, while recognizing the grandeur of the varied panorama of life, was too great a mind to be dazzled by its scattered secondary causes to desist from probing the totality of the links that make up its entire chain and not discover the truth of that subtle but impenetrable essence underlying the whole. If He refrained from defining this *Causeless Cause,* or described It as what it was *not* in terms of Its effects, it was only to stress the impossibility of verifying *the Absolute* by any known yardstick. That He did acknowledge the unity of Its essence as the generating force, the primal cause for the whole scheme-of-things, there can be no doubt.

And as all things originate from one essence, so they are developing according to one law and they are destined to one aim which is Nirvana. Nirvana comes to thee, Kassapa[151] *when thou understandest thoroughly, and when thou livest according to thy understanding, that all things are of one essence and that there is but one law. Hence, there is but one Nirvana as there is but one truth, not two or three. And the Tathagata is the same unto all beings differing in his attitude only in so far as all beings are different. The Tathagata, however, O Kassapa, knows the law whose essence is salvation, and whose end is the peace of Nirvana. He is the same to all, and yet knowing the requirements of every single being, he does not reveal himself to all alike. He does not impart to them at once the fulness of omniscience, but pays attention to the disposition of various beings.*[152]

He is all, what has been and what shall be. He is eternal. By knowing Him one conquers death. There is no other way to liberation (Nirvana). He is Brahma (the creator); He is Siva (the judge), He is Indra, He is the imperishable, supreme, the Lord of Himself. He is Visnu (the Preserver), He is life, He is time. He is fire, He is the moon. From Him are born life, mind and all the senses; sky, air, light, water and earth which is the support of all existence. From Him all proceed, in Him all exist, and to Him all return. That Brahma without a second, He is. He is subtler than the subtle, greater than the great. He is this manifold universe. He is the ancient, the person. He is the lord of golden hue. He is Siva. He is without hands and feet, of inconceivable powers. He sees without eyes. He hears without ears. He knows (all). He is of one form. None knows Him. He is always pure consciousness.

> *Taittiriya Upanishad,* III.10,5
> (8,9,15,19,20,21,22,23)

---

[151] Kassapa, one of the foremost disciples of the Buddha *(see* Glossary for details).

[152] SDP. V. also *Aditta-pariyaya Sutta* (Sermon on the lessons to be drawn from burning); Also *Jataka Tales,* p. 82; Bigandet; 130-144.

And this one Cause or one *Essence* from which all things originate is the *Unoriginated.*

It should be noted from the above that the Buddha is succinctly acknowledging the four fundamental pillars of all great Faiths, which cover the whole range of spiritual life. To paraphrase the Buddha's discourse: The origin of all things is one—*the Unoriginated, the Uncreated, the Uncaused*—or whatever name we wish to give It, including Creator or God. From the *Unoriginated* emanate all things and they are subject to one law by whatever name it is called, Dharma, or Karma, or Religion. Those sentient beings who understand this and adhere strictly to the path enjoined by Dharma attain to that ineffable bliss of Nirvana which is not compartmentalized, but is the all pervading aura of light and joy, open to all who undeviatingly tread the path of the Dharma, which is revealed to humanity in perfect accord with its capacity to understand it (Dharma), by the perfect Teacher, the Tathagata, who knows the ability of each person to grasp its meaning. So, we see that there are four distinct concepts involved here: (1) the *Essence* of all is one; (2) from this *Essence* emanates the 'One Law' to envelope everything in Creation; (3) knowing this, and acting upon this knowledge according to its requirements, one can attain the end of all suffering born of ignorance; and (4) this can only be accomplished by recognizing the Teacher of the Law (the Buddha) who conveys the requirements of the Law according to the capacity of each to receive and act on it. The reader will appreciate that all four terms are separately listed by the Buddha, and, therefore, understand that, if they were all meant to be taken as one, the Buddha would have simply not listed them separately, since on other occasions, He has, in order to make a point, equated Dharma with Nirvana and with Truth, while in the above case He has also separated Truth from Nirvana and Dharma. Moreover, it should be noted that neither here nor anywhere else is Dharma or Nirvana spoken of as the essence from which all things originate. They are spoken of as the path or the goal, but never the 'source' from which all things originate, never the ground of being, or the underlying Reality. Nor is 'truth' that absolute entity, since a little thought on the use of the term 'truth' will indicate that it is simply an affirmation here and not a separate entity, e.g. (*a*) the truth is that all things are originated from one essence, or (*b*) the truth is that all are developing according to one law, or (*c*) the truth is that they are all destined towards one goal, and (*d*) the truth is that the Tathagata knows the Law (Dharma), whose essence is salvation and whose end is the peace of Nirvana, and imparts this knowledge to all, in perfect accordance with each person's capacity to receive it. It is interesting to note that the Tathagata makes no claim to knowing the *Essence* from which all things originate, but He claims only to know the Law. He, nevertheless, acknowledges that the recognition of the *one essence* or the underlying Reality is an *a priori* condition for effecting the transformation from the passing or perishable existence to the realm of the imperishable, the eternal, *Unborn, Unoriginated, Uncreated, Unformed.* No one with the Buddha's unique awareness of the failings of human existence and the transitory nature of the world could have devoted His whole life to the task of liberating man from the things of time, the mutable, without a positive experience of the time-less, *the Eternal.* It is with that Eternal Reality in mind that the Buddha constantly tells us of the unreal nature of the world and of all our desires for it.

It is hard to realize the essential, the truth is not easily perceived; desire is mastered by him who knows, and to him who sees aright all things are naught. There is, O monks, an unborn, unoriginated, uncreated, unformed. Were there not, O monks, this unborn, un-originated, uncreated, unformed, there would be no escape from the world of the born, originated, created, formed. Since, O monks, there is an unborn, unoriginated, uncreated, and unformed, therefore is there an escape from the born, originated, created, formed. What is dependent, that also moves; what is independent does not move. Where there is no movement there is rest; where rest is there is no desire; where there is no desire, there is neither coming nor going, no ceasing-to-be, no further coming to-be.

When there is no darkness, then there is neither day nor night, neither being nor non-being, only the auspicious One alone. He is the Imperishable. From Him proceeds the Ancient Wisdom.

He is the God of forms infinite in whose glory all things are, smaller than the smallest atom, and yet the Creator of all, ever-living in the mystery of his creation. In the vision of this God of love there is eternal peace. The mind cannot grasp Him above, or below, or in the space in between. With whom shall we compare Him whose glory is the whole universe? Far beyond the range of vision, He cannot be seen by mortal eyes; but He can be known by the heart and the mind and those who know Him attain immortality.

Svetasvatara Upanishad,
IV.18,19,20

Where there is no ceasing-to-be, nor further coming-to-be, there is neither this shore nor the other[153] shore, nor anything between them. Even this is the end of Sorrow.

Udana, v. 81

He who knows Me in reality as without birth and without beginning, and as the Supreme Lord of the universe, he, undeluded among men, is purged of all sins.

Bhagavad Gita, X.3

Among the letters, I am the first letter of the alphabet; of the different kinds of compounds in grammar, I am the copulative compound. I am verily the endless Time (the devourer of Time, God); I am the sustainer of all, having My face on all sides.

Bhagavad Gita, X.33

Here, the Buddha shows us that the negative character of expressing our cognition of *the Absolute* should not be equated with the fallacy of Its non-existence. There are no existing qualities in the entire scheme-of-things which

---

[153]Nirvana is known as the 'other shore'. However, the above verse from the *Udana* mentions a condition where there is 'neither this shore nor the *other* shore'—beyond Nirvana. The Hindu scriptures also mention this condition.

can be related to *the Absolute,* for It is outside any plane of thought or generation. The *Unborn, Unoriginated, Uncreated, Unformed* is *the Absolute.* But it is not possible to equate It with Dharma, since the phenomenon of Buddhahood is not dependent on any Dharma and, by definition, *the Absolute* must be the cause of all conditions and phenomena. Nor can Nirvana be equated with *the Absolute,* for Nirvana is not the ground of being. Nor is Karma 'the unconditioned Absolute' since Karma is only a cause-effect relationship totally dependent on conditions. Hence, while *the Absolute, the Uncreated,* must be sought and discovered in order to gain freedom from sorrow, yet, as the Buddha cautions, one must not be gullible to accept as the *Uncreated* anything without a great deal of reflection.

The man who is free from credulity, who knows the uncreated, who has severed all ties, who has put an end to all occasions, who has renounced all desires, he, indeed, is exalted among men.

Dhammapada, v. 97

Verily he is the seer, who sees the Supreme Lord as the only imperishable substance abiding equally in all perishable beings. Whenever he perceives the diversified existence of beings rooted in the One Supreme Being, and the projection of all beings from Him, that very moment he attains Brahma.

Bhagavad Gita, XIII.27,30

And, while He warns against the practices prevailing in His time of accepting any multitude of beings, objects and gods, as the *Uncreated* or the *Unoriginated,* the Buddha, in the following verses, strongly implies that the acknowledgement of the underlying Reality is imperative for recognizing the futility of the mundane life and, thereby, for detaching ourselves from the ephemeral so as to reach the *depth of the eternal.* Ignorance or disbelief in *the Uncreated,* or *Unmade,* is the cause of all error and sorrow. By denying *the Uncreated, the Absolute,* we make existence itself into an 'unmeaning' and, thereby, negate any purpose for our own life, while the discovery of the *Uncreated* and belief in It gives us the most joyful experience of serene certitude that quells our doubts and fears and imparts meaning and direction to our existence. As the *Chandogya Upanishad* states, "where there is the Infinite there is joy. There is no joy in the finite."[154] And we can all understand this if we recognize that the mind of man is the only entity we know that is conscious of on-coming death—death, which for each and everyone of us writes 'finis' to our earthly gains and possessions, snatching away for all time the things that seem so dear to us in our delusive ignorance. Those that see this life as death and everything in creation as perishable, long for *the Eternal, the Uncreated.* The Buddha, too, recognizes this distinction and shows us the path to immortality.

---

[154]VII.23.

Whenever he comprehends the origin and destruction of the elements of the body he obtains joy and happiness, which is life eternal to those who know.

Dhammapada, v. 374

When a man has heard and has understood and finding the essence, reaches the Inmost, then he finds joy in the source of joy.

Katha Upanishad, 2.14

Him I call a Brahmin who has no desires, who is free from doubt by knowledge (of the truth), who has reached the depth of the eternal.

Dhammapada, v. 411

He is not moved by evil: he removes evil. He is not burned by sin: he burns all sin: And he goes beyond evil, beyond passion, and beyond doubts, for he sees the Eternal.

Brihadaranyaka Upanishad 4.3-4

O Brahmin, cut off the stream, be energetic, drive away desires. Knowing the destruction of all that is made you will know the uncreated, O Brahmin.

Dhammapada, v. 383

One should deligently seek that Supreme State, having reached which one never returns; and saying to himself, "I seek refuge in the Primal Person, from whom has emanated this beginningless flow of creation", one should meditate on Him.

Bhagavad Gita, XV.4

The Buddha acknowledged *the Uncreated, the Absolute,* that is totally apart and different from all Creation. And it was His glimpse of *the Uncreated* that established Him on the pedestal of unshakeable certitude, lifting Him into the plane of Nirvanic bliss, away from the delusions and sorrows of existence. This perspective is almost mandatory to gain a fuller comprehension of those momentous first verses[155] that Gautama uttered upon achieving enlightenment (Buddhahood).

I have run through a course of many births looking for the maker of this dwelling and finding him not; painful is birth again and again. (anekajatisamsaram sandhavissam anibbisam gahakarakam gavesanto dukkhajati punappunam)

When all the desires that dwell in the heart are cast away, then does the mortal become immortal then he attains Brahma here (in this very body).

Brihadaranyaka Upanishad, IV.4,7

Now are you seen, O builder of the house, you will not build the house again. All your rafters are broken, your ridgepole is destroyed, the mind, set on the attainment of nirvana, has attained the extinction of desires, (gahakaraka! dittho si, puna geham na kahasi sabha te phasuka bhagga, gahakutam visankhitam visankharagatam cittam tanhanam khayam ajjhaga)

When a man knows God, he is free: his sorrows have an end, and birth and death are no more. When in inner union he is beyond the world of the body, then the third world, the world of the Spirit, is found, where the power of the All is, and man has all: for he is one with the One.

Svetasvatara Upanishad, I.11

Here, in the first verse, the *maker of the dwelling* is mentioned as a person *(him)* and not having found *him* has, according to the Buddha, resulted in the

---

[155]*Dhammapada, vv. 153, 154.*

painful cycle of rebirths. In the following verse Gautama proclaims His triumph in having discovered this *builder of the house* and declares to *him* that he will not build this house again (at least as far as Gautama is concerned, meaning, His earthly form and personality will not continue to repeat the cycle of births and deaths). To continue with these same celebrated verses, the now enlightened Gautama, the Buddha, proclaims that the conditions born of delusion, which previous to His discovery of the *builder of the house* held Him to the cycle of *becomings,* have now been totally destroyed and His *mind, set on the attainment of nirvana, has attained the extinction of desires*—which, as we have seen from the Buddha's description in the last chapter, is precisely what Nirvana is. *(The stopping of becoming is Nirvana. Nirvana is called getting rid of craving. Nirvana is the realm of self-realization. Nirvana is where one realizes that there is nothing but what is seen of the mind itself, etc.)* Some commentators on this verse have claimed that 'craving' or 'desire' *(tanha)* is the *maker of the dwelling* or *builder of the house* which is being addressed by the newly become Buddha. This is not likely since this word *tanha* is mentioned only once and only at the end of the verse in relation to *the extinction of desires (tanhanam khayam ajjhaga),* and is nowhere referred to as a person *(him).* Moreover, the Buddha clearly tells us that craving is simply a by-product of ignorance and not the fundamental cause of holding us in bondage within the *cycle of becoming.*

"Monks, what is the provenance, what the origin, what the birth, what the source of these four graspings?[156] *Craving, monks, is the provenance, craving is the origin, craving is the birth, craving is the source of these four graspings. And what, monks, is the provenance, what the origin, what the birth, what the source of craving? Feeling, monks . . . is the source of craving. And what is . . . the source of feeling? Contact is . . . the source of feeling. And what is the . . . source of contact? The six*[157] *bases of sense-impression . . . are the source of contact. And what is the . . . source of the six bases of sense-impression? The psycho-physical . . . is the source of the six bases of sense-impression. And what is . . . the source of the psycho-physical? Consciousness is . . . the source of the psycho-physical. And what . . . is the source of consciousness? The formative tendencies are the source of consciousness.*

When a wise man has withdrawn his mind from all things without, and when his spirit of life has peacefully left inner sensations, let him rest in peace, free from the movements of will and desire. Since the living being called the spirit of life has come from that which is greater than the spirit of life, let the spirit of life surrender itself into what is called 'turya', the fourth condition of consciousness. For it has been said: 'There is something beyond our mind which abides in silence within our mind. It is the supreme mystery beyond thought. Let one's mind and one's subtle body rest upon that and not rest on anything else'.
Maitri Upanishad, 6.19

When the wise man knows that the material senses come not from the Spirit, and that their waking and sleeping belong to their own nature, then he grieves no more. Beyond the

---

[156]The four graspings are: the grasping of sense-pleasures, the grasping of views, the grasping of rite and ritual, the grasping of the theory of self. The last 'grasping' is the 'grasping of the theory of self' but not of *self.*

[157]The six bases of sense impression are the five senses and the mind.

And what is the source of the formative tendencies? Delusive ignorance, monks, is the provenance, delusive ignorance is the origin, delusive ignorance is the birth, delusive ignorance is the source of the formative tendencies.

When, monks, a monk has got rid of delusive ignorance, and insight-knowledge has arisen, he, by the diminishing of delusive ignorance and by the arising of insight-knowledge, does not grasp after sense-pleasures, nor views, nor rite and ritual nor the theory of self. Not grasping, he is not perturbed; being unperturbed he himself individually attains to Nibbana, and he comprehends: "Destroyed is birth, brought to a close is the holy life, done is what was to be done, there is no more of being for me."

Thus spoke the Exalted One and the monks rejoiced in what he had said.

Majjhima-nikaya
(Culasihanada Sutta)

senses is the mind, and beyond mind is reason, its essence. Beyond reason is the Spirit in man, and beyond this is the Spirit of the universe, the evolver of all. And beyond is Purush (the Supreme), all-pervading, beyond definitions. When a mortal knows Him, he attains liberation and reaches immortality.

Katha Upanishad, I. (8-11)

The Buddha tells us that, by eradicating *delusive ignorance* through *insight-knowledge*, we can make an end of all *graspings* and their causes and attain to the serenity of Nirvanic bliss. The point that must be noted is that the liberation of the mind is not based on a nothingness (the end of all *delusive ignorance* which is merely a negation, a non-reality) but on a reality beyond, *insight-knowledge*, something positive. The question here is, what *insight-knowledge*? Or *insight-knowledge* of what? Of whom? It is clear that *craving* or its origin, *delusive ignorance*, cannot be the cause of enlightenment, just as darkness cannot give birth to light. Light cannot come from the absence of light but only from the source of light. Likewise *insight-knowledge* must either emanate from the source of knowledge or be about that source of knowledge. But, in either case, the source of *insight-knowledge* must be outside and above the seeker, who upon being endowed with it attains Nirvana. We must also remember that the Buddha was in quest of the imperishable, *the Eternal*. Hence, it is much more likely that his exultance was directed at a power (some 'thing' or some 'one') above Him whom He addresses as *him, the builder of the house* (the 'house' being the physical and psychological personality of Gautama) and that these first verses are a joyous proclamation expressing gratitude to the *builder of the house* for at last having shown 'himself' to Gautama's questing mind. Nor could the Buddha, who was inspired from the *wholly beyond*, state that others could also try out their own fanciful concepts of achieving Buddhahood. Otherwise, He could not claim that His was the only doctrine to tread the path of the newly discovered Dharma.

We have seen from preceding chapters that the preponderence of evidence for Gautama's attainment of enlightenment is in the direction of divine bestowal, an act of grace from the *wholly beyond*. Hence, He could not entertain any admission of having had any human teacher or guru for winning this unique prize and discovering the peerless Dharma, to wit, His rejection of the teachings of His two mentors, Alara and Uddaka, as well as His response[158] to the questions of Upaka the Jain whom He met on His way to Benares soon after achieving Buddhahood.

I have conquered all, I know all, in all conditions of life I am free from taint. I have renounced all and with the destruction of craving I am freed. Having learnt myself, to whom shall I point as teacher?

However, this was not always so, for the Buddha admits that He, too, was one of *those beings shut up as it were in the egg-shell of ignorance.*[159] And this claim of His of being at one time 'ignorant' and then becoming 'all knowing', while not incongruous within the context of divine bestowal *(exaltation from the Absolute)*, yet, in the light of the fact that there had been other such 'all knowing' Buddhas before Him, only strengthens our premise that the omniscient mass of knowledge—*the Absolute*—must have had to exist prior to and independent of all *Buddha risings*. It is the eternal omniscient ground of being, that is the underlying Reality behind all *Buddha risings*, and there could be no Buddha without It.

Hail to thee, womb of the void, who art free of all conceits, omniscient one, thou mass of knowledge, knowledge personified, all Hail to thee! Thou, teacher of the pure essence of truth which makes an end of worldly knowledge, O Vajrasattva, born of the non-substantiality of all things, Hail to thee! From you, O Lord, there ever rise into existence Buddhas and Bodhisattvas, who possess as their good qualities the great perfections, O Thought of Enlightenment, Hail to thee!
Prajnopaya-viniscaya-siddhi,
III.9-11, G.O.S. Vol. 44, 1929

My Prakriti (Nature) in her primordial, undeveloped state is the womb of all creatures; in that I place the seed of consciousness. The birth of all beings follows from this combination of Matter and Spirit, O decendant of Bharata. Of all the bodies that take birth from different wombs, this Primordial Matter is the Mother, and I am the procreating Father, O son of Kunti (Arjuna).
Bhagavad Gita, XIV.3,4

To have glimpsed *the Eternal*, the underlying Reality, is in itself to rise above the ephemeral and go beyond to the farther shore of *no becoming, Nirvana*. This eternal Reality reveals Itself to the Buddhas in accordance with Its own law of Divine Manifestation and the Buddhas in turn as perfect mirrors reflect Its truth (Dharma) in their whole being. As the Buddha states, *establish the Truth in your mind for the Truth is the image of the Eternal, it*

[158]*Dhammapada,* v. 353.

[159]*Parajika Suttavibhanga,* I.1.4.

portrays the immutable. I was born into the world as the king[160] *of Truth for the salvation of the world. The subject on which I meditate is Truth. The practice to which I devote myself is Truth. The topic of my conversation is Truth. My thoughts are always in the Truth. For lo! my self has become the Truth.*[161] Now some may argue that, as the Buddha on previous occasions has called Dharma the *King of Kings,* and since He Himself after attaining enlightenment promises to live *honoring and respecting it,* Dharma is the *Eternal* mentioned by the Budda in the above passage. This is not possible because of the following reasons: The Buddha specifically states that He is the ordained Dharmaraja (King of Truth) for bringing about the salvation of the world. Hence, if by *the Eternal* is also meant the Dharma then the Buddha is higher than *the Eternal.* Moreover, nowhere in the Buddhist scriptures has Dharma been endowed with perception or mind; thus, the Buddha, possessing both mind and claiming omniscience, would again be in a category different and higher than Dharma.

The more rational explanation for these excerpts from the *Digha-nikaya* involves the clear separation of the three entities as the Buddha has listed in the text itself, namely, the incomprehensible and unknown *Eternal;* the Truth (Dharma) forever emanating from *the Eternal* and portraying *the Eternal* as Its very image; and the Buddha, the expounder of the Truth (Dharma), who in His life and teaching exemplifies it so perfectly that no distinction could be made between Him and the Truth—*whosoever see me sees Dhamma, seeing Dhamma, he sees me.*[162] *For lo! my self has become the Truth.*

The Buddha, as we saw, is not conditioned by Dharma, Karma or Nirvana, and this is easily understandable, since the Buddha possessed that one 'thing' totally absent in Dharma, Karma or Nirvana—the Mind. But the Buddha Himself, though not conditioned by Dharma or Nirvana, is *not the creator, guardian, or lord of the world; He has not decreed its laws, nor is he able to alter them. He cannot stop the change of all things, nor can he dissolve the law of Causality.*[163] *He is not even the discoverer of the teachings He proclaims.*[164] Hence, while Buddhahood is dependent on *the Absolute, the Absolute* is not bound by any condition and is totally outside any frame or concept. It is 'Sunyata' (voidness). It is not 'joined' with Buddhas, *since it is not related to any known experience.* As the Buddha[165] states in reply to a question:

---

[160]Dharmaraja, one of the titles of the Buddha, Dharma meaning religion or truth and raja, king.

[161]*Digha-nikaya,* I.46.

[162]*Samyutta-nikaya,* III.22, 87, 13.

[163]*Katha-vatthu,* 214.

[164]*Mahaprajnaparamita-Shastra,* I.p. 157. This further alludes to a revelation from a higher plane.

[165]*Tevijja Sutta,* I.i.

THE GOD OF BUDDHA

If by the Absolute is meant something out of relation to all known things, its existence cannot be established by any known reasoning. How can we know that anything unrelated to other relations: we know nothing that is, or can be related.

What cannot be thought with the mind, but that whereby the mind can think: Know that alone to be Brahma, the Spirit; and not what people here adore.

Kena Upanishad, i.6

Then Buddha said: "Subhuti, words cannot explain the real nature of the cosmos. Only common people fettered with desire make use of this arbitrary method."
Vajra-Sattva, XXX (The Integral Principle)

The Supreme (tad ekam) is without qualities and attributes, 'neither existent (Sat) nor non-existent (Asat)'.

Rig Veda, X.129

There is nothing else besides Me, Arjuna. Like clusters of yarn-beads formed by knots on a thread, all this is threaded on Me.

Bhagavad Gita, VII.7

This, again, emphasizes that puny man cannot really unravel the mystery of the universe by any kind of reasoning on his part, since any fixed proposition on the real nature of the cosmos can be refuted by dialectic. Only a higher plane can look down and comprehend the essence of the lower and not those who are themselves within the parameters (space and time) of that plane.

The Tathagata sees the triple world (the world of the Uncreated and Causeless Cause, the world of the Spirit-Mind and the world of matter) as it really is: 'It is not born, it dies not; it is not conceived; it springs not into existence; it moves not in a whirl, it becomes not extinct; it is not real, nor unreal, it is not existing nor non-existing; it is not such, not otherwise, nor false. The Tathagata sees . . . in His position no laws are concealed.[166]

. . . That beginningless supreme Brahma is said to be neither Sat (real) nor Asat (non-real). It has hands and feet everywhere, eyes, head and face everywhere, ears everywhere. It stands pervading all. It is the perceiver of all sense-objects, though devoid of all senses; though unattached and attributeless, It is the sustainer of all and enjoyer of the qualities. It is without and within all beings, and constitutes both animate and inanimate creation. By reason of its subtlety, It is incomprehensible; both at hand and far away is *That.*

Bhagavad Gita, XIII.12,13,14,15

However, when questioned concerning the nature of the underlying Reality, the Buddha could only respond by a calm silence, just like the teacher of the Upanishads, who, when asked to describe the attributes of the Supreme, replies that he (Baskali) is answering (by his silence) but that the pupil (Bahva) understands not. Thus, the Buddha's own near total, but not complete, silence in the realm of affirming *the Absolute* was simply the result of the truth that the Absolute Reality is above all determinations. The first condition of the Infinite is that It cannot be rationalized by the finite mind and, since It is not a matter capable of logical proof, the Buddha did not

---

[166]*The Lotus Sutra,* Ch. XV.

emphasize *the Absolute* as the ground of being, but left no doubt of the reality of Its existence by His condemnation of the empirical world and His unequivocal admonitions concerning the ephemeral nature of the mundane.

Despite the well-nigh God-saturated psyche of India from the earliest time, Indian thought has always been reticent in defining the nature of the Supreme. The Upanishads do not demonstrate any tendency towards containing the Absolute Reality within any framework of human logic or definition. Like the person who, when asked to write an essay on God, turned in a blank page, the Upanishads, too, when asked to recount the attributes of the Supreme, maintain silence. Apart from the impossibility of giving any description or attribute to *the Absolute,* the Buddha's own reason for negative definitions concerning the Supreme Being becomes clear if one views it in the context of the India of His time, when every kind of claim was being advanced by the Brahmins and religious leaders to knowing the nature, the form, as well as the dictates of God, Who by then had been made to appear in many instances as a silent accomplice of those advancing such claims of intimacy with Him—claims which continued in endless futility without serving the real needs of the time, and led only to frayed tempers and discord. The Buddha refuted such claims by rational dialogue not merely to discredit those impossible notions, but also to oblige them, and through them the masses, to demonstrate by their deeds their assertions of piety. It is not surprising that the Buddha was easily revolted at those various anthropomorphic concepts of *the Absolute.* He realized only too clearly that any being that could be comprehended or imagined by the mind of man was less than the mind that comprehends it. To Him that 'God' of man's conjecture was as alien to the *Eternal Essence, the Uncreated,* as unreality is to the Real. He proclaimed that those who talk about Brahma, and say that Brahma is this and Brahma is that, had never seen Brahma face to face and were like the blind in love with a beloved whom they have never seen. It was such touting of various claims of easy familiarity with God by the theologians and charlatans of His times, for furthering their own prestige and authority over the masses by the alleged efficacy of their own sundry systems for salvation, that obliged the Buddha to uncompromisingly oppose the concept of a personal God, who was reputed to be swayed by supplications and subject to human emotions and who interfered in the workings of his own laws within the universe, thus proving that neither he nor his laws are perfect. Hence, by simple logic, He was able to show that, if the Supreme is merely an irascible victim of his own emotions, who rules the universe according to whim rather than through perfect laws, then such a being is better relegated to oblivion. For men could then have no certainty of salvation, *no safe refuge* from such an unpredictable supernatural tyrant. If, on the other hand, He exists in the plenitude of His perfection, then there is, indeed, an escape for *the born, the originated, the created, the formed,* and the escape is through unswerving devotion and strict adherence in thought, word and deed to His law—the Dharma. In confirmation of this latter concept, the *Tevijja Sutta*[167] relates that any attempt at a unity of spirit with the Absolute Brahma is pointless, since it is impossible to know what we are looking for. However, we can draw near to the experience of Him, that underlying Reality of all things, only by striving on the road of Dharma to attain Nirvana. Personal striving, and not surrender to or dependence on an external power, is the gist of the Buddha's message. But this is also a reiteration of the age-old truth preached by every Religion, namely, that heaven or hell are the products of our own acts and 'as we sow, so shall we reap'. For, endowed by our Creator with the rational soul and the freedom to choose, the world of humanity can have it no other way if it must, in justice, conform to this great and unique gift as well as fulfil its highest responsibility in exercising this freedom of choice. It was the Buddha's mission to renew once again for the world of His time that vision of *the Eternal,* to provide a glimpse of that ineffable state of existence beyond the passing entanglements of this physical world, and to lift humanity out of the quagmire of ignorance and craving and to set its feet on the sure road of righteousness (Dharma), which alone would bring that true freedom of detachment and lead mankind beyond the pale of the cycle of *births and deaths* on to the heights of Nirvanic bliss or Brahmaloka. And, despite the aspersions that have been cast by Buddhist theologians on the concept of Brahma as either a ground of being or the state of eternal bliss, the Buddha Himself clearly acknowledged the world of Brahma[168] as His very own native land, since He was truly a denizen of that higher spiritual abode to which every pious Hindu aspired:

We are told, Gautama, that the Sakyamuni knows the path to a union with Brahma. And the Blessed One said: "What do you think, O Brahmins, of a man born and brought up in Manasakata? Would he be in doubt about the most direct way from this spot to Manasakata?" "Certainly not, Gautama," replied the Brahmins. *"Thus," stated the Buddha, "the Tathagata knows the straight path that leads to a union with Brahma. He knows it as one who has entered the world of Brahma and has been born in it. There can be no doubt in the Tathagata."*

Digha-nikaya, 9,35

You are Vayu (Wind-God), Yama (God of Death), Agni (Fire-God), Moon God, Brahma (the Creator of beings), nay, the father of Brahma himself.

Bhagavad Gita, XI.39

Though unborn and immortal, and also the Lord of all beings, I manifest Myself through My own Yogamaya (divine potency), keeping My nature(Prakriti) under control.

Bhagavad Gita, IV.6

For, I am the abode of the imperishable Brahma, of immortality, of everlasting virtue and of unending bliss.

Bhagavad Gita, XIV.27

---

[167] *'Tevijja Sutta', Digha-nikaya,* i.235.
[168] See also (pp. 105-14) for a more detailed explanation.

His message, as stated, was directed constantly at the Hindus, and especially the Brahmins, and it should be evident that He had to speak to them in their terms and from their perspective if He was to be understood and accepted by them. His main emphasis was on righteous conduct in this world so as to attain Brahma's world (Brahmaloka) in the existence beyond. Thus, He repeatedly used the words 'Brahma-faring' (living according to the precepts of Brahma), which, on other occasions (page 32), He equates with Dharma itself. And, at times, He Himself is called Brahma in human form.[169]

The Buddha is an embodied Brahma. *Anguttara-nikaya, V.4*	There is a Spirit hidden in the mystery of the Upanishads and the Vedas; and Brahma, the God of creation, owns Him as his own Creator. It is the Spirit of God, seen by gods and seers of olden times who, when one with Him, become immortal. *Svetasvatara Upanishad, V.6*

It is unthinkable, therefore, that He could have made any headway in gaining converts from among the Hindus had He denied Brahma and negated the very existence of the Supreme. This He did not do; on the contrary, He repeatedly asserted that He had come not to negate but to *utterly purify and completely fulfill the Brahma-faring and explain its meaning in the spirit and the letter.*[170]

Gautama says: This itself is the whole of the Brahma-faring: friendship, association and intimacy with the Lovely. Because of my friendship with the Lovely, beings liable to birth are freed from birth, beings liable to ageing, decaying and dying are freed therefrom. Thus must you train: I will become a friend, associate and intimate of the Lovely. In order to do so this one thing must be closely observed, namely diligence among wholesome mental states. *Samyutta-nikaya, I, 88-89*	I am the One to be known through the many Vedas, I am the maker of the Vedanta and the knower of the Vedas. Merit or demerit I have none. There is no destruction for me, no birth or body, senses or intellect. I have not earth, water, fire, air, ether. Knowing the nature of the Supreme Self, dwelling in the cave of the heart, stainless without a second; the witness of all, free from (the duality of) existence and non-existence, he obtains the pure nature of the Supreme Self. *Taittiriya Upanishad III, 10.5*
	Thoroughly abandoning all duties, come thou unto Me alone for shelter; it is I who will liberate thee from all sins. *Bhagavad Gita, XVIII.66*

---

[169]*Digha-nikaya, 27, 8, III, p. 84.* (Dhamma-kayo iti pi Brahma-kayo iti pi, Brahma-bhuto iti pi). See also *Anguttara-nikaya, V.10, 115, p. 226.* (He has fully become a divine being of moral purity.)

[170]*Samyutta-nikaya, IV.314-16.*

It is important to understand the meaning of this *Lovely*, referred to by the Buddha. As He states, the whole of Brahma-faring is friendship, association and intimacy with *the Lovely*. Now, while Brahma-faring culminates[171] in Nirvana and is synonymous with Nirvana, it cannot be equated with *the Lovely* because of the following distinction: Brahma-faring can lead to friendship, association and intimacy with *the Lovely*, but friendship, or association, or intimacy, is not the same as identity with *the Lovely*. The Buddha, too, who on occasions has claimed identity with Dharma and also that He had attained the highest Nirvana, makes no claim of identity with *the Lovely*, but states that, because of His friendship with *the Lovely*, beings are able to enter Nirvana (witness the condition for Nirvana: freedom from birth, ageing, decaying and dying). Hence this *Lovely* is higher than the Buddha, since friendship, association and intimacy with It is vital for the Buddha's task of salvation. Moreover, since the Buddha, too, had to seek salvation, one could logically assume that *the Lovely* was also instrumental for the Buddha's own enlightenment. Once again, as in His address to 'him', *the builder of the house*, the Buddha uses words ('friendship', 'association', 'intimacy') implying relationship with a sentient entity and not something inanimate such as Dharma, Karma, or Nirvana. While in an earlier passage,[172] the Buddha says that *Dharma is lovely in the beginning, lovely at the middle, lovely at the ending*, in the above passage from *Samyutta-nikaya* no mention is made of Dharma and, if by *Lovely* is meant Dharma, then this *Lovely* should not be necessary for attaining Buddhahood or Nirvana or even to be freed from ageing and dying, as no Dharma was necessary for Gautama's attainment to Buddhahood or Nirvana. Now, as the Buddha's friendship with this *Lovely* was imperative for freeing men from sorrow, this *Lovely* is not Dharma and, since the Buddha did not regard either Dharma or Nirvana or Karma as the ground of being, it is difficult to identify this *Lovely* with either Dharma or Nirvana[173] or Karma. Instead, this *Lovely* has some of the same attributes as the *Unoriginated, Uncreated, Unborn and Unformed*,[174] the knowledge and discovery of which liberates one from the sorrow and pain of *all becomings*. And, if we can recognize that the *Unoriginated, Uncreated* etc. are aspects uniquely associated with *the Absolute*, then we can understand that the *Lovely* talked of here is the ineffable Reality, by associating with which the Buddha derived the unbounded bliss of Nirvana. As He tells us, we, too, by diligent effort, must direct our path towards becoming *a friend, associate and intimate of the*

---

[171]*Samyutta-nikaya*, III.189.

[172]*Vinaya-pitaka*, I.20-21.

[173]Na samsarasya nirvanat kimcid asti visheshanam (In truth there is neither Samsara nor Nirvana, nor is there any difference between them).

[174]Mentioned in the famous passage from *Udana* (see p. 133).

Lovely. But, as to any description of this *Lovely, the Absolute,* He leaves us no clues. While acknowledging Its 'all-conditioning' power He makes no mention of Its essence, since none is possible. For there, as the Upanishad[175] states, "the eye goes not, nor words, nor mind. We know not, we cannot understand, how then can He be explained. He is above the known and also above the unknown." No echo returns to us from the depths of *the Eternal,* and any effort to probe Its essence is doomed in futility. We are as bats in the cave of infinity, or as the poet wrote:

> "The six blind men of Hindustan, who learning much inclined,
> That went to see the elephant,[176] though all of them were blind."

Each, groping at and feeling the different parts of the elephant—its trunk, its legs, its tail—confidently proclaimed that the elephant was very like a snake, a tree, a trunk, a rope! The elephant is all that and much more. For fear of being called the seventh blind man of Hindustan, it is not the writer's intention to say what the elephant is like, but only to state that there is the elephant. Even if one could open one's eyes and see the whole elephant, how could one really describe it to those still blind? As the Upanishad states, "From it speech turns back along with the mind, . . . words and thoughts cannot reach Him and He cannot be seen by the eye. How can He then be perceived except by him who says, He is?"[177]

Hence, every belief in Ultimate Reality or God is restricted by its very nature, and however attractive or natural the idea of a personal or anthropomorphic Creator as the source of all creation and the 'ground' of being might appear to our mind, it nevertheless becomes the first impediment to the development of our mind to that truer and grander vision of the Supreme. We must, at all cost, desist from making God out in our image since any belief in such a concept is very strictly limited! Nor can we hope to gain any meaningful concept of *the Absolute* by linking words upon words to It, such as God is love or God is truth, or God is just, implying, once again, a thrust, all too natural for us but also totally fallacious, in the direction of attaching to the Supreme these various attributes, e.g. love, truth, strength, etc. conceived by our finite human minds. Here, again, these same attributes, of which we ourselves have only the vaguest understanding, often-times smothered by our own personalized standards concerning these attributes, constitute the greatest obstacles to our gaining any clear vision of the Supreme. And through the contradictions created in our own minds by

---

[175]*Kena Upanishad,* I.3,4.

[176]The reader may kindly excuse these few lines on the elephant, as the *Dhammapada* has a whole chapter on it (XXIII, Nagavaggo)!

[177]*Katha Upanishad,* II, 3.12,13.

ignorantly applying such parameters to *the Absolute,* we, too, like the ancient Buddhist poet *(Why triumph, falsehood, truth, and justice fail?),* may be led to a rejection of Its existence or to the denial of God.

We must understand that the Sun does not shine by our definitions of light. It is its own standard. The greatest truth that the finite mind can ever hope to grasp is that one cannot really know the Supreme except through Its effects and that, too, only in part, for the Ultimate Reality is outside and beyond anything and everything and comprises all things—the manifest and the unmanifest, time and eternity, Samsara and Nirvana. "There the sun shines not, nor moon, nor the stars; lightnings shine not there and much less earthly fire. From His light all these give light, and His radiance illumines all creation."[178] Our logic, which is predicated on our own experience and knowledge, is totally useless in determining anything outside the narrow limits of our own dull faculties. The Buddha, better than all others, realized that the Supreme not only transcends Time and Space but also what we know as logic. *The Absolute* is supra-logical and Its reality is as alien to the world of physical and even metaphysical phenomena as 'nothingness'. Intuition, and not deductive thought, is the vehicle for approaching It. "He comes to the mind of those who know Him beyond thought, not to those who imagine He can be attained by thought."[179] Only through Its attributes can we sense the presence of *the Absolute,* and for Its attributes we are told to look around and within us.

How can the truth which is inexpressible be taught and heard? It is through It's attributes that It is taught and heard.
Madhyamika Vitti, p. 264

Who sends the mind to wander afar? Who first drives life to start on its journey? Who impels us to utter these words? Who is the Spirit behind the eye and the ear?
Kena Upanishad, I.1

Silent are the Tathagatas, O Blessed One.
Lankavatara Sutta

There is no likeness of Him whose glory is infinite.
Yajur Veda, 32

As the Buddha states, *the Law permeates the universe;* hence, by whatever name we call the Supreme, to every discerning mind the evidence presented by the cosmos is overwhelmingly in the direction of order. Even seemingly chaotic phenomena, when probed beneath their surface, present clear proof of the universality of this law of order and organization. And order and organization denote intelligent guidance, if not within the body of such

---

[178]*Katha Upanishad,* II.2,15. Also *Mundaka Upanishad,* II.2,11.
[179]*Kena Upanishad,* II.3.

phenomena, then outside and above these. Whether one looks to the world of matter or to man's mind, to reason or to religion, one cannot escape from acknowledging the presence of a single universal Reality underlying the scheme of things entire. From the investigation of the minutest increments of energy and on to the giant galaxies, the intelligent mind recognizes an universal Reality demonstrating Its presence through intelligibly operating laws and permeating the whole realm of phenomena. Intelligence or its workings is the underlying thread running through the entire cosmos, and intelligence means Mind.

The Buddha, too, acknowledges this. *The Mind is everything,* He says, and *the Cosmos is replete with mind.* But Karma, Dharma and Nirvana are not possessed of Mind. And it is precisely because Mind exists that Karma, Dharma, and Nirvana are not regarded as the ground of being by the Buddha.

Intelligent guidance and creative thought can only emanate from the mind, and the more comprehensive the law and organization that is evident in a phenomenon, the higher the intelligence required to bring it about and the greater the mind behind it. Hence, Universal Law must come from Universal Mind. But what is the Universal Mind? What is our own finite mind? Well, if we cannot visualize the nature and form of our own mind, which surely exists, how can we visualize that Mind from which time and space and all else originate? Our mind demonstrates its presence by the effects of its creative thought which we see in our discoveries and inventions, while every aspect of creation, not the least being we ourselves possessed of mind, stands as eternal testimony of the Universal Mind.

No one can be content at the thought of an existence without purpose—a universe of chaos, where woe and weal, disaster and security are bereft of any meaning. While we may imagine on occasion that the universe is devoid of feeling for our ethical strivings, or without cognizance of our presence, yet, in our inmost being and as expressed in the every day run of life, our thoughts and acts are based on the belief or assumption that the universe is a manifestation of law predicated on a Reality possessed of Will and Mind. The greater our progress in unravelling the mysteries of the phenomenal world, the greater becomes our conviction that mind is the only essential, the only reality and the only instrument for determining and controlling the cosmos. *There is nothing but what is seen of the mind.* Sooner or later the third and the greatest aspect of this truth must also dawn on us, namely, that the mind is the only Creator. The Universal Mind is 'everything' and from it everything is generated. But, whatever the image conceived by us of the Supreme, it is, in the final analysis, merely a symbol, absolutely unable to give us any precise description of the Ultimate Reality, nor can such imagery in the framework of creation convey to us any intrinsic meaning concerning the operation of Its sovereign will, which we describe as the Law.[180] And just as we are cautioned not to conceive of the Universal Mind as something merely different in degree but resembling in essence our own finite minds, the Buddha also shows us the abysmal difference between the Supreme Will and our own exercise of free choice predicated on 'self'. *There is self and there is truth. Where self is, truth is not. Where truth is, self is not. Self is death and truth is life.*

It would be gross error to think that the Supreme Will dabbles in an endless series of possibilities possessed of an infinite variety of choices, all equally valid. Absolute Truth emanating from the Supreme is not a compound of facts but a singular non-composite reality. In our understanding of this indivisible unity *(that all things originate from one essence and that there is but one law and hence but one truth, not two or three)* lies our own freedom from error. Those who burn away their own fanciful notions about other paths to salvation and desist from exercising their own free will and submerge their will in the Supreme attain enlightenment. *When the selves break like soap bubbles, their contents will be preserved and in the truth they will lead a life everlasting. In the truth thou shalt live forever.* Choice, free or otherwise can only be present when there is doubt. Alternatives only have meaning because all of us, to a greater or lesser degree, are ignorant. There are no alternatives in the face of 'All-Knowledge', nor can there by any choice in the presence of 'Perfection'. Hence, absolute freedom can only be possessed by Universal Mind as It is not conditioned by any choice or alternatives and manifests Itself through Its Sovereign Will in bringing forth and directing the entire creation, with its immanent laws of Dharma and Karma, of beings and Buddhas, the 'led' and the 'leading', the 'going' (road) and the 'goal' (Nirvana).

The Supreme Will and Absolute Truth are in perfect harmony. And as we strive to recognize and adhere to Its purpose we ourselves will achieve a greater measure of freedom. For true freedom consists only in harmony with the will of *the Absolute* as exemplified by the *one Law.* Our minds must grow to an awareness of the Universal Mind and we will find in it our *safe refuge,* for we are products of that Mind.

A time may come in the remote future when we will have learnt to compress Time and Space and manipulate Life itself, since these are not limits forbidden us by the Power that brought us into being. Nor will we take away anything from Its greatness and glory when we do reach those heights. For, what limits can the Almighty, the All Knowing Creator Mind, place on

---

[180]The student of the Upanishads may recognize here the glint of two indivisible aspects of a singular Reality, the supraexistential denoting the Absolute and Its immanent Will within the cosmos indicating the Law. Buddhism, too, mentions both these aspects, the first as the state of Sunyata (Voidness) and the second as the Dharma.

Its handiwork within the entire frame of creation if It has no fear of Its handiwork? None, of course. It has done much more. It has continued to help the minds that It brings into being to reach the highest and It has imparted to these myriads of minds the secret for achieving these heights through the path of 'harmony'. We are taught to be in harmony with the entire cosmos but, most important of all, in harmony with the highest life in the cosmos, the life of the mind—other minds, our fellow beings. This is the perennial Message of the Universal Mind, conveyed to us throughout the ages, through the periodic *rising of the Buddhas*. And, finally, were we to pass all states[181] and arrive at the *other shore, replete with mind,* and in a sense all-knowing, our 'all-knowledge' would only reveal to us more than ever before the Reality of that Universal Mind. We would know that there was a time when we were not, but Time was, and we would know also about the Creator of Time, *the Absolute, the Unoriginated, the Lovely,* the Universal Mind—the God of Buddha.

This I have said to you, O Kalamas, but you may only accept it O Kalamas not because it is written, not because it is tradition, not because of its authority in the past or in the scriptures, not for the sake of any particular method, not for the sake of careful consideration, not for the sake of forebearing with wrong views, not because of its apparent suitability, not because your teacher is spiritual, but if you yourselves understand that this is so meritorious and perfect that when accepted it is for the weal of all then you may accept it.[182]

---

[181] See also p. 24 "But it will be like a flame in a great body of blazing fire."

[182] *Anguttara,* III, 653. *'Kalamas Sutta'.*

EPILOGUE

In his book, *The Discovery of India,* Jawaharlal Nehru states, in his reply to Andre Malraux's question to him as to "why Buddhism was absorbed and finally exiled from India by Hinduism," that, "while there were explanations and answers, they all seemed to miss the real reason for this phenomenon," which he went on to imply was one of the greatest tragedies in the 5000 year history of the brilliant, spiritual and cultural life of India. This sad episode has been a double-edge misfortune. For, while Indian thought was deprived of its fairest fruit, Buddhism, too, uprooted from its native soil, became spiritually detached from its cultural springs, developing concepts and practices alien to the metaphysics of Hindu India in which the Buddha had found both His physical as well as His spiritual birth and growth.

Hence, in order to arrive at the true meaning of the Buddha's words, we have had to recognize the vital need for examining them within the context of the thought of Hindu India. No foreign scholar of Buddhism, however well-versed in the mere mechanics of the Pali and Sanskrit languages, can fully discern the true meaning of the Buddha's concepts and teachings without a complete understanding of the cultural essence embedded in the Vedas and the Upanishads, especially as expressed by the *Bhagavad Gita,* with which the Buddha demonstrated a remarkable identity of views and from the sources of which He naturally derived not merely His formative inspiration but also a continuing impetus for propounding the reforms and enlarging the concepts of His doctrine, which was destined to infuse a new breath of life in the stagnating body of religion in His day.

Since the last century, many western ideologies and 'isms', such as humanism, agnosticism, atheism, etc., have either tried to espouse the Buddha or recruit Him into their ranks as their 'champion' or have quoted Him as an example for boosting their theories. Such efforts at 'drafting' the Buddha as 'champion' or 'chairman' by these ideologies and 'isms' have failed. None of

150

these movements have shown any capability for transforming their 'panaceas' into the practicality of cure for the ills which beset the human race today. These movements, one and all, already fragmented among themselves, are powerless to meet the challenges of the present.

Those writers and scholars who have tried to put the Buddha into the frame of their ideological canvasses have missed the point and do not understand Him or His message. It is simply not possible to take the Buddha apart and fit Him into some man-made lattice created to display a particular bill-board proclaiming some circumscribed ideology. Because they have overlooked His essential divinity, they are at a loss to understand with what argument or alchemy the Buddha was able to marshal, move and transform the spirit of His followers into an instrument for the spiritual conquest of humanity, comparable in its achievements only to that of the other great religions. If they who wish to view the Buddha from the correct perspective would accept Him as what He Himself claimed to be, *a unique and noblest of being,* a Prophet, a Divine Manifestation, then the secret of His power and accomplishments in the affairs of humanity would become clear. For, it is nothing less than one of the great religions. Claiming a station higher than human, *which no worldling can attain,* He brought a message of assurance for those who saw the ephemeral and the mundane as of no intrinsic worth, and desiring the permanent, were willing to renounce the transitory in exchange for the eternal. His the call to lead them from "death into immortality." This was the magic of His appeal which, sustained by His claim of divinity, generated in the hearts of His disciples that inexplicable brand of faith found only within the realm of religion. Those who seek proof, look around.

Hence, western scholars who could no longer stomach the Judaeo-Christian concepts of an anthropomorphic Creator or God would have found it easier to direct their urge for self-satisfaction, coupled with their desire to enlighten others, in propounding arguments for dialectical materialism and its dead-ends rather than anchoring their hopes on providing proofs for atheism in the Buddha's doctrine. Unlike the limited options enunciated by some western philosophers on the concept of the Primal Being—wavering between a capricious anthropomorphic creator God, and an inanimate super-cause effecting the workings of the whole physical cosmos, but unconcerned with the existence of the mind or sentient beings within that same cosmos, modern[183] western thinkers have finally come to appreciate the thought of Indian re-

---

[183]". . . A rapturous amazement at the harmony of natural law, which reveals of an intelligence of such superiority, that, compared with it, all the systematic thinking and acting of human beings is an utterly insignificant reflection." (Albert Einstein, *The World As I See It,* pp. 28-29). "That deeply emotional conviction of the presence of a superior reasoning power which is revealed in the incomprehensible universe, forms my idea of God." (*The Universe and Dr. Einstein,* p. 15, ed. 1949). Also see *Origin of Species* by Charles Darwin, and *Where Science is Going* by Max Plank.

ligion proclaimed at least three thousand years earlier. These modern savants, like the philosophers of ancient India, recognize that the choice of belief in the Supreme does not lie between an anthropomorphic Creator and no Creator at all but enters a domain both above and beyond such spatio-temporal limits into the realm of pure Mind, infinite and not subject to any analysis by the crucible of human intellect, but undeniably demonstrating Its presence through intelligibly operating laws[184] covering the gamut of existence, physical and metaphysical. The very nature of the Infinite Mind must be to bring forth uncounted myriads of minds and nurture them into ever expanding dimensions of awareness and freedom. As we have seen from the preceding chapters, the Buddha not only infers the existence of such a Mind as the underlying Reality but also acknowledges It as the ground of being from which must emanate the entire cosmos. He gave IT no name or form but, then, neither did the Vedas or Upanishads. Nor, for that matter, did any other Religion pronounce upon It. *The Absolute* can never be known *except through its attributes* and, therefore, *silent are the Tathagatas.*

Those who have written at length on the Buddha's concepts concerning these subjects and found them at variance with the thought of Hinduism should have been more persistent in the direction of identity on the larger meaning of religion and life's purpose contained in both these Faiths, in order to detect the true reason for the Buddha's constrained similes and negative descriptions of *The Absolute,* rather than to have concentrated their efforts in the search for peculiarities. It is concerning this manner of coming to conclusions about the Buddha's rejection of a non-sensible concept of God, to which Mahatma Gandhi[185] addressed himself in his Forward to *The Way of the Buddha:*

"I have heard it contended times without number and I have read in books claiming to express the spirit of Buddhism, that the Buddha did not believe in God. In my humble opinion such a belief contradicts the very central fact of the Buddha's teaching. Confusion has arisen over his rejection, and just rejection, of the base things that passed in his generation under the name of God. He undoubtedly rejected the notion that a being called God could be actuated by malice, could repent of his actions, and like the kings of the earth could possibly be open to temptations and bribes, and could have favorites.

"God's laws are eternal and unalterable and not separable from God himself. It is an indispensable condition of His very perfection. Hence the great confusion that the Buddha disbelieved in God and simply believed in the moral law.

---

[184]Also defined by Laotzu and his disciple Chuang-tze and later echoed in the West by Plotinus and Augustine.

[185]*The Way of the Buddha,* pp. 2-3.

"Because of this confusion about God Himself arose the confusion about the proper understanding of the great word Nirvana. Nirvana is undoubtedly not utter extinction. So far as I understand the central fact of the Buddha's life, Nirvana is utter extinction of all that is base in us, all that is vicious in us, all that is corrupt and corruptible in us. Nirvana is not like the black dead peace of the grave, but the living peace, the living happiness of a soul which is conscious of itself and conscious of having found its own abode in the heart of the Eternal.

"Great as the Buddha's contribution to humanity was in restoring God to His eternal place, in my opinion, greater still was His contribution to humanity in His exacting regard for all life, be it ever so low.

"His whole soul rose up in mighty indignation against a belief that a being called God required for His satisfaction the living blood of animals in order that He might be pleased—animals who were His own creation.

"The one thing that the Buddha showed India was that God was not a God who can be appeased by sacrificing innocent animals. On the contrary, He held that those who sacrificed animals in the hope of pleasing God were guilty of a double sin."

Far too long has the Message of the Buddha remained uprooted from its native soil from which it had originally derived its motivation and succour. Endowed with that spark of the Divine, Buddhism, however, was able, like every other divinely ordained Faith, to continue its growth and spread its branches over the surface of Asia until its shade enveloped nearly a fourth of the human race. Nevertheless, as in *all component things,* the centuries have not left it unscathed, but, as with all other religions, worked their ravages upon it, inexorably altering its pristine character, fragmenting its meaning and confusing its purpose, more so because of its long and virtually complete and tragic exile from the land of its birth. However, as spring gives way to winter, so winter in its turn becomes a prelude to a new planting and the blossoming of new life. A new spring-time is beckoning the Dharma. But for it to blossom again the Faith of the Buddha must retrace its steps in the 'Way of the Buddha,' not only to its pristine purity in time, not merely a return to the geographical location of its birth, not even to its roots in the metaphysical concepts of the India of the Upanishads. These things are both non-realizable and, even worse, futile. For the things of time and matter have no permanency. No, if the Dharma is to be rejuvenated, it must do more than merely return to the soil of its birth, more than relate itself with the things of time. It must lift its gaze above these things and beyond to that timeless Cause which, by the Buddha's own admission, gave to Him a Message and a Purpose:

That Cause without beginning in time. That common foundation of all

> *dharmas. Because It exists there also exist all places of rebirth as well as the full attainment of Nirvana.*[186]

> *There is O monks, an Unborn, Unoriginated, Uncreated, Unformed. Were there not, O monks, this Unborn, Unoriginated, Uncreated, Unformed, there would be no escape from the world of the born, originated, created, formed.*[187]

> *Establish the Truth in your mind, for the Truth is the image of the eternal, it portrays the immutable; it reveals the everlasting; the Truth gives unto mortals the boon of immortality. The Buddha has proclaimed the Truth, the Buddha our Lord has revealed the Truth.*[188]

Hence, O monks and true followers of the Buddha, there is no *escape* for you if you cannot understand that the Buddha came to proclaim and reveal that truth which *portrayed the Immutable,* but which was not of itself unchanging—that truth which was only *the image of the Eternal* but not of itself everlasting. The Buddha only revealed what every other Buddha before Him (as well as Rama and Krishna), has also clearly proclaimed concerning the Divine and its purpose:

> Fools, not knowing my supreme nature, think low of Me, the Lord of creation, who has put on the human body for the deliverance of the world, to be an ordinary mortal.[189]

> On the other hand, Arjuna, great souls, who possess a divine nature knowing Me as the prime cause of creation and imperishable, worship Me constantly with undivided mind.[190]

> There is nothing else besides Me, Arjuna.[191]

Only another *Buddha-rising* like a new spiritual dawn can sweep away the morass and light once again the pure *Dharma* leading to that *One Essence.* Buddhism must re-affirm and proclaim this underlying Reality—the Universal Mind, God. It must anchor itself to this true 'Ground' for its being, this *Causeless Cause,* behind all *Buddha-risings.* How can there exist the truth

---

[186] *Ratnagotravibhaga,* pp. 72-73 (*Abhidhamma-Mahayanasutra*).

[187] *Udana,* 80-81.

[188] *Digha-nikaya,* 1.46.

[189] *Bhagavad Gita,* IX.11

[190] *Bhagavad Gita,* IX.13.

[191] *Bhagavad Gita,* VII.7.

which 'portrays' and is only the image of the *Essence* if there did not first exist that *Unborn, Unoriginated, Uncreated, Unformed?* And if this 'Uncaused Reality' did not exist, how could there be a Tathagata or a Buddha to show the path to Nirvana by proclaiming the truth of the Dharma which is itself only an emanation from *the Eternal.* Then indeed, there would be no escape from this *world of the born, originated, created, formed.*

A BRIEF GLOSSARY OF HINDU

AND BUDDHIST TERMS*

Abhidhamma	Metaphysics.
Abhidhamma-pitaka	A collection of treatises in which Buddhist philosophy is systematically elaborated according to Theravada teachings.
Abhi-jna	Superknowledge, Six: *(1)* Wonder-working powers, *(2)* heavenly ear, *(3)* knowledge of the thoughts of others, *(4)* ability to recollect one's own previous rebirths, *(5)* knowledge of other beings' rebirths, *(6)* knowledge that the outflows are extinct.
Abhuta	Uncreate.
Acata pabbajja	Renounced the world for good.
Adityas	Vedic gods.
Ahetu-ja	Without any original cause.
Ahimsa	Non-violence. This teaching, especially prominent in Buddhism, proscribes the taking of life and inculcates a gentle attitude to all living creatures.
Ajata	Unborn.
Akasha	Empty space.
Akathamkathi	Free from doubt.
Akata	Unmade.
Amatogadha	The deathless state.

*It is felt that the descriptions and concepts related to most of these terms constitute generally accepted ideas concerning these and hence no effort has been made to change their terminology or definitions.

156

Amitabha	One of the best-known Buddhas of devotional Buddhism, who has created a paradise (the Pure Land far to the West) into which those who call upon his name with faith will be reborn.
Amoha	(Pali) Correct understanding. Knowledge.
Anagamin	A venerable one who will never be reborn as a mortal, but only in a higher world or in heaven.
Ananda	The foremost disciple of Siddharta (the Buddha) and also one of his cousins.
Ananuvejjo	That inconceivable deeper mode of life.
Anatta	Unreality. This is the Pali form of the Sanskrit *anatman*, i.e. non-Atman. The Buddhist doctrine of *anatta* is that there is no Self or Atman, either in the cosmos or in individuals; there is no permanent underlying Self behind psychological phenomena, but a person is simply a stream of impermanent states, experiences, etc. *Anatta* is, with Anicca and Dukkha, one of the characteristics of all individual experience.
Anguttara-nikaya	'Enumerating' (Dialogue, Pali canon). 'Gradual Sayings', a section of the *Sutta-pitaka*.
Anicca	'Impermanent' (Pali). The Buddha's teaching is that all things are impermanent, a constant succession of changes, with nothing permanent underlying them. However, this view is modified in the Mahayana with the elaboration of the concept of an Absolute. *(see also* Dharmakaya.) These two concepts are not mutually contradictory. (Sanskrit: Anitya).
Aniccata	Death.
Anupadhishesa	Unbounded liberation. Nirvana.
Anussutam	Pure, without lustful appetites.
Anuttara	Unsurpassable, incomparable, the most perfect being.
Anuttara Samyaksambodhi	Consummation of incomparable enlightenment.
Apadam	Trackless. He who defies all description, who has no mark or track by which he can be described. The Buddha.
Apadana	Stories about Buddhist saints in the *Khuddaka-nikaya*.

157

Aparam	Beyond.
Apratishthita	Without ceasing. (Also meaning 'altruistic' or 'dynamic Nirvana').
Apsara	Celestial nymph.
Arahat	The perfect disciple; one who has completed the discipline required to attain liberation. One who has destroyed the spokes (ara) of the wheel of life (hata).
Aranyakas	'Forest Texts' composed around 600 B.C. (Symbolic interpretations of rituals and sacred formulas). Also known as 'abider in joyful peace.'
Ariyan	Noble, saintly. Variant of Aryan.
Ariyanam	Those who tread on the path of sanctity.
Aruparaga	Desire for life in heaven.
Asamskrita	Unconditioned, uncompounded. (Pali: Asamkhata). 'Nibbana is the only Dhamma not conditioned by any cause'. Also called Asankhata.
Asat	False. That which is non-existent. Unreal.
Asavas	The 'cankers' which obstruct spiritual achievement, e.g. sensual longing, desire for continued separate existence, ignorance.
Ashvaghosha	Famous Buddhist poet, author of a biography of the Buddha in Sanskrit, first century.
Ashoka	First Buddhist emperor of India (B.C. 274-232). Grandson of Chandragupta Maurya. After his conversion to the Buddhist Faith, Ashoka assumed the royal title 'Piyadassi' (of benevolent aspect). Under his auspices, the third Buddhist Council was held in Pataliputra. Buddhism lost royal patronage after the death of Ashoka. The Mauryas were succeeded by the Sungas and the latter by the Kanvas, who were all staunch supporters of Brahmanism. However, Buddhism by then had already become a mass religion and hence continued to remain popular. Variant: Asoka.
Asrava	'Influence', a factor of being.
Asura	Demonic power. Gigantic being.
Atman	The soul, conceived as one in reality with Brahma. Self, as an imperishable spiritual entity.

Attadipa	The self as our light.
Attasayana	The self as our refuge.
Avatara	*(Lit.* Descent). One who has descended. Divine manifesting (descending) itself in human form. Variant: Avatar.
Avacya	Ineffable.
Avijja	Ignorance, delusion, a synonym of Moha.
Bala	Fool, unwise person.
Bhagavan	The Lord. Creator-God. Also called Ishvara.
Bhagavad Gita	'Song of God': Song (Gita) of the Lord (Bhagavad). Perhaps the most famous religious writing of Hinduism. Recognized as an orthodox scripture of the Hindu religion and possessing equal authority with the Vedas, Upanishads and the *Brahma Sutra.* Forming the triple canon (prasthanatraya) of Hinduism and the most consistent among these three. Sixth book of the *Mahabharata.* The *Bhagavadgita* does not represent any specific school of Hindu Thought but the whole warp and woof of Hinduism and beyond Hinduism, religion in its universality ever continuous, conveying worth and direction to human life. As the message it conveys also acknowledges the past traditions and values of the background from which it speaks, the *Gita* is officially designated as one of the Upanishads, deriving its main inspiration from that tremendous series of scriptures called the Upanishads upon whose ancient wisdom, 'Prajna-purani', the *Gita* is essentially predicated and enunciated by the divine seer Krishna who elucidates the multifaceted and priceless diamond of truth and its powers of redemption for humanity. As the oft-quoted analogy from the *Vaishnaviya Tantrasara* relates, "the Upanishads are the cows and the cowherd's son Krishna is the milker; Arjuna is the calf, the nectar-like *Gita* is the excellent milk and the wise man is its drinker."
Bhakti	Devotion to God.
Bhante	Respected sir. Formal manner of addressing a bhikku.
Bhavana	Meditation and development of mind and insight. Contemplation, concentration.
Bhikku	Mendicant monk. (Pali: Bhikshu).

THE GOD OF BUDDHA

Bhikkuni	Nun. (Pali: Bhikshuni).
Bhuta	Spirit, ghost.
Bimba	Image.
Bodhi	Enlightenment, the profound insight and illumination attained by a Buddha.
Bodh Gaya	The place where Gautama attained enlightenment, later came to be known as Bodh Gaya (six miles south of Gaya) and is regarded as the most important centre of Buddhist pilgrimage.
Bodhisattva	One moved by compassionate zeal to aid his fellow men toward salvation, hence willing to postpone his own entrance into Nirvana to this end. A Buddha-to-be. A spiritual hero. (Pali: Bodhisatta).
Brahma	The neuter word is used in the Upanishads and elsewhere for the Sacred Power sustaining the cosmos. Deeper investigation as well as references in the *Bhagavad Gita* and the Buddhist texts of *Samyutta-nikaya* strongly imply that it (Brahma) is a 'state' or a 'condition' more akin to the Buddhist concept of Nirvana. It is not of 'itself' the Ultimate Divine Reality, the Supreme Person, the determining power behind the universe. It cannot of itself be regarded as personal and something to which love and reverence is directed. Also viewed as the 'creator' aspect of the Hindu Trinity. *Variant.* Brahman.
Brahmabhuta	Brahma-become.
Brahmachari	Moving or dwelling in Brahma.
Brahmavihara	Living like Brahma. Divine state.
Brahmin	A Hindu of the highest class, namely the priestly class. The other three classes in order: Kshaitrya (King or warrior class), Vaisyas (Traders or artisan class); Sudras (Labourers).
Buddha	The Enlightened One. From Bodhi.
Buddhacarita	'The Acts of the Buddha'. The first full-length biography of the Buddha by the first century Indian poet Ashvaghosha.
Buddhaghosa	Pali author, Fifth century; *Visuddhimagga*.
Buddha-vamsa	Treatise on lives of 24 preceding Buddhas and also of Gautama.

160

Buddham

The Awakened. Anyone who has arrived at complete knowledge. There are many Buddhas, some lived in the dim past; others may rise in the future.

Buddhankura

Presumptive Buddha, Buddhabija.

Buddhiyoga

The method by which one gets beyond Vedic ritualism and performance of one's duty without any attachment for the results of one's action.

Chakravarti

Sovereign Lord. World Ruler.

Chanda

Will, resolve.

Citta

Memory, recognition: the faculty of systematic cognition. Consciousness. Thought. Mind. The word is sometimes used for the Atman, which can be looked on as pure consciousness.

Dana

Benevolence, loving charity.

Deva

Heavenly being. Literally 'shining one.' In no sense a creator, neither omniscient nor omnipotent. Simply a denizen of another world.

Dhammapada

Way of Truth; Path of virtue; Words of the doctrine; Utterances of Religion. The *Dhammapada* proper is a part of the *Khuddaka-nikaya* of the *Sutta-pitaka*. The Pali version contains 423 verses divided into 26 chapters. The version in Chinese has 39 chapters and 502 verses.

Dhammadana

'Gift of the Law'. The discipline of grounding in the Buddhist religion.

Dhammassa guto

Guardian of the law, or guarded by law. One whose acts are directed by a sense of justice.

Dhamma-tthitata

Rule of Law.

Dharma

Rule of duty or of social obligation, the Reality. Religion, Law, Doctrine, Truth, The Pali form of this Sanskrit word is Dhamma. *Lit:* Mode of being.

Dharmakaya

'Body of the Law.'

Dhatu

Principle.

Dhyana

Meditation. (Pali: Jhana).

Digha-nikaya

Collection of 'long' dialogues which is probably the oldest and most authentic part of the *Sutta-pitaka* (Pali canon).

THE GOD OF BUDDHA

Dipankara	The Buddha preceding Gautama. *Lit:* Dipa means 'Lamp' and Kara means to 'become'. Dipankara means 'to make a lamp of one's self', or to become a beacon. Buddha Gautama was also called dipankara. This word is more a title than a proper name.
Dosa	Malice, anger.
Dukkha	Sorrow, suffering, grief, pain.
Eight-fold Path	The Noble Eight-fold Path sums up the Buddha's prescription on how to attain Nirvana. The first two 'stages' of the Path, Right View and Right Aspiration, refer to the attitude to be taken up by the aspirant for Nirvana; the next Right Speech, Right Conduct and Right Means of Livelihood, refer to the moral and social requirements to be met by the aspirant; while the last three, Right Endeavor, Right Mindfulness (Sati) and Right Contemplation, refer to the mental and spiritual disciplines that are needed.
Four Stages	The four stages of the Noble Eight-fold Path are: *(1)* Conversion to the Dharma. This act frees one from the delusion of self; from doubt as to the Buddha and His Doctrine, and from reliance on rites and ceremonies. *(2)* The state of those who will only return once to this life. *(3)* The state of those who will never return to this world. *(4)* The state of Arahat, the Holy One.
Gatha	Verses (Indo-Iranian origin).
Gandharva	Heavenly musician. A class of beings.
Gosala	Contemporary of the Buddha, founder of the Ajivikas.
Gotra	Clan.
Guru	Master, teacher.
Hinayana	The Lesser Vehicle. (Theravada—path of the Elders).
Indra	One of the chiefs among the gods.
Iti-vuttaka	Sacred writings of southern Buddhists consisting of one hundred and ten extracts, beginning "Thus it was spoken by the Blessed One." Part of the *Khuddaka-pitaka.*
Itthataya	This state.

Jains	Members of the Jain sect, a religious movement that arose in India contemporary with Buddhism.
Jambudvipa	India. Ancient name of India used by the Buddha as well as in the *Mahabharata* (Ch. II, p. 314). According to the ancient Indian concept a continent in the centre of the world's surface.
Jarata	Existence.
Jataka Tales	Five hundred and fifty old stories, fairy tales and fables, the most important collection of ancient folk-lore extant. These stories, a part of the *Khuddaka-nikaya,* were composed around 200 A.D. by Aryasura, a gifted poet.
Jati	Rebirth. Individual existence.
Jina	Victor, conquerer.
Jivanmukti	Liberation realized within this life.
Jivatman	The soul as a separate individual.
Jnana	Gnosis.
Kalpa	Aeon, an age or epoch of time. (Pali: Kappa).
Kama	Desires. Sensuality, bodily passions.
Kaniska	The best known of the Kusan kings, flourished in the second century A.D. and ruled over a large part of India from his capital Purusapura (Peshawar). Under his auspices was held the Fourth Buddhist Council.
Kanthaka	Name of Siddharta's horse.
Karana	Cause, origin.
Karaniyam	One's duty. What ought to be done.
Karma	Volitional action, which is either wholesome or unwholesome. It is that which passes in unbroken continuity from one momentary heap (mass) of the skandhas to another, either during the life of a person or after his death, until the result (vipaka) of every volitional activity of body, speech or thought, is arrived at. Pali. Kriya.
Kassapa	(Sanskrit: Kasyapa). The name Kassapa applies mainly to Kassapa of Uruvella, one of the great pillars of the Buddhistic brotherhood. However, according to the *Anguttara-nikaya,* he is not the same person as Maha-Kassapa who presided over the first Council at Rajgriha.

Khina	Terminated.
Khuddaka-nikaya	Collection of minor texts, part of the *Sutta-pitaka*.
Klesa	Sin.
Koti	One koti is ten million world cycles.
Krishna	Krishna, the eighth manifestation (avatar) of Vishnu. The most widely revered and most beloved figure in the Hindu pantheon. While little can be authenticated of the historical Krishna, He is mentioned in the *Chandogya Upanishad* as one who taught man's life as a sacrifice: "As Ghora Angirasa told this to Krishna, the son of Devaki, he also added, since he had become free from desire, that in the final hour, one should take refuge in these three beliefs: Thou art the indestructible (aksitamasi); thou art the unshakeable (acyotam asi); Thou art the essence of life (pramasamsitam asiti)". By 6th century B.C. we already see Krishna elevated to Godhood. Krishna worship is also mentioned in the earliest Pali Canon, (in the Buddhist work *Niddesa)*. Panini, the great grammarian and a senior contemporary of the Buddha names Vasudeva and Arjuna as those who are being worshipped (The affix 'Vun' comes in the sense of 'this is his object of veneration' after the word Vasudeva and Arjuna—Vasudevar-junabhyam). Also, Patanjali in his *Mahabhasya,* commenting on Panini (IV.3,-98) calls Krishna (Vasudeva) Bhagavad. May the power of Krishna assisted by Sankarsana increase. (Patanjali's *Mahabhasya* on *Panini Sutra,* II. 2, 24).
Kusinara	A town in the Gorakhpur district of Uttar Pradesh, where the Buddha passed into Nirvana in His eightieth year.
Lalita Vistara	Standard Sanskrit work of the Northern Buddhists on the Buddha's life down to the time when He openly came forward as a teacher.
Lankavatara Sutra	The proclamation of the teaching in 'Lanka' (Ceylon). Mahayana scripture.
Loba	Desire, craving, lust.
Loka-dhatu	One world cycle.
Lokattora	Supramundane.

Madhyamika	Middle Way.
Mahabhinishkramana Sutra	'Book of the Great Renunciation' is a Sanskrit work of around the second century A.D. on the story of the Buddha leaving His home and family.
Mahabrahma	Great Brahma.
Mahaparinibbana Sutta	The Pali account from the second Pitaka of the passing of the Buddha. This is the oldest and most reliable of all authorities. It cannot be dated later than the end of the fourth century B.C. nor earlier than the time when Patna had become an important center of the Buddhist Church.
Mahaparinirvana Sutra	A Mahayana work, quite different from the Pali work *Mahaparinibbana Sutta.*
Mahaprajnaparamita Shastra	The book of the Great Teaching of Complete Enlightenment, attributed to Nagarjuna.
Mahavagga	Part of the *Vinaya-pitaka.*
Mahavamsa	'Great-Chronicle,' Pali historical work.
Mahavastu	'Book of the great events' Hinayana work in hybrid Sanskrit.
Mahavira	The last of the Tirthankaras of the Jainas, who emphasized an ascetic life. He was a senior contemporary of the Buddha.
Mahayana	The Greater Vehicle, or the broad path to salvation. The cardinal tenet of the Mahayana is that the Buddha is not just a human teacher but an eternal phenomenon that manifests itself on earth at intervals of time for the salvation of mankind.
Mahishasaka	Hinayana School.
Maitri	Friendliness.
Majjhima-nikaya	'Medium-length' (Dialogues, Pali Canon). Part of *Sutta-pitaka.*
Majjhima Patipada	Middle Path.
Mamayitam	The unattached person.
Manas	The discriminative and deliberative faculty of mind. Faculty of perception.
Mano	Pride.
Manovijnava	Discriminative knowledge.
Mara	The Evil One. The Great Tempter. Death. At times equated with the five Skandhas.

165

Marga	Way leading to sorrow.
Maya	Illusion.
Mettavihari	He who lives in friendliness.
Milinda	The Indo-Greek king Menander or Menandros (B.C. 115-90). The *Milindapanha,* or 'Questions of Milinda' (which is a non-canonical Buddhist text), shows clearly this ruler's great interest in the Buddhist Faith.
Milinda Prasnaya	*Milinda Prasnaya* or 'Questions of King Milinda'. A very ancient Pali work dated around the first century of the Christian era. It is a discourse between Milinda and Nagasena (or Nagarjuna), the founder of the Madhyamika school of Northern Buddhism. (Also called *Milindapanha).*
Moksha	Ultimate or final liberation of the soul from the cycle of birth and death.
Muni	A sage.
Nagarjuna	Also called Nagasena. One of the greatest Buddhist philosophers. He lived in the Kaniska period and was chiefly responsible for formulating the Mahayana doctrine. Author of *Madhyamika-karikas.*
Namarupa	Nama means name, rupa means form.
Niraya Hell	The hell of filth.
Nidanakatha	Biography of the Buddha in Pali attributed to Buddhaghosa, fifth century.
Niddesa	An old commentary, ascribed to Sariputra, on the latter half of *Sutta-nipata,* itself a section of the *Khuddaka-nikaya.*
Nirmanakaya	Transformation body.
Nirodha	Extinction—Removal of sorrow. (Nirodha-Sumapatti: Extinction of all conscious process).
Nirvana	The state achieved by the conquest of craving. The spiritual goal of Buddhism. (Pali form: Nibbana, which literally means 'the going out', as of a flame). According to the Buddha it can also be attained here in this life.
Padam Santam	The path of tranquility or peaceful abode.
Pali	The word means 'text'. Hence the language of the Buddhist Canonical texts and also the commentaries on those texts which are collec-

tively called Tipitaka, of the Theravada Buddhist scriptures. The term 'palibhasa' originally meant the language of the canonical texts of the Theravada. These texts, which originated and were compiled in north India between the first and second Buddhist Councils, were subsequently (after Ashoka's time) carried to Ceylon, then Burma and Thailand more than a thousand years later. We cannot yet with certainty assign a locality of origin to Pali and, while it seems to have evolved from Sanskrit and other dialects, including Magadhi (or Maghada Prakrit, the language in which the Buddha preached) and is in many respects closely related to Vedic and Sanskrit, its actual origins may lie in some other old Indo-Iranian dialect. It is, however, fairly certain that the Buddha himself, who taught in Magadha Prakrit and was, of course, fully conversant in Sanskrit, did not speak Pali, since it was not in use as a language at that time in the area of His activities. Pali has a great mixture of divergent dialects caused by the need to assimilate the different views of the great wandering Buddhist teachers whose versions in various dialects of the Buddha's teachings were not always identical. The Pali scriptures (Tipitaka) were long preserved orally, being committed to writing under King Vattagamini of Ceylon around 80 B.C.

Pali Canon

Tipitaka ('three baskets'), collection of Hinayana scriptures transmitted to Ceylon, Burma, Thailand etc., consisting of *Sutta-pitaka, Vinaya-pitaka,* and *Abhidhamma-pitaka.*

Pana

Faith.

Panch Sila

As a means of adhering to the noble eight-fold path, the Buddhists, by popular convention adopted the following five Pali stanzas. These five stanzas direct each person to dedicate one's self to their adherence:

(1) Panatipata veramani sikkhapadam samadiyami (I resolve to observe the precept to refrain from destroying life).

(2) Adinnadana veramani sikkhapadam samadiyami (I resolve to observe the precept to refrain from stealing others' property).

(3) Kamesu micchacara veramani sikkha-padam samadiyami (I resolve to observe the precept to refrain from sexual immorality).

(4) Musavada veramani sikkhapadam samadiyami (I resolve to observe the precept to refrain from falsehood).

(5) Sura—meraya-majja-pamadatthana veramani sikkhapadam samadiyami (I resolve to observe the precept to refrain from taking intoxicants).

Paramatma

Ultimate soul, Final Reality.

Paramattha

Pali: The ultimate form of natural phenomena (truth in the ultimate sense).

Paramita

Perfection, ideal virtue. It is derived from Parama; superlative, Best, Alpha, often translated as 'gone over to the other shore', reached Nirvana.

Paranirvana

'Beyond Nirvana,' the state into which one who has attained Nirvana passes at death. Complete or Final Nirvana.

Paratantra

Dependent reality.

Parinishpanna

Highest reality.

Parjna

Or Prajna. Transcendental wisdom or insight.

Parsva

Parsva, who flourished in the 8th century B.C., is regarded as the twenty-third Jaina Tirthankara. He taught the Four Fundamental principles constituting the basic code of conduct, namely: Truth, Non-Violence, Non-Covetousness, Non-Acquisitiveness (Caturyana Dharma: Satya, Ahimsa, Asteya, Aparigraha). These were later embodied in Buddhism.

Pathama Maha Sangayana

First Buddhist Council held at Saptapani Guha, 100 days after the Buddha's passing, and attended by 500 Arahats, presided over by Arahat Maha Kasyapa and included both Arahat Ananda and Arahat Upati. This council sat for three months and collated the following which were to be popularly known as the Pali Canon: *Abhidhamma-pitaka* (The Higher Doctrine); *Vinaya-pitaka* (Discipline for the Order); *Sutta-pitaka* (General Discourses).

Paticcasamuppada

Law of Conditioned Origin.

Patigha

Hatred.

Patimokkha

The disciplinary code of the bhikkus.

Patthana

'The Book of Origins', on the causes of existence.

Prajna-paramita	'Perfection of Insight'. Also name of a group of Mahayana texts, and of the philosophical teachings of Nagarjuna. Wisdom of the highest and clearest kind.
Prakriti	Nature. Phenomenal.
Prana	Breath. The life principle.
Prapti	A force maintaining the living equilibrium of the factors composing a personality.
Pitakas	Collections, as the canonical books of the southern Buddhists are called. The Mahayana teaches five instead of the four stages found in the Pitakas and the *Lalita Vistara*.
Pratyeka-Buddha	One seeking salvation independently of others.
Prithagjana	Worldling. (Pali: Puthujjana).
Puggala-pannatti	Discipline for those who have entered the Path.
Purush	The soul, conceived as individual or (sometimes) as universal (the soul of the universe). The Spirit Supreme.
Rahula	'Impediment'. Siddharta's son.
Rama	Seventh incarnation of Vishnu. Hero of the Hindu epic *Ramayana*.
Ratna	Jewel (also Ratan).
Rishi	A sage, ascetic.
Rita	Vedic for Law.
Rupa	Shape, form. Material properties or attributes, of which, according to Buddhism, there are twenty-eight in number.
Ruparaga	Love for earthly existence.
Saddha	Conviction. Faith.
Sad-dharma-pundarika	'Lotus book'. 'Lotus of the Good Law'. Mahayana scripture, second century.
Sadhu	Lit: 'Very good'. A sage.
Sakka	King of the Gods, e.g. Brahma, Indra.
Sakkaya-ditthi	Delusion of self.
Sakra	Indra, chief of the Aryan pantheon.
Sakya	Lit: 'Oak-hearted'. A royal race on the northern frontiers of Magadha a region of Bihar, claiming descent from Rama and Lachman, the exiled sons of King Okkaka of

the Solar dynasty. Suddhodana Gotama, father of Siddharta (the Buddha), claimed descent from Ikshvaku of the solar dynasty (Sanskrit: Ikshvaku. Pali: Okkaka).

Sakyamuni — The sage of the Sakyas, i.e. the Buddha.

Samadhi — Complete concentration. The object with which the mind is in communion with the Divine.

Samana — An ascetic, religious man. Pali word derived from 'sam'—to quiet, i.e. he who quiets the senses. (Sanskrit: Sramana—he who works hard.)

Samata — Altogether everywhere, universal sameness, having no partiality.

Sambhara — The achievement of merit and knowledge during previous lives.

Samjna — Perception, notion, conscious volition.

Sammitiyas — Hinayana school.

Samsara — Karma-formations, conditioned things, impulses, predisposition (Samska). The ocean of birth and death, i.e. of successive individual existences in transmigration. The cycle of becoming. (Pali: Sankhara or Samskara—predisposition, stirring of volition). In Buddhism these are divided into 52 parts.

Samskrita laksanani — All phenomenal existence. Conditioned factor of being (Samskrita Dharma).

Samuddaya — Cause of sorrow.

Samyaksambuddha — The completely and perfectly enlightened.

Samyutta — 'Classified'.

Samyutta-nikaya — 'Collection of Discourses of related content', part of the Sutta-pitaka (Pali canon).

Sangha — The order of Buddhist monks. Assembly, community, order.

Sankhya — One of the traditional systems of Indian metaphysics, closely associated with Yoga. Its main teachings are as follows: *(1)* There is a fundamental distinction between matter 'prakriti' and soul 'purusa'; *(2)* there are innumerable souls, and these are involved in matter and, therefore, with the endless round of Samsara; *(3)* liberation consists in the individual soul isolating itself from matter and thereby escaping further entanglement in rebirth; *(4)* liberation accrues upon insight (viveka), whereby the soul perceives its essential distinctness from matter. Yoga adopts the general metaphysical system of Sankhya, but asserts that liberation requires a certain form of physical and mental discipline.

Sanna

Abstract ideas. According to Buddhism these are divided into six classes corresponding to the six classes of sensations.

Sannyasin

One who has retired from active life to devote himself to spiritual concerns. This possibility is controlled in Hinduism by the doctrine of four stages of life: that of being a student, that of the householder (i.e. family man), that of one who withdraws from the householder's duties, and, finally, that of the homeless wanderer or religious mendicant. (Variant: Samnyasin).

Sariputta

One of the Buddha's foremost disciples, distinguished for his faith.

Sarnath

A township near Benaras, acquired fame as the venue of the Buddha's First Sermon.

Sarvadharma

Revealed standards. Whole realm of formulations.

Sarva-jnata

Omniscience.

Sasana

Religion. The Teaching of the Buddha.

Sati

The Pali word for 'recollection' or 'mindfulness'. Right 'sati' typifies one of the last three stages of the Eightfold Path. It is a central part of Buddhist mental and spiritual training always to be 'mindful' or 'aware' of what one is doing, one's motives, etc.

Satya

Truth.

Satya-siddhi

Name of Hinayana school of followers of Harivarman.

Shantiparamita

Perfection of Patience.

Shastra

Book of teachings.

Shrada

Faith, devotion, reverence, humility.

Shravasti

Known from ancient times as the 'city of wonders', located in Northern India near the Nepalese border. Ruled from earliest times by the Ikshvaku kings and perhaps also founded by Lava, elder of the two sons of Rama. Shravasti became the capital of Oudh (Ayodhya) at the time of the Buddha and is located only a short distance northwest of Kapilavastu, the Buddha's birthplace. (Variant. Sravasti).

Siddharta — Proper name of the Buddha. He was Siddharta Gotama (or Gautáma), son of Suddhodana Gotama, king of Kapilavastu.

Sila — Good Conduct. Discipline.

Silabbata-paramasa — Dependence on rites.

Sirima — Sirima is the Buddhist counterpart of the Brahmanic goddess Stri.

Shiva — Vedic god. The 'destroyer' aspect of the Hindu Trinity. Variant: Siva.

Skandhas — The five factors constituting an individual person: i.e. body, feelings, perceptions, impulses, consciousness: Aggregates (Upadi).

Sramana — An ascetic.

Sravaka — 'Hearer,' a disciple not yet capable of independent progress.

Sthityanyathatvam — Change of state.

Stupa — A reliquary, often bell-shaped and built in the open to contain relics of the Buddha or his disciples, or to commemorate the scene of their acts. In the course of time it came to symbolize the Buddhist doctrine.

Sugata — A wholesome path, 'well-gone', an epithet of the Buddha.

Sumeru — (Pali: Sineru). The legendary central mountain of the world.

Sunya — The void, emptiness. The Madhyamika philosophy emphasizes the voidness (Sunyata) of the Absolute, for it cannot be described in empirical terms and all theories or views about it fall into self-contradiction.

Sunyata — 'Voidness', used to characterize the Absolute in certain Mahayanist teachings.

Sutta — A text or teaching supposedly spoken of by the Buddha. (Sanskrit: Sutra).

Sutta-nipata — A collection of 70 didactic poems of the Theravadin Buddhist canon.

Sutta-pitaka — 'Basket of Discourses', part of the Pali Canon or 'discourses for the laity.' These sacred books of the southern Buddhists consist of the following 5 parts:

(1) Digha-nikaya. The collection of 34 long treatises; one of which is the *Maha-Parinibbana Sutta.*
(2) Majjhima-nikaya. The collection of 152 treatises of moderate size.
(3) Samyutta-nikaya. Continuation.
(4) Anguttara-nikaya. Miscellaneous, the largest book in the three Pitakas.
(5) Khuddaka-nikaya. The collection of short treatises. This is added by one school to the next Pitaka. It contains the following short books: *(1) Khuddaka-Patha* and *(2) Dhammapada.*

Svayambhu	One who has attained by himself alone. Buddha.
Tanha	Craving for existence, selfish or blind greed. (Sanskrit: trisna).
Tantra	'Woven'. System of rites and doctrines.
Tathata	'Thusness'. 'Suchness'—a word used in the Mahayana for the Absolute or Ultimate Reality. The use of the word 'Suchness' indicates that it cannot be described in ordinary language.
Tathagata	He who has fully arrived, i.e. the Perfect One. A title of the Buddha. One who has arrived at a condition which cannot be described, but can only be said to be 'thus' or 'like this'.
Tath'eva	'That is exactly so'. The utterances of a Tathagata.
Theragatha	'Songs of the Monks'. *Therigatha:* 'Songs of the Nuns'. These are parts of the *Khuddaka-nikaya.*
Theravada	Pali term meaning 'The Way of the Elders.' Strictly, the Theravada is only one among the many original Hinayana schools, the rest having disappeared.
Thiti	Prime of existence (Sanskrit: Stithi).
Tirthankara	A Jain teacher.
Triratna	Three jewels; the three essential things, i.e. Buddha, Dharma, Sangha.
Tripitaka	'The Three Baskets.' Canonical Buddhist scriptures. (Pali: Tipitaka), is arranged in three parts: *Vinaya-pitaka; Sutta-pitaka;* and *Abhidhamma-pitaka*

Triple world	The world of sense-desire; the world of form; the formless world.
Tusita heaven	The heaven of delight, the third-lowest heaven, where Bodhisattvas await their last birth.
Udana	'Song of exultation' (inspired words of the Buddha), ancient Buddhist work of second century Buddhist era consisting of eighty-two short lyrics, supposed to have been uttered by Gautama under strong emotion, at important crises in his life. Each lyric is accompanied by details of the circumstances under which it arose. Literally, spontaneous verse. Part of the *Khuddaka-nikaya*.
Udanavarga	Sanskrit version of the *Dhammapada*.
Uddhacca	Self-righteousness.
Upacaya	Birth.
Upadana	Grasping. Desire.
Upanishads	Philosophical dialogues of treatises on the Vedas of ancient India. Written from B.C. 1000 to B.C. 500. The word 'Upanishad' is derived from the combinations Upa (near), ni (down) and sad (to sit); i.e. sitting down near, such as a group sitting down near their teacher to learn secret doctrine.
Upeksha	Equanimity.
Uposatha	Fasting.
Utpada	Origin.
Vajji	Name of a people living in the neighbourhood of Magadha, before whom the Buddha had preached and most of whom had become followers of His Dharma.
Vajra	Adamantine.
Vajrayana	'Diamond Vehicle', youngest stream of Buddhism.
Vajrach'chedika- Prajna paramita Sutta	Diamond Cutter Sutra, a small book belonging to the *Maha-Prajnaparamita* (Perfection of Transcendental Wisdom). One of the many books in the Canon of Mahayana Buddhism and by far the largest, running into many volumes.
Vajra-Sattva	The 'diamond being', or the 'imperishable truth'.
Vasubandhu	Traditionally thought to be the brother of

Asanga, fourth century. Hinayana teacher of the Sarvastivadin school, author of the *Abhidharma Kosha;* in the light of recent research, not identical with the Mahayana author Vasubandhu.

Veda
'Knowledge'.

Vedas
Lit: Books of Knowledge. Oldest (B.C. 1500-1000) scriptures of the Hindu Aryans. Principle Vedas are four: *Rig Veda, Sam Veda, Athar Veda, Yajur Veda.*

Vedana
Feelings, sensations. Divided into six classes according to Buddhism, those received by each of the five senses and sixthly by the mind.

Vedanta
'End of Veda', the Upanishads at the end of the Veda; also the name of the system based upon them, especially that of Shankara.

Vessantara Jataka
The *Vessantara Jataka* tells the story of the Bodhisattva's life as prince Vessantara in his last but one incarnation before he became Gautama Buddha. As Vessantara, he practised the perfection of charity. One by one, he gave away all the things he possessed and was banished by his father for his excessive charity. While he was in exile, he even gave away his wife and children who were, however, restored to him at the intervention of Indra.

Vicikiccha
Doubt.

Vidya
Rapt contemplation. Wisdom.

Vidya-carana-sampana
Possessing knowledge and virtue.

Vijnana
Thought, covering the whole group of mental activities from the most concrete ideation to the most abstract meditation. Intelligence.

Vimana-vatthu
'Celestial Mansion'. Also part of the Pali Canon by same name, which lists the good deeds for being reborn as a deva.

Vinaya
Discipline.

Vinaya-pitaka
Discipline for the Order, (Pali Canon)—early Buddhist sacred books of the southern Buddhists consisting of 5 sections of 227 rules of the monastic doctrine:
(1) Parajika. On sins involving expulsion.
(2) Pacitti. On sins requiring forgiveness.
(3) Mahavagga. (Collectively called Khandaka) and

(4) Cula-vagga. (Contains rules for the daily life of the monks.)

(5) Parivara-patha. A resume of the preceding books.

Vishnu

The 'preserver' aspect of the Hindu Trinity: Brahma (Creator), Vishnu (Preserver) Shiva (Destroyer). Vishnu is generally considered to incarnate from time to time to preserve righteousness and reinstate the spiritual goal for the salvation of humanity. Rama, Krishna and Buddha are considered by the Hindus to be the seventh, eighth and ninth incarnations respectively of Vishnu. Variant: Visnu.

Visuddhimagga

'The Path of Purification', work of Buddhaghosa.

Vyakarana

Prediction, Prophecy.

Vyaya

Cessation.

Yaksha

(Sanskrit: Raksha), Demoniac being, demon.

Yama

Death personified. Ruler of the Underworld.

Yamaka

'The Pairs'. The apparent contradictions of contrasts.

Yoga

'Yoking' of Thought, spiritual discipline. One of the traditional Indian metaphysical systems, closely associated with Sankhya, from which it derives its fundamental ideas. But it differs from Sankhya in stressing the need for meditative practices in order to attain liberation, and also in elevating one of the souls (purusas) into the position of Supreme Soul or Lord (Isvara) who assists other souls towards liberation. But it should be noted that isolation from matter is the ultimate objective, not union with the Isvara. The meditative practices can be divided into physical and mental ones, the former being preparation for the latter. The term yoga is also used more generally for any such system of meditation (e.g. we can speak of Buddhist yoga, etc.).

Yogacara

A philosophical school of Buddhism, arising out of the Madhyamika, from which it differs (1) in emphasizing the need for yoga in order to attain to final truth and (2) in adopting an idealist position in regard to reality—the Absolute being conceived as Absolute Mind, in line with the description of the highest states of trance as being the realization of pure consciousness.

Yojana

A distance of about seven miles. Figuratively, 'a great distance', e.g. miles and miles; very long.

SELECTED BIBLIOGRAPHY

The Dhammapada, by S. Radhakrishnan, Madras, 1968.

The Dhammapada, translated from Pali by F. Max Muller, Vol. X, Part I of *The Sacred Books of the East*, Oxford, 1881.

Anguttara-nikaya, Warren's Buddhism in Translation.

Buddhism, by T.W. Rhys Davids, in the Series on Non-Christian Religious Systems, New York, 1880.

Garland of Birth Stories (Jataka Tales), translated by F. Fausboll.

Buddhist Birth Stories (Jataka Tales), translated by T.W. Rhys Davids.

The Buddha's Explanation of the Universe, by C.P. Ranasinghe, Colombo, 1957.

The Mahaparinibbana Suttanta; (The Book of the Great Decease), Vol. XI of *The Sacred Books of the East*, Oxford, 1881.

The Mahavagga. I-IV (Vol. XIII): V-X (Vol. XVII) of *The Sacred Books of the East*, Oxford, 1881-1887.

The Questions of King Milinda, translated from Pali by T.W. Rhys Davids, Vol. XXXV of *The Sacred Books of the East*, Oxford, 1890.

The Sutra of Forty-two Sections, Kyoto, Japan.

The Way of the Buddha, Publication of Government of India.

The Buddhist Scriptures, A New Translation, by Edward Conze, The Penguin Classics, 1959.

The Gospel of Buddha, by Paul Carus (G.O.B.P.C.).

The Lion's Roar, by David Maurice (U Ohn Ghine), London, 1962.

Sutta-nipata, translated from the Pali by V. Fausboll, Part II, Vol. X of *The Sacred Books of the East*, Oxford, 1881.

The Buddhist Texts, excerpts by Conze, Horner, Snellgrove, Valey, New York, 1964.

The Udana, by Major General D.M. Strong.

The Ramayana and Mahabharata, condensed English verse by Romesh C. Dutt, Great Britain, 1955.

The Bhagavad Gita, with Sanskrit text and English translation and introduction by Gita Press, Gorakhpur, 1961.

The Bhagavad Gita, with Sanskrit text, English translation, introduction and notes by S. Radhakrishnan, London, 1960.

The Bhagavad Gita, by L.D. Barnett, London, 1905.

The Upanishads, by F. Max Muller, *The Sacred Books of the East*, Vol. 1, 1879.

SELECTED BIBLIOGRAPHY

The Thirteen Principal Upanishads, by R.G. Hume, London, 1931.

Katha Upanishad. by R.L. Pelly. Text, translation, introduction and notes, 1924.

Chandogya Upanishad, by S.C. Vasu with commentary of Sri Madhvacarya, 1917.

Brihadaranyaka Upanishad, by Swami Madhavananda, with Sankara's commentary, 1934.

The Upanishads, with an introduction by Juan Marasco, Penguin Books, Great Britain, 1967.

The Essence of the Vedas, by Basdeo Bissoondoyal, Bombay, 1966.

The Vendanta Sutras of Badaryana, by George Thibaut, Parts I & II, with commentary by Sankara.

INDEX

ABHIDHAMMA, meaning of, 156
Abhidhamma-pitaka, 156
Abhidharma Kosho, 73
Abhidharma Mahayanasutra, concept of the
 Cause in, 131
Abhi-Jna, meaning of, 156
Abhisambodhi, 23
Adi-Buddha, 110
Ahimsa, in Buddhism, 156
Alara Kalama, 7, 11, 97, 138
Amara Sinha, 8n
Amaravati, 17
Amitabha, 157
Ananda, viii, 157
Anatta, meaning of, 157
Anath-pindika, 66
Anguttara-nikaya, 14, 69, 72, 92, 124, 157;
 concept of Brahma in, 92; concept of Dharma
 in, 31; reference to Buddha as Brahma in,
 143
Anicca, meaning of, 157
Anuruddha, 108, 109
Anuttara Samyaksambodhi, meaning of, 157
Apadana, 157
Arahat, 106, 158; Arahats, Anuruddha, 108,
 109
Aranyakas, 158
Ariyapariyesana Sutta, 107
Aryadharma, 30; span of, 30
Ashvaghosha, 158
Ashvaghosha Buddhacarita, account of Sid-
 dharta's vision in, 4, 5
Ashoka, Emperor, 1n, 158; title of, 1n
Atman, 63, 64, 158; meaning of, 63, 64
Attavada, 65, 72; concept of, 72
Avatars (Divine Manifestation), 13, 27, 159;
 meaning of, 159

BAHA'U'LLAH, 2, 20
Bhagavad Gita, vii, 7, 47, 48, 52-4, 71, 74, 75,
 88-90, 120, 129, 150, 159; attributes of Soul
 according to, 71; concept of Brahma in, 88-
 90, of self in, 74; on doing one's duty, 54; on
 right action, 52, 53; selfless action in, 47, 48;
 subject matter of, 159; theory regarding the
 Creation in, 120; transmigration of soul in,
 75
Bimbisara (King), 6
Bo Tree, significance for the Buddhists, 8n
Bodh-Gaya, 8n, 160;
Bodhisattva, 4, 105, 160; meaning of, 4, 160
Brahma, reference to the Unmanifest Brahma in
 the Hindu scriptures, 81, 88-90, 105; traces of
 Unmanifest Brahma in the Buddhist texts,
 106-9, 120, 121, 160
Brahma Wheel, 25n
Brahma-faring, 143, 144
Brahmabhuta, 85, 90, 103, 130
Brahmajala Sutta, 9; account of Gautama's
 enlightenment in, 9
Brahmaloka, concept of, 92, 130, 142
Brahmanirvana, 85, 87
Brahmin, 61-3, 141-3, 160; concept of Brah-
 minhood in Buddhist writings, 61-3, in
 Dhammapada, 135
Brahminical Hinduism, state of Hinduism be-
 fore the advent of Buddha, vi, ix
Brihadaranyaka Upanishad, concept of self in,
 76
Buddha, Gautama, iv, 5-13, 15-17, 19n, 30-3,
 36, 38-40, 45-57, 59, 63, 67, 68, 72, 73, 85,
 91, 93, 96, 97, 146; achievements of, 79, 85,
 91, 93, 96, 97; acknowledgement of the
 existence of *Uncreated,* the *Absolute,* 134,
 135, 138, 140, 152; acknowledgement of the

180